D1613247

Networked Nonproliferation

NETWORKED NONPROLIFERATION

MAKING THE NPT PERMANENT

Michal Onderco

STANFORD UNIVERSITY PRESS

STANFORD, CALIFORNIA

STANFORD UNIVERSITY PRESS
Stanford, California

Printed in the United States of America on acid-free, archival-quality paper

Library of Congress Cataloging-in-Publication Data

Names: Onderco, Michal, author.
Title: Networked nonproliferation : making the NPT permanent / Michal Onderco.
Description: Stanford, California : Stanford University Press, 2021. | Includes bibliographical references and index.
Identifiers: LCCN 2021016211 (print) | LCCN 2021016212 (ebook) | ISBN 9781503628922 (cloth) | ISBN 9781503629646 (epub)
Subjects: LCSH: Treaty on the Non-proliferation of Nuclear Weapons (1968 June 12)—History. | Nuclear nonproliferation—International cooperation—History. | Nuclear nonproliferation—Government policy— United States—History. | United States—Foreign relations—1993–2001.
Classification: LCC KZ5675 .O53 2021 (print) | LCC KZ5675 (ebook) | DDC 341.7/34—dc23
LC record available at https://lccn.loc.gov/2021016211
LC ebook record available at https://lccn.loc.gov/2021016212

Cover design: Rob Ehle

Typeset by Kevin Barrett Kane in 11/15 Adobe Garamond Pro

Contents

Foreword

Twenty-twenty should have been the year of the celebration of the fiftieth anniversary of the NPT and the twenty-fifth anniversary of its indefinite extension. Things turned out differently, with the Review Conference—at which the celebration would have taken place—being postponed to 2021 due to the impossibility of meeting during the pandemic.

At NPT Review Conferences, typically over a thousand diplomats and members of civil society gather for four weeks of meetings. When preparing for my first participation as a Dutch Vienna-based diplomat in such a meeting in 2010, I have to admit that, at first, I thought of all this talk about "1995" as the talk of an in-crowd of veterans. However, I quickly learned how the decisions and diplomacy of the conference in 1995 still very much affect our work on the NPT today. I would have benefited tremendously if I had then had access to the publication now in front of you. Who were—and still are—the key players and why? What was the power of diplomacy and its cooperation with civil society? How can it be that such massive processes can still have surprising outcomes? And what was the context of the decisions and what do they really mean?

It was a privilege to attend the 2018 critical oral history conference on the 1995 NPT extension in Rotterdam and to listen to those veterans, recounting not only their countries' positions but also how they felt about those stances and what some of the internal struggles were.

The importance of diplomatic networks cannot be overstated. These networks are built within the diplomatic world but also, crucially, through think tanks and civil society providing a platform for informal discussions. These sessions increase common understanding and build personal relations, a prerequisite for effective multilateralism. This is even more necessary a year into the pandemic, with only limited possibilities for such interaction. However, there is also a more formal side to diplomatic cooperation, and this publication sets out the good example of US-EU cooperation in multilateral arms control.

The NPT is rightfully called the cornerstone of the international nuclear nonproliferation and disarmament architecture—an architecture that is under stress. The NPT therefore deserves our utmost efforts for successful Review Conferences. It is a positive sign that younger generations are engaging on the NPT. To them, I would recommend this publication especially in order to understand why it is that this cornerstone survived its original deadline and to be inspired by how the impossible was made possible.

AMBASSADOR MARJOLIJN VAN DEELEN
*European Union Special Envoy for
Disarmament and Non-proliferation**

---

* The views expressed are purely those of the writer and may not in any circumstances be regarded as stating an official position of the European External Action Service.

Acknowledgments

This book started in the summer of 2015. After one wonderful year, my postdoctoral fellowship at the European University Institute was drawing to a close. It was raining heavily, which was unusual for Tuscany in June. Sitting in Arezzo's famous *Caffè Dei Costanti* across from the equally famous Leopoldo Nuti, I was explaining to him how surprising it was that there were so many references to the extension of the Non-Proliferation Treaty in my previous research on the Global South and Iran's nuclear program. "You should go research it," Leopoldo said.

The book you hold in your hands is a result of that research. It is obvious that the journey was long, because for most of the period, I did not work on the book full time and there were months when I did not work on it at all. Two things pushed me to finish the book: in 2018–19, I was privileged to spend a one-year sabbatical at Stanford University's Center for International Security and Cooperation (CISAC), where I had promised (a year earlier) to work on this project. At CISAC, I produced a lengthy paper, which I judged to be missing much crucial detail, despite being almost 15,000 words long. The desire to furnish that detail persuaded me to write a book. The second push came during the 2019 preparatory committee for the next NPT Review Conference. The Dutch Ministry of Foreign Affairs agreed to sponsor a side event on the NPT extension, which I helped organize. Diplomats and experts participating in the event were intrigued but wanted more detail. Magically, around the same time, a number of my archival requests from the US National Archives started coming through, and there was no longer an excuse to not finish this project.

A number of people were instrumental to the project's success. Leopoldo Nuti not only encouraged me to pursue it, he also kindly agreed to include it in the funding application from the Nuclear Proliferation International History Project (NPIHP). Since 2015, I exchanged dozens of emails with Leopoldo, and he has always been a voice of sound advice. Matias Spektor was a rising star when I met him for the first time, and he has been nothing but generous with his time, advice, contacts, and insight. In spring 2016, he hosted me at Fundação Getúlio Vargas in Brazil as I was starting the project, thus giving me space to think about it (and then grilled me on my ideas over *caipirinhas*). Scott Sagan was my mentor at CISAC. From my first day at Stanford, he was a source of much insight, tough love, and generous feedback. He has read the long draft more times than I dare to admit, pushing me to craft the argument that you can read in these pages. Harald Müller's unique experience of being an academic and a government adviser led me to regularly call on his expertise.

Within the NPIHP, I benefited from the advice of many wise academics. Chuck Kraus, Christian Ostermann, Carlo Patti, Joe Pilat, and Elisabeth Röhrlich were particularly helpful. Anna-Mart van Wyk deserves a special place—with her, we filed the Promotion of Access to Information Act requests in South African archives, the results of which in 2016 were the first indication that this project was worth pursuing. Our joint paper is the basis for chapter 5 in this book. In Robin Möser I found a second-to-none partner for talking about South Africa's foreign policy, the country's nuclear program, and the historical documents that often officially do not exist (not to mention our shared passion for oaked pinotage).

At Stanford, I discussed different parts of the book with various people. All of these conversations shaped this project in some form. Jeffrey Knopf was an enormously smart person to talk to about everything nuclear (and he also happened to suggest the title for this book). David Holloway (who is also a part of the NPIHP network) helped my understanding of the historical setting and was a great sounding board for my ideas. Walks with Gabrielle Hecht were as much about scholarship as about scholarly life. In my chats with Steven Pifer, I've learned a huge amount about arms control and US relations with Eastern Europe around the end of the Cold War. I've learned a lot from talking to (and learning about the exciting work of) Fiona Cunningham, François Diaz-Maurin, Sidra Hamidi, Yogesh Joshi, Erik Lin-Greenberg, Chantelle Murphy, Max Polleri, Kristin Ven Bruusgaard, and Yeajin Yoon. CISAC's team was enormously helpful in making my stay there as smooth and as enjoyable as humanely possible.

Other colleagues read various drafts that became part of this book and provided generous feedback. Robert Jervis was the first person I told about my plan to write a book, and he provided crucial advice on the book proposal. Benoît Pelopidas read an early draft and provided scorching criticism that helped make this project much sharper. Mohamed-Ali Adraoui, Thierry Balzacq, Tomisha Bino, Wyn Bowen, Rebecca Davis Gibbons, Stephen Grand, Christian Lequesne, Gregoire Mallard, Anna Péczeli, Clara Portela, Bill Potter, Farzan Sabet, Michal Smetana, Arturo Sotomayor, and William Kindred Winecoff helped make this book better through their advice.

Markus Haverland has been my manager (yes, that's where neoliberal academia has reached in the Netherlands), but more importantly, provided copious amount of insightful suggestions that helped make this book more readable. He was immensely supportive of this project since day one and helped fight many administrative battles alongside (and sometimes for) me. Rik Joosen produced Figure 3 when my computer could not output the data.

Part of this book rests on interviews that were conducted with three dozen former officials. I am not going to name them all here—they are noted in the References—but I am greatly indebted to their incredible generosity with time and insight. One interviewee who deserves special mention, however, is Ben Sanders. He welcomed me into his home in rural Connecticut in the midst of the worst snowstorm the US Northeast had experienced in a decade (this included driving forty-five minutes to the nearest train station to pick me up, and another drive back); he shared his personal archive with me and let me take the originals to have them copied and return later.

In addition to all those who contributed their time and insight, some capital was also needed for the success of this project. The collection of oral history interviews, archival materials, and the oral history conference were supported by the Nuclear Proliferation International History Project and funding from Carnegie Corporation of New York. Additional funding for these efforts was provided by the Erasmus School of Social and Behavioral Sciences, Erasmus Trustfonds, and the Dutch Ministry of Foreign Affairs. Portions of this research were also supported by Charles University Research Centre program UNCE/HUM/028 (Peace Research Center Prague/Faculty of Social Sciences).

Throughout the project, I benefited from the help of numerous talented young students. Aliaa Ali and Nathaniel Stuart helped me with the translation of documents from Arabic into English. Johanna Melsheimer and Madeline Zutt provided helpful research and editorial assistance during the finalization of the manuscript.

Stanford University Press could not have been more helpful in making the experience of publishing this book more pleasant. I am very thankful to Caroline McKusick and Jessica Ling for their help in the process, and to Mary Carman Barbosa, who edited the manuscript with so much care, for making this text much more readable.

And then, there is Martina. She was the one I dragged halfway across the world to Stanford, uprooting her from her work and her circle of friends. She was the one to whom I always gave the last call before going to sleep in faraway lands when scouting for documents, interviewing people, or presenting papers. Not a single time did she hold my frequent absences against me, in what was either a sign of resignation or support (I choose to see it as the latter). Without her unending love, I would have never started—let alone finished—this book.

Abbreviations

ABM	Anti-Ballistic Missile (Treaty)
ACDA	Arms Control and Disarmament Agency
ACRS	Arms Control and Regional Security (working group)
ANC	African National Congress
CEND	Creating an Environment for Nuclear Disarmament
CFE	(Treaty on) Conventional Armed Forces in Europe
CFSP	Common Foreign and Security Policy
CTBT	Comprehensive Test Ban Treaty
CTBTO	Comprehensive Nuclear-Test-Ban Treaty Organization
DFA	Department of Foreign Affairs (South Africa)
ENDC	Eighteen-Nation Disarmament Committee
EPC	European Political Co-operation
FCO	Foreign and Commonwealth Office (UK)
FMCT	Fissile Material Cut-Off Treaty
IAEA	International Atomic Energy Agency
ICRC	International Committee of the Red Cross and Red Crescent
INF	Intermediate-Range Nuclear Forces (Treaty)
JCPOA	Joint Comprehensive Plan of Action
MEWMDFZ	Middle East Weapons of Mass Destruction Free Zone

NAC	New Agenda Coalition
NAM	Non-Aligned Movement
NATO	North Atlantic Treaty Organization
NNWS	Non-Nuclear-Weapon States
NPIHP	Nuclear Proliferation International History Project
NPT	Non-Proliferation Treaty (Treaty on Non-Proliferation of Nuclear Weapons)
NPTREC	NPT Review and Extension Conference
NSC	National Security Council
NSG	Nuclear Suppliers Group
NSS	National Security Strategy
NWFZ	Nuclear-Weapon-Free Zone
NWS	Nuclear-Weapon States
OAU	Organization of African Unity
OEWG	Open-Ended Working Group
PPNN	Programme for Promoting Nuclear Non-Proliferation
PrepCom	Preparatory Committee
RevCon	Review Conference
SADC	Southern African Development Community
SCFA	Sub-Council on Foreign Affairs (South Africa)
START	Strategic Arms Reduction Treaty
TPNW	Treaty on the Prohibition of Nuclear Weapons
UNGA	United Nations General Assembly
UNSC	United Nations Security Council
WEOG	Western Europe and Others Group

Networked Nonproliferation

The "hammer down" moment of the extension, May 11, 1995, at the United Nations, New York. Author: Onno Kervers, reprinted with permission. Processed by *d/arch digitaliseert* Rotterdam.

Introduction

SHORTLY AFTER NOON ON MAY 11, 1995, Jayantha Dhanapala, after a dry diplomatic introduction, proceeded to the most important part of his speech.

> The documents before representatives provide, in my humble opinion, an excellent basis for an understanding on principles and objectives for nuclear non-proliferation and disarmament, the strengthening of the review process for the Treaty and for the extension of our Treaty. It is also clear that a majority exists in terms of article X, paragraph 2, relating to the extension. This leads me to conclude that it will not be necessary to resort to a vote on the three draft decisions before us . . . as they command the general support of the Conference.
>
> Accordingly, if I hear no objection, I will take it that the draft decisions may be adopted without a vote.[1]

And then, after what direct witnesses describe as the shortest pause, the hammer went down. Leaders of various delegations jumped and hugged, congratulating each other. The Treaty on the Non-Proliferation of Nuclear Weapons (the Non-Proliferation Treaty, or the NPT) was extended indefinitely.

Then Dhanapala took to the floor again and requested waiving procedural rule for a mandatory twenty-four-hour waiting time, and to pass the resolution on the Middle East immediately. Similarly to his action just minutes before, the resolution was passed. Then, six of the supporters of indefinite extension were allowed to speak in its favor. In the order of speakers, the People's Republic of China, Algeria, France (also on behalf of the EU and its associated countries), South Africa, Japan, and Canada took the floor. Six opponents of the extension were also given an opportunity to express that they were not part of the majority in favor of the extension: Syria, Jordan, Malaysia, Nigeria, Iran, and Egypt spoke. And then, at 1:50 p.m., the meeting was adjourned. The deed was done.

Indefinite extension was not the preferred course of action for a majority of the countries. Many countries from the Global South and members of the Non-Aligned Movement (NAM) were skeptical about the treaty's indefinite extension and complained of the lack of progress on nuclear disarmament. This disagreement continues still today. So, why was the treaty, in the end, extended indefinitely? For anyone who follows global nuclear politics, the indefinite extension of the NPT is a feat worth explaining.

The Treaty on the Non-Proliferation of Nuclear Weapons is the most widely ratified multilateral disarmament agreement in the world. Initially signed for a period of just twenty-five years, it was extended indefinitely against the expectations of diplomats and experts alike. Even a quarter of a century later, there are still conflicting accounts of why this happened. The question of *why* is fundamentally important for our understanding of the nonproliferation regime but also, more broadly, in understanding how the US exercises its power in global governance.

The NPT Review and Extension Conference (NPTREC) was held in New York City starting on April 17, 1995, and NPT members decided to extend the treaty indefinitely in a final package adopted on May 11, 1995. The package consisted of three decisions: the Decision on Strengthening the Review Process for the Treaty, the Decision on Principles and Objectives for Nuclear Non-Proliferation and Disarmament, and the Decision on the Extension of the Treaty.[2] In addition, the NPTREC adopted a resolution on the Middle East, which endorsed the establishment of a Middle East zone free of weapons of mass destruction (WMD).

The fact that the extension was passed without a vote is an important detail. Serious disagreements arose about the voting in the Rules of Procedure, particularly about whether the vote should be open or secret. The Western countries argued that a decision as momentous as the one about extending the NPT must be open. The nonaligned countries pushed for a secret vote. The Western countries feared that a secret vote would allow for defections away from indefinite extension.[3] Therefore, making the rules about voting would be as divisive as the voting itself. The discussion on open or secret voting opened questions about possible last-minute vote switches. Although the proposal in favor of indefinite extension had over one hundred signatories, it simply was not certain that all would vote in favor in a secret ballot.

The deliberations that led to the three decisions were negotiated in a small group of the most important countries at the conference—the so-called Friends of President—convened by conference president Jayantha Dhanapala. The resolution on the Middle East was negotiated separately by the US and Egypt, with only limited influence and input of other countries (this negotiation is discussed in detail in chapter 5).

From a theoretical standpoint, explaining the NPT's indefinite extension is about how a leading world power—the United States—managed to navigate and influence a global regime in which a majority of parties held opposing preferences. This, in turn, helps us to better understand how power works within global governance in general, and within the nonproliferation regime in particular.

This book provides a novel argument (outlined in chapter 2) about US *multilateral* nonproliferation policy and contends that the extension happened because its chief proponent, the US, was able to leverage the many connections it held with other influential members of the nonproliferation regime outside the regime. This position enabled the US to draw on varied resources and allowed it both to persuade some parties and to pass responsibility on to other actors. In the language of social network theory, the US enjoys high *eigenvector centrality*—it is connected to many other well-connected states.

The Puzzle of Extension

To say that the indefinite extension of the treaty—and without a vote—was unexpected would be an understatement. Throughout the late 1980s and early 1990s, scholars broadly recognized that *indefinite* extension of the NPT was not forthcoming. As will be discussed in chapter 1, the treaty's text did not permit termination in 1995. Whatever the outcome, the treaty would not "end" in 1995. However, the text did permit a very short extension that would automatically lead to termination. The question of the 1990s was therefore not whether the treaty would be extended or not, but what form of extension it would take.

The discussion about the NPT's indefinite extension happened against the backdrop of what an expert at the Los Alamos National Laboratory, Joseph Pilat, labeled as the "golden age of arms control."[4] The early post–Cold War period saw numerous arms control agreements negotiated, signed, ratified, and implemented. In 1991, the nuclear stockpiles of the two largest superpowers—the US and the Soviet Union—while still relatively high, started to decline significantly as a result of the first Strategic Arms Reduction Treaty (START).[5] The relationships between the former adversaries was improving—including among the scientists in both countries' nuclear labs.[6] In 1991, after the first Gulf War, Iraq's nuclear program appeared to be reined in. The same year, South Africa, a former pariah, joined the NPT (though it would not be until 1993 that information about its past nuclear program would become public). In 1992, France and China joined the NPT, and three post-Soviet republics, in which leftover elements of the Soviet nuclear arsenal were located, decided to disarm. In 1993, START II was signed. In 1994, the Agreed Framework was concluded with North Korea. In addition, progress was achieved in the area of conventional armaments—the Treaty on Conventional Armed Forces in Europe entered into force. In other areas of nonconventional arms control, negotiations on the Chemical Weapons Convention were concluded in 1993.

Yet the indefinite extension of the NPT was not expected. During a workshop with leading diplomats and experts from both the Global North and Global South in 1985, the rapporteur wrote that "the Treaty appears very fragile . . . On balance, the probability appears to be that the Treaty will be extended for a five year period."[7] British academics John Simpson and Darryl Howlett expected a contentious conference.[8] Joseph Pilat wrote in 1994 that the process of the NPT Review Conferences was idiosyncratic and that whatever progress on arms control was to be achieved, the process could still end in negative outcomes.[9] In a later paper, while praising the NPT as a "stabilizing force in an unstable, uncertain world . . . a *sine qua non* of future stability,"[10] he clearly highlighted the uncertainty about the extension. Contrary to Pilat's recommendations, German academic and disarmament expert (and a long-time scientific adviser to the German federal government) Harald Müller wrote, in a number of papers, that the NPT was unlikely to be extended absent major changes to it, including new disarmament and nonproliferation steps.[11] Benjamin (Ben) Sanders, a former UN official and the executive director of the Programme for Promoting Nuclear Non-proliferation (PPNN), argued that the NPT is subject to much criticism from members and nonmembers alike.[12]

In the face of this uncertainty, a massive civil society mobilization in favor of extension was organized. The PPNN, mentioned above, was established in 1986 with the express goal of preparing diplomats for the NPTREC, giving them the substantive expertise needed to meaningfully participate in the conference. As part of this effort, PPNN organized workshops for experts in different continents, published papers and regular newsletters distributed for free, and convened a group of experts and diplomats to discuss development in the nuclear field.[13] However, there was an even broader activation of civil society, not least by the Campaign for the Non-Proliferation Treaty, led by Joseph Cirincione. US academic institutions, such as the Monterey Institute for International Studies based in California, organized workshops in Central Asia, working with local diplomats and experts on promoting nuclear nonproliferation. The Ford Foundation and Carnegie Corporation, together with the W. Alton Jones Foundation, became leading funders in this field, giving grants to a broad range of academic institutions and NGOs.[14] George Bunn and Roland Timerbaev, as US and Soviet negotiators of the NPT, spoke out (both individually and jointly) in favor of the NPT's indefinite extension.[15]

Academics and nongovernmental experts were not the only ones fearful for the treaty's extension. Throughout the preparatory process for the NPTREC, diplomats reported uncertainty about the number of countries in favor of the extension. During the February 1995 meeting of the Western group, the US diplomats argued that seventy countries were in favor of indefinite extension (well below one half of the NPT parties), yet German diplomats called this assessment "optimistic," and French and Russian diplomats "warned against [such] optimism."[16] Less than two weeks before the conference itself, the director of the Arms Control and Disarmament Agency (ACDA), John Holum,

told the president-designate of the conference Jayantha Dhanapala that the
US believed that an indefinite extension without a vote (or any decision without a vote, for that matter) was impossible.[17] At the time of the conference's
start, according to the *New York Times* ex post summary, "the United States
and its allies, among them Russia, faced formidable opposition to an indefinite extension, and did not have enough declared votes for a simple majority
had there been a ballot."[18] Even a week after the start of the conference, the
NGOs in favor of indefinite extension counted less than half of the treaty
parties as being in favor.[19]

That the indefinite extension happened at all, with or without a vote,
is therefore puzzling. It is clear that the US was the chief proponent of indefinite extension. But if a majority of states opposed it, how did it come to
pass? What did all the academics of the 1990s get wrong? And what did the
diplomats underestimate? This is the basic puzzle this book seeks to answer.

This puzzle also presents another, equally important question: How is it
possible that the US attained its preferences in a global governance regime
in the face of opposition? The question about the extension of the NPT is,
after all, one about the exercise of power in global governance by great powers, as will be discussed in chapter 2. Existing explanations regarding global
governance present a lacuna that does not explain the exercise of power in
situations where voting is not present. This book fills this lacuna.

Existing Explanations

In previous scholarship, extension of the NPT has often been noted but not really scrutinized. The explanations offered tend to fall into three broad families
of international relations theory: realism, institutionalism, and constructivism.

Realist Explanation

Realist scholarship has studied how the US has pressured friends and allies
to forego nuclear weapons as well as to join existing nonproliferation agreements.[20] Such studies broadly confirm the accepted view in nuclear proliferation scholarship, that the US has pursued nuclear nonproliferation as one of
its chief national interests.[21] References to preventing the spread of nuclear
weapons can be found repeatedly in the National Security Strategy (NSS) reports.[22] The pursuit of nuclear weapons was always at the core of the charges

by the US against the so-called "rogue states."[23] In addition to bilateral pressure, however, the US has vigorously supported multilateral measures aimed at preventing the proliferation of nuclear weapons, chief among them the NPT.[24] In a way, this argument fits the neorealist argument about state power driving international institutions. Realists have long considered that great powers establish the international institutions to fit their preferences, and that these institutions are largely their instruments.[25]

Scholars have drawn on a similar logic, explaining the emergence of the multilateral NPT regime as a result of superpower collusion, in which states with small opportunity costs are compensated and states with large opportunity costs are punished.[26] Naturally, such a system works as long as a majority of countries become members of the regime voluntarily, but that still leaves open the possibility that the superpower will use the regime to coerce or bribe the intransigent countries.[27] Historical scholarship focusing on the foundation of the NPT supports this reading, confirming both that the superpowers colluded in crafting the regime[28] and that they built the regime with an expectation that it would be useful to curb certain countries' nuclear aspirations. Recent work has added to this argument by advancing the notion that the US coerces countries into compliance in the regime via bilateral threats and side payments.[29]

There is undoubtedly some evidence that at least some power play took place at the NPTREC. The US managed to have the head of the Venezuelan delegation, Adolfo Taylhardat, removed during the conference and to have the head of the Mexican delegation, Miguel Marin-Bosch, effectively muzzled.[30] In both cases the national leaders understood that bilateral relations with the US would turn sour if they did not fall into line. These countries exercised what David Lake called "symbolic obeisance."[31]

The situation was similar in South Africa. In chapter 4 I explain in more detail the genesis of US attempts to recruit South Africa to campaign for the NPT's indefinite extension, but here, suffice it to say that long-term payoffs helped guide the thinking of South Africa's Vice President Thabo Mbeki, who was responsible for this dossier.[32]

Yet coercion is possible only if a sufficiently large number of states are willing to comply voluntarily—otherwise enforcement becomes too costly and thus impossible.[33] Constructivist scholars working on legitimacy have long argued that however powerful the hegemon, it cannot force *all* other members of the community to comply. At some point, someone will be opposed to even the most powerful hegemon's preferences.[34] As stated above, shortly before the conference, the German and French diplomats estimated that about half of the countries were opposed to indefinite extension and that it would be infeasible to coerce them all. Therefore, while threats and side payments may explain *some* countries' behaviors, the fact that indefinite extension occurred without a vote remains to be explained.

Institutionalist Explanation

In her rational institutionalist account of the NPT's extension, Barbara Koremenos argues that institutional learning is key to understanding the extension of the NPT.[35] Upon entering the treaty, many nations were concerned about its future distributional consequences and thus preferred that the treaty be concluded for a limited period of time. Nonetheless, Koremenos argues, through mutual interaction within the NPT the parties ultimately learned that concerns about the distributional effects (or the potential hindrance of European integration) were baseless and that the treaty was useful insofar as it prevented the spread of nuclear weapons.[36]

This approach certainly has empirical purchase on the NPT extension when it comes to the absence of proposals to end the treaty. As Koremenos maintains, and as all observers can recognize, no proposal was advanced to abolish the treaty upon its twenty-five-year anniversary in 1995. Not even its critics were in favor of its termination (or brief extension, since termination was not in fact possible).

This theory, however, does not explain why indefinite extension was chosen over other options, such as a one-off extension or rollover extensions. Koremenos recognizes that these alternatives existed but treats them as a confirmation of her theory that none of the parties sought termination of the NPT. Yet the fact that the countries shared a fundamental interest in maintaining the NPT does not presuppose that they would ultimately agree with indefinite extension. In fact, they might still view another type of extension as superior if they perceived the main goal of the NPT as pressuring the five nuclear-weapon states (China, France, Russia, the UK, and the US) to take steps toward nuclear disarmament. Therefore, while the institutionalist theory can explain why the NPT did not *end* in 1995, it cannot explain the hard-policy question of the early 1990s' nonproliferation regime: How long should the extension of the NPT last?

Constructivist Explanation

The argument that the NPT was extended indefinitely because of a grand bargain rests on the balance between, on the one hand, the political commitments of both nuclear-weapon states (NWS) and non-nuclear-weapon states (NNWS; in the form of the Decision on Principles and Objectives) as well as the commitment to bolster the review process of the NPT (in the form of the Decision on Strengthening the Review Process) and, on the other hand, indefinite extension. Often, the argument is enlarged by the attention given to the international environment, in which other cooperative steps—such as massive reductions in nuclear arsenals and successful negotiation of arms control agreements discussed above—are given a role of magnifier, increasing the willingness of the states to accept the bargain leading to indefinite extension. Practitioners and former participants in the NPT Review Conference often argue as well that "the bargain" made the extension of the NPT possible.[37]

In academic circles, this argument was popularized by Cecilia Albin in her groundbreaking work on justice and fairness in negotiations. Albin argues that a just solution is delineated along five criteria: negotiation structure, process, procedures, allocation of costs and benefits from the agreement, and implementation and compliance.[38] These criteria fall broadly within what Harald Müller would call procedural justice (the former three) and distributive justice (the latter two).[39] In her analysis of the NPT extension, Albin ultimately argues that indefinite extension captured a "*fair balance* between the concerns, interests and obligations of the various parties."[40]

This argument may explain the adoption of the three decisions, but it ultimately points to a minimally just solution, rather than delineating the particular form of the extension.[41] It is important to recall that the treaty was extended by a single-line resolution. The operative paragraph of the Decision on Extension reads simply:

> The Conference of the Parties to the Treaty on the Non-Proliferation of Nuclear Weapons . . . [d]ecides that, as a majority exists among States party to

the Treaty for its indefinite extension, in accordance with article X, paragraph 2, the Treaty shall continue in force indefinitely.[42]

There is no discussion of conditionality or commitment undertaken by parties. In fact, the three decisions are reported in the conference record in such a way that they are listed as three separate (and not intrinsically linked) documents precisely because the US wanted to avoid any semblance of conditionality. The record was clarified on this account upon the request of German ambassador Wolfgang Hoffmann, who submitted an appeal at the urging of the US delegation.[43] Still, the constructivist explanation leaves unclear exactly why other possible outcomes were not adopted—alternative outcomes that, at least from the perspective of distributive justice, would be fairer in terms of the distribution of burdens and benefits.

As will be discussed in more detail in chapter 1, three basic alternatives to the agreement were adopted by the conference: *green-light rolling extension,* requiring a periodical positive vote for rollover of the treaty; *red-light rolling extension,* requiring a periodical vote but granting a negative vote by a majority the power to prevent rollover; and *extension with strings attached.* It thus remains confounding why the treaty was adopted with the given package, and why other packages that were fairer or equally as fair were not adopted.

How This Book Was Researched

This book follows what political scientists call Y-oriented research. It seeks to explain a certain outcome (the dependent variable, or "Y").[44] The case was selected because of its real-world relevance and the gaps in the existing scientific explanations. Explaining why the NPT was extended helps us to understand how US multilateral arms control policy works. At a time when arms control—including its multilateral aspects—is in crisis, we need to understand whether any lessons of the past can help us find future paths.

Methodologically, this book falls in between what political scientists Derek Beach and Rasmus Brun Pedersen call "theory-testing process-tracing" and "explaining-outcome process-tracing."[45] On the one hand, it provides a theoretical explanation and then examines if and how this explanation fits the historical reality.[46] On the other hand, the book is also substantively interested in explaining the outcome and offers new evidence not published or even discovered before. It therefore contributes both to the scholarship on

US foreign policy in general and to nonproliferation policy in particular; it also adds to the history of the nuclear era and the study of the NPT regime.

So, what is this new evidence? When I started researching this book, it quickly became obvious that scholarship on the NPT extension was scarce. Numerous participant memoirs had been published, but serious academic scholarship was minimal, and generally focused on only a particular slice of the puzzle—e.g., on a single-country case. One of the key goals in this project was to collect more evidence, gather more historical material, and provide a more comprehensive explanation.

In addition to the extensive work with secondary sources—other academics' work—I collected new primary data using three methods. First, I conducted in-depth oral history interviews with over thirty key diplomats. Whenever possible, I met them in person, but in a few instances in which the distance was too far or the expense unjustifiable (our university's finance administration would have had a field day grilling me over a three-day business trip to Venezuela), I reached out to the interviewees by phone or Skype, depending on where they resided and which option they felt more comfortable with. These interviews were semistructured in that I used the same basic interview script and questions in all of the interviews. However, as usually happens in elite interviews, we recurrently wandered into other unexplored areas. Interviewees often wanted to share particular insights or details they thought were important. An average interview lasted around two hours, but it was not uncommon to have much longer ones (the record was four hours). The shortest interview cited in this book ended after fifteen minutes, when the interviewee became fed up with my questions and hung up the phone.[47]

These individual interviews were combined with a Critical Oral History Conference with a dozen key participants, which took place in March 2018 in Rotterdam, the Netherlands. Representatives of the key countries at the NPTREC were invited, and during two days of discussions, we explored six topics: the mood and expectations for the conference, hurdles for the agreement, overcoming the obstacles for agreement, the Middle East question, the origins of the Final Documents of the conference, and the extension's impact. The conference was supported by an extensive reading packet of primary documents that was distributed to the participants ahead of the conference, as well as by the participation of about a dozen academic experts.

The Critical Oral History Conference was originally meant to be the leading element of my research, but it emerged over time that the interviews I conducted ahead of the conference were equally important. Thus to avoid any negative feedback, the earlier interviews were not distributed to the conference participants prior to the conference.[48] In structuring the Critical Oral History Conference, I followed the methodology developed by Christian Ostermann and Leopoldo Nuti from the Nuclear Proliferation International History Project (NPIHP), which was tried and tested in other conferences within the NPIHP.[49] The interviews, as well as the conference, were conducted in English.

Finally, I collected primary historical materials. Through the freedom of information access (or its equivalent in other countries), relevant documents were requested from the National Archives and Records Administration in Washington, DC; the Clinton Presidential Library in Little Rock, Arkansas; the archive of the Department of International Relations and Cooperation in Pretoria; the Political Archive of the German Federal Foreign Office in Berlin; and the archives of the European Council in Brussels. In addition to the archives I myself accessed, colleagues were at times kind enough to share primary diplomatic documents from other countries' archives. Accessing documents from archives on three continents allowed me to put together a complex puzzle. Often, the documents complemented each other. Occasionally, however, they revealed obvious inconsistencies. For example, South African diplomats' efforts to mislead other countries about their true preference for the NPT extension was not unmasked by many. In addition to the diplomatic documents, I accessed the archives of the Programme for Promoting Nuclear Nonproliferation, which gave me insight into the discussions about arms control at the end of the Cold War and the expectations that individuals had at that time. I accessed these archives at the Special Collections of the University of Southampton in the UK (where PPNN was administratively anchored), as well as in the Rockefeller Archive Center in Sleepy Hollow, New York (this gave me access to a wide collection of documents on other arms control initiatives funded by the Ford Foundation in the 1990s). I also benefited enormously from access to the private papers of Ben Sanders, a former senior UN official in the field of disarmament and later the executive director of PPNN. Naturally, not every single piece of historical material is cited in this book. However, the argument presented here builds on thousands of individual documents, which I read over a period of more than five years.

I recognize that political scientists may only infrequently conduct in-depth historical research. However, this aspect of the work on the present book afforded me enormous pleasure, allowed me to meet dozens of bright interviewees, made it possible to scrutinize theoretical arguments in light of empirical evidence, and most importantly, gave me a more tangible picture of how nonproliferation policy is implemented in the real world. This is what this book is about.

Structure of This Book

This book consists of six chapters as well as this introduction. Chapter 1 provides a gentle introduction to the history of the NPT's indefinite extension, by asking "why indefinite extension?" This chapter exploits the fact that not every reader is familiar with the historical setting of the NPT's extension. In this chapter, I discuss the origins of the provisions for limited duration in the NPT—how these provisions made their way into the treaty, and what the parties originally thought about these provisions. I also offer a brief history of the NPT between 1970 and 1995, including its gradual expansion and the successes (and failures) of the review conferences, with particular emphasis on the topics that emerged as key in the NPT discussions during that period. The chapter then provides a historical and legal sketch of the possible extension options, including their meanings and justifications. Additionally, chapter 1 provides an overview of the US position, with an emphasis on decision-making within the US Arms Control and Disarmament Agency, at the State Department, and at the White House.

Chapter 2 introduces the reader to the theoretical argument. This chapter discusses in depth the premise based on social network theory, tying it to the diplomatic position of the US in global networks. In this chapter, I explain how this theory differs from other explanations of states' influence in international organizations. The chapter also provides evidence for the argument that the US did, indeed, possess a unique position in diplomatic, commercial, and military networks in the mid-1990s, unparalleled by any other nation.

The US was able to achieve indefinite extension of the treaty thanks to its relationship with three major actors: the European Union (EU), South

Africa, and Egypt. These partnerships allowed the US to reach the countries in the neighborhood of the EU, break the opposition within the Non-Aligned Movement, and garner the support of the Arab countries in the Middle East. With this in mind, the book's primary empirical chapters focus on these relationships.

Chapter 3 focuses on the cooperation between the US and Europe. While US cooperation with the European countries happened primarily within the framework of the Western European and Others Group (WEOG) of the United Nations General Assembly (UNGA), this cooperation allowed the US to leverage the economic power of the EU (which was the tool the European countries chose to utilize) in its part of the globe to the advancement of the US goal of furthering nuclear nonproliferation. While the EU supported indefinite extension on its own, teaming up with the EU allowed the US to advance its interests more efficiently. Empirically, the focus of this chapter is twofold. Initially, it discusses the negotiations between the US and the European countries (sometimes joined by Russia), especially within the framework of the WEOG. These negotiations primarily focused on the exchange of information and the plotting of strategy for various meetings. Furthermore, the chapter examines the activities of the European countries, primarily regarding the démarches, threats, and inducements toward the third countries. These activities in favor of indefinite extension started with the preparation of the first-ever Joint Action, a new instrument that the EU gained after the Treaty of Maastricht. Based on the Joint Action, the EU proceeded with démarches and a diplomatic push for indefinite extension in bilateral settings as well as in individual member states.

Chapter 4 discusses the cooperation between the US and South Africa.[50] This relationship was significantly newer than the one with the EU. While US efforts to "co-opt" South Africa can be traced back to late 1994, the cooperation gained force only after a meeting between the then vice president of South Africa, Thabo Mbeki, and US vice president Al Gore in late February 1995. Mbeki was instrumental in reversing the position of South Africa that until then favored a green-light rolling extension. He also overruled his own party, which supported a one-off, short-term extension. By breaking from both his diplomats and his party, Mbeki created a situation that helped to break the anti-extension block within the Non-Aligned Movement and to pave the position toward extension. In this chapter, I scrutinize the domestic process within South Africa in late 1994 and early 1995 as well as the interactions between Mbeki and Gore.

This chapter demonstrates that US cooperation with South Africa was important also because it allowed the US to put something on the table in exchange for support of indefinite extension. The Decision on the Principles and Objectives, proposed by South Africa, in theory reflected a bargain. However, because the extension conference formally adopted a series of freestanding documents that were not explicitly linked, South Africa did not sponsor the resolution in favor of the treaty's indefinite extension. This is exactly what network theory would expect: the US managed to leverage the power of weak ties.

Chapter 5 studies the cooperation with Egypt that allowed the US to co-opt Arab countries and diminish opposition to the extension among the nonaligned countries. The chapter will focus on Egypt's diplomacy related to Israel's nuclear program prior to the 1995 NPT Review and Extension Conference; the discussions within Egypt held between its foreign ministry and the Council presidency (which held opposite preferences, driven by different motivations); and, ultimately, the negotiations in New York leading to the adoption of the Resolution on the Middle East, one of the key documents that emerged from the conference.

Since 1981, when Egypt joined the NPT, there had been a group of diplomats within the Egyptian foreign ministry that opposed the treaty. By 1995, these diplomats were all in positions of power: Amr Moussa was the foreign minister and Nabil Elaraby was ambassador to the UN (and thus the head of the delegation to the NPT conference). These diplomats opposed indefinite extension unless the conference (and by proxy, the US) adopted tough action on Israel. Egypt came to the conference with a resolution on a nuclear-weapon-free zone in the Middle East, targeting Israel. But for procedural reasons, the US had to enter into negotiations with Egypt on the latter's acquiescence to extension without a vote. The price Egypt exacted for this was a resolution on the Middle East, negotiated bilaterally between Egypt and the US. No other two countries could have negotiated this resolution: the US was able to make a commitment on the part of Russia and the UK, while Egypt brought the whole group of Middle Eastern countries on board. This not only underscores the network logic but also demonstrates that the US was forced to make yet another concession to a weaker, regional power. The chapter focuses empirically on the negotiations in New York (based on interviews with both sides) and on the parallel discussions between Washington, DC, and Cairo (based on documents acquired from the Clinton Presidential Library).

Chapter 6 wraps up with a look at the postextension politics of the NPT. In particular, this chapter looks at the interpretation and reinterpretation of the commitments undertaken in 1995. It provides a brief history of the post-1995 policy innovations within the NPT regime, with a focus on the additional commitments adopted in 2000 and 2010. It also looks at how these commitments adopted in 1995 have held up twenty-five years after the vote for indefinite extension.

1

Why Indefinite Extension?

THAT THE INDEFINITE EXTENSION of the NPT arose as an issue in the mid-1990s was a result of the terms of the treaty as well as of the broader history of the nuclear nonproliferation regime since the NPT's entry into force in 1970. Therefore, in an effort to answer the question this chapter addresses, four related questions must be addressed: Why was the treaty of limited duration in the first place? What shape was the regime in twenty-five years after its inception? Were there were any serious alternatives to indefinite extension? and, Why did the US emerge as the leader of indefinite extension?

The extension conference was convened because Article X.2 of the treaty stipulates that

> Twenty-five years after the entry into force of the Treaty, a conference shall be convened to decide whether the Treaty shall continue in force indefinitely, or shall be extended for an additional fixed period or periods. This decision shall be taken by a majority of the Parties to the Treaty.[1]

This original limit to the duration of the NPT was inserted into the treaty to accommodate the European allies of the US, who felt they had been targeted and straightjacketed by the treaty. These countries originally insisted on limiting the duration of the NPT as an insurance against possible adverse future developments. By the time of the conference, however, these countries were not the ones opposed to the extension.

Opponents of the extension questioned more closely whether the NPT had been successful in advancing the state of global nuclear disarmament—one of the chief goals of the treaty—than whether it was successful in preventing the spread of nuclear weapons.[2] Although the treaty attracted numerous new signatories—by 1995 it was signed by almost all countries in the world save for a handful of exceptions—critics claimed that it achieved too little to lead to the goal of a world without nuclear weapons, which the nuclear-weapon states had agreed to in Article VI of the treaty. To keep the nuclear states' feet to the fire, three alternatives had been proposed in line with the wording of Article X.2 above: a green-light rolling extension, a red-light rolling extension, and a conditional extension.

As mentioned above, by 1995 the European allies of the US had dropped their opposition to indefinite extension, with the result being that the mantle of the opposition was carried by the Non-Aligned Movement (NAM). As the NAM largely acts as a bloc, the fear was real that it would block the NPT's indefinite extension.[3] Thus, from early on, the US emerged as a champion of indefinite extension, in line with its original designs for the treaty.

This chapter will discuss the origins of the limited duration of the NPT, the review conferences (RevCons) until 1995, and the alternatives to indefinite extension, as well as a description of how and why the US became the chief champion of the treaty's indefinite extension.

Limited Duration

Time-limited duration of international treaties is not unusual. According to Barbara Koremenos's study, about half of international security treaties are of limited duration, with the average period being five years.[4] Why do states put these provisions in the treaties? Because of uncertainty.

Two sources of uncertainty for states predominate in international politics: first, stemming from the international system itself, and second, regarding the distribution of benefits from international treaties. International relations scholars' starting point for analysis of international cooperation is that there is no higher authority in the international system beyond states, a feature labeled as "anarchy." Because of the anarchic nature of the international system, states have no assurance of reciprocation or cooperation. Without enforcement of cooperative agreements, uncertainty makes cooperation difficult. Even if states can trust their counterparts' motivations and willingness today, they have no way of knowing what will happen in the future.[5] At the beginning of an agreement, states have a poor understanding of who will benefit from cooperation in the future, therefore they are unwilling to tie their hands for an indefinite term. In the language of Barbara Koremenos, "when uncertainty about the state of the world is high, flexibility is more likely to be incorporated."[6] In the case of the NPT, this is reflected in the fact that the more severe security threat a state faces (or perceives to face), the less likely it has been to sign the treaty.[7]

At the same time, and relatedly, the uncertainty about the distribution of benefits from international treaties is also tethered to the uncertainty about the state of technology. In treaties such as the NPT, the institutional measures put in place end up governing much of the technology. Thus there is uncertainty about whether states will lose out on the technological end of the bargain, which would be detrimental not only to their security but also to their economic well-being. For this reason, states are unwilling to enter into long-term, inflexible agreements.

Have these concerns been reflected in the NPT discussions as well? It turns out, remarkably, yes. The original limited duration of the treaty—the twenty-five years stipulated in Article X.2—was included at the express demand of the US's European allies, which were concerned about the consequences of the treaty on their security and their economies.

The initial draft of the treaty, submitted in 1965 by the US, spoke of its indefinite duration, and the initial Soviet submission in 1967 spoke of an "unlimited duration."[8] The initial US assumption was that the provision for review conferences would appease the opponents of indefinite duration. The US background paper for the February 1967 meeting of the Eighteen-Nation Disarmament Committee (ENDC) stated:

> The non-nuclear countries will probably object to signing a non-proliferation treaty of unlimited duration containing no obligations upon the nuclear-weapon powers to halt the nuclear arms race within any specified period. The review clause, however, provides for an automatic conference at the end of five years to review the operation of the treaty "with a view to assuring

that the purposes and provisions of the Treaty are being realized." We have advised some of our allies that at this conference the non-nuclear-weapon states can call upon the nuclear-weapon states to show whether the treaty is living up to its stated purpose of leading toward the easing of tensions and the facilitating of disarmament rather than merely being a step to preserve nuclear monopoly.[9]

However, opposition to indefinite duration was palpable. In a bilateral meeting with ACDA's assistant director Samuel de Palma in January 1967, Germany's foreign ministry's director of planning Gunther Diehl expressed "serious concern . . . that the treaty would further restrict the capability of Germany industry [sic] to stay abreast of modern technology."[10] Mohamed Shaker wrote in his definitive study of the NPT's negotiation, citing a Swiss submission to the ENDC, that "such a commitment seemed hardly conceivable in a field where development was as rapid and unpredictable as that of nuclear science and its technical, economic, political and military implications."[11] The Italian representative to the conference Roberto Caracciolo famously said that "[t]o imprison [future generations] in an iron corset, which could not be adjusted to the changing conditions of history, would in our opinion expose that corset to the danger of bursting."[12]

Italy, therefore, submitted a formal proposal that would see the NPT as valid for a duration of X number of years, after which the treaty should be automatically extended for the same period unless states withdraw from the agreement subject to a six-month notice.[13] That Italy lifted this mantle was not accidental—as Italian historian Leopoldo Nuti writes, the Italian reaction to the initial US draft of the treaty was that of "visceral resentment."[14] As Nuti explains, Italy was concerned both about the consequences of the NPT for European political cooperation and, more importantly, about the regional balance of power and security in Europe. Italian leaders held close discussions with Germany but also with Asian powers such as Japan and India. The Italians demanded that the treaty introduce a measure of flexibility, either by changing the duration or by introducing a possibility for amendments. The possibility for withdrawal included in Italy's proposal was, in the view of the Italian delegation, the escape clause in case of especially grave circumstances. Italy, however, preferred to have different governments express themselves on this point more explicitly.

Other delegations, particularly the European NATO allies, were similarly not in favor. The Swiss delegation sent an aide-memoire to the ENDC in late 1967, spelling out that "[t]he non-nuclear-weapon states certainly cannot take the responsibility of tying their hands indefinitely if the nuclear-weapon states fail to arrive at positive results in [the direction of limitation of armaments]."[15]

The Americans tried to engage the Soviets bilaterally on this issue. However, the Soviets rejected the idea that the NPT parties would be able to get out of the treaty easily after the initial period of duration.[16] For this reason, the reference to the potential easy withdrawal at the end of the initial period was dropped, and the period of "X years" was replaced in the final joint treaty draft by a period of "twenty-five years." Shaker argues that this duration reflected the fact that the nuclear era was, at that time, barely twenty-five years old.[17]

The period was not warmly welcomed. Germany preferred a period of five to ten years, India and Brazil decried legitimation of vertical proliferation, Tanzania lamented that developing countries were left in "comparative technological backwardness for twenty-five years." Italy tried smuggling the easy-escape clause back in.[18] Canada and the US heavily criticized Italy for this step; Dean Rusk himself wrote an agitated note to Italy's then foreign minister Amintore Fanfani arguing that the US had accommodated all Italian demands.[19] As the withdrawal provisions were dealt with in another portion of the treaty, the Italian easy-escape clause was removed. Italy voted in favor of the treaty draft.

Despite the discussions within the NPT setting (outlined in the next section), the situation among US allies changed over the treaty's first quarter-century. The explanation for this lies partly in the fact that the US "compensated" the allies for their security concerns by providing conventional military assistance.[20] Normative change set in, which made nuclear weapons seem undesirable for a number of European countries, particularly Germany.[21] European countries were offered credible assurances, including in the form of external deterrence and nuclear sharing.[22] By 1995, the gap in the views of the NPT among the European countries decreased markedly, demonstrated by the progress made at the NPT RevCons.

NPT and the Review Conferences until 1995

Having been negotiated in 1968, the NPT entered into force on March 5, 1970, when the US and the Soviet Union ratified the treaty (after forty other countries had already done so, including the other state depositary of the treaty, the UK). The first forty signatories of the treaty were mainly small and middle powers from across the world.

Over time, participation in the treaty grew steadily to almost 180 countries in 1995 (see Figure 1). At the same time, participation in the review conferences remained unequal and rather low. In the last RevCon before the extension, in 1990, only 83 countries sent participants to the conference. Over time, the conferences became much more technical and specialized, with main committees and subcommittees. Despite the growing complexity, state delegations to these conferences remained rather small, with a median of three to four delegates. It is therefore not surprising that the technologically more advanced countries and those with larger economic and strategic stakes became more dominant, as they could field bigger delegations to the conference.[23]

The NPT Review Conferences have been meant to provide the non-nuclear-weapon states, in particular, with a means "both to express their views on the implementation of the Treaty and to discuss means of improving [the] implementation where necessary."[24] Because the goal of the RevCons was meant to be "limited and indirect," the goal was to have all of the decisions within this setting passed as "a product of the entire membership."[25]

In line with Article VIII.3, five years after the treaty's entry into force, the first review conference was convened in Geneva in May 1975. Presided over by Swedish diplomat and disarmament negotiator Inga Thorsson, the conference welcomed representatives from 57 states. This number may appear small, but the NPT had at that time just 91 state parties. The interest in the conference was not high, most of the participants were represented at the level of their specialized disarmament diplomats (in stark opposition to the high level of participation in more recent years). The conference demonstrated relatively high cooperation among the blocs—despite the Cold War setting, the East and West cooperated quite actively during the

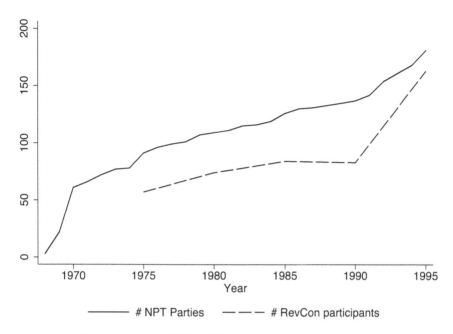

FIGURE I Participation in the NPT and NPT Review Conferences over time

conference. This cooperation happened both at the superpower level as well as among the middle and small powers; for example, through cosponsorship of proposals and working papers.[26] Reading the accounts of the discussions in 1975, one is eerily reminded of the issues dividing the actors at that time. Members of the Western bloc as well as those of the socialist bloc argued that the state parties had sufficiently fulfilled their obligations under disarmament (the SALT I discussions had at the time just been completed) and were focused instead on reaching a universal definition of nuclear safeguards. The NAM considered that universal safeguards would put them at a technological disadvantage and claimed the nuclear-weapon states had fallen short of their nuclear disarmament commitments.[27] The effort to complete the Comprehensive Test Ban Treaty (CTBT) was already well under way at the time.[28] However, the review conference was also remarkable because it was the first—and last—time the member states adopted a statement certifying that parties to the treaty are in good standing in their obligations with regard to the nonproliferation obligations.[29] The conference was able to agree on a final declaration, a political statement at the end of the conference. This declaration was adopted by consensus, the decision-making method used within the NPT setting ever since.[30] Only the RevCons in 1985, 2000, and 2010 have been able to reach other final political statements by consensus. The 1995 RevCon technically did not reach a final declaration, but given that the treaty was formally extended, no observer considers that conference a failure.

The subsequent 1980 RevCon, attended by 74 out of 109 NPT state parties at the time, was not as successful. While the conference agenda was not markedly different from that of five years earlier, members were unable to reach consensus on the Final Document. During this conference, the goal of universalization of the treaty was an important factor discussed.[31] Conference president Ismet Kittani of Iraq suspended negotiations during the conference to focus on nuclear disarmament, noting that there was a near-universal agreement in other areas.[32] However, the conference also noted with concern the "introduction unilaterally of supply conditions without consultations among Parties," a reference to the London Club (later known as the Nuclear Suppliers Group; NSG) guidelines published two years prior.[33] The London Club was often hailed as the highlight of US-Soviet nuclear cooperation, as it established a de facto cartel on the export of nuclear technologies from countries aligned with the two superpowers (that is, all countries capable of delivering nuclear technologies at that time).[34] At the same time, developing countries—including some allies of the US—deeply resented the London Club, as they considered it a stitch-up against their interests.[35] This sentiment has not abated since and is still today a staple of the NPT Review Conferences.

The 1985 RevCon was—similarly to the first conference—successful. The conference took place during the height of the Cold War, and cooperation between the US and the Soviet Union (or between their allies and satellites, as was also the case during the 1975 RevCon) was minimal.[36] The conference, chaired by Mohamed Shaker of Egypt (who by that time was Egypt's ambassador in London), took place during a time of heightened tension: in the period since the previous review conference, Israel had bombed Iraq's nuclear facilities in Osirak, and concerns about the Israeli and South African nuclear programs had increased.[37] The issues of nuclear assistance and safeguards continued to be points of contention, and the absence of the CTBT was still discussed as a relevant topic.[38] Especially on safeguards, the 1985 RevCon was revolutionary, as it broached the discussion of full-scope safeguards (also later known as comprehensive safeguards) to be applied to both non-nuclear-weapon states and nuclear-weapon states, as well as issues related to transport of nuclear materials.[39]

The 1985 RevCon introduced an institutional innovation: formation of the group called "Friends of President." The Friends group consisted of the chairs of the main conference committees, the treaty depositaries, selected other countries, and the secretary general of the conference.[40] The Friends of President group was useful because it allowed Shaker (as the conference president) to sidestep the negotiations in the plenary and focus instead on hammering out the deal with a small number of heavyweight actors. However, it also fueled resentment and feelings of yet further exclusion among those who found themselves outside of the group. Nonetheless, thanks to this institutional innovation, Shaker was able to produce the Final Document at an event that was fraught with potential for conflict.

The last review conference prior to the extension conference was the 1990 RevCon. This conference, convened in late summer 1990, attracted 84 out of 140 parties to the treaty. Presided over by Oswaldo de Rivero of Peru, the conference ended in failure. The issues around the peaceful uses of nuclear energy—particularly the complaints of the developing countries that export controls unduly limit their rights under the treaty—were combined with discussions about the effectiveness of the International Atomic Energy Agency (IAEA) safeguards regime.[41] The conference participants also endorsed and encouraged nuclear-weapon-free zones. However, the biggest problem that emerged during this conference was related to nuclear disarmament. While the Western European countries (and former Soviet satellites) praised the steps made toward the end of the Cold War, the nonaligned countries were still unhappy with the pace of disarmament. The nonaligned states demanded extension of the negative security assurances, legally binding commitments not to use nuclear weapons against any nuclear-weapon states. This demand, was, however, a smaller sticking point compared to the lack of progress on the CTBT issues.[42] The absence of the CTBT turned out to be a breaking point for the conference. The US diplomat Thomas Graham, Jr., argued that the conference was "single-handedly wrecked" over this topic by the Mexican delegate Miguel Marin-Bosch.[43]

As it is clear, the NPT was not heading toward an easy extension. In the first twenty-five years of its existence, tensions among the countries of the former Western camp and the former Eastern camp regarding preferences, as well as the goals of the NAM, became harder to ignore: while the former Western and former Eastern camps focused mainly on nuclear safeguards and nonproliferation, the NAM focused mainly on access to nuclear technologies and nuclear disarmament. The extension of the treaty created a moment when the nonaligned countries felt they had an opportunity to extract more concessions from the West and the East in exchange for extension. Already in the late 1980s, an expert group discussing the nuclear relations between the Global North and the Global South concluded that the extension was likely for a maximum of five years, precisely because of the concerns related to nuclear disarmament.[44] Other academics expected that the treaty would not be extended unless major changes to it were made.[45] As the international community began approaching the year 1995, the question became: What kind of future was possible for the NPT?

Alternatives to Indefinite Extension

Inquiring about other options aside from indefinite extension is not as straightforward as it may appear. For institutionalists, such as Barbara Koremenos, the alternative to indefinite extension was the termination of the treaty.[46] This view was also raised by some treaty proponents as the natural alternative to indefinite extension.[47] Nevertheless, collapse of the NPT was not an option that was seriously considered by state parties as the 1995 NPT Review and Extension Conference was drawing near. It was also broadly accepted that if the conference was not able to adopt any decision, the treaty would remain in power, provisionally, until a majority of state parties came together to make a decision about the treaty's extension.[48]

Here it may be useful to think about both the alternatives that were actually raised at the conference as well as the alternatives that were theoretically possible but not brought up during the conference. While termination of the treaty was not an option—in fact, the wording of Article X.2 does not permit termination—it could have been extended for a single, short period, which would effectively mean termination at the end of that time. However, none of the parties came up with this suggestion. Indeed, while Venezuela mentioned such a proposal in its speech to the conference, it did not ultimately formally table such a proposal.

At the conference itself, two other alternatives to indefinite extension were raised: a proposal tabled by Mexico, which was basically an extension "with strings attached," and a proposal tabled by a number of nonaligned countries for a rolling extension of twenty-five years, which would require a negative vote at the end of the rollover period to prevent yet another rollover (henceforth, this alternative will be referred to as a red-light rolling extension).[49]

The proposal that did not make it through to the end of the conference was South Africa's green-light rolling extension proposal, which did not survive the domestic political process but which South Africa pursued until late in the process.

If we are to engage the idea of why the NPT was extended indefinitely, we need to critically explore the alternatives. This is especially true if we want to assess whether the fairness of the deal underlying indefinite extension was what drove countries to accept it.

Red-Light Rolling Extension

The red-light rolling extension is also known as the Bunn–Van Doren extension, named after the American lawyers who discussed it in the twin working papers published in the early 1990s (though this name is somewhat unfair, because George Bunn and Charles N. Van Doren argue that although this option is consistent with the treaty, they do not advocate it).[50] This option stems from the wording of Article X.2. Since that article states that extension for "an additional fixed period or periods" was a valid option, the question arose as to how this option could emerge. Bunn and Van Doren's starting point was that if the NPT were to be extended for additional fixed periods, there would have to be some sort of a rollover mechanism between periods. In the absence of such a mechanism, there would be no difference between an extension for a single period and an extension for successive periods. Using their own example, in the absence of a rollover mechanism, what difference does it make if the treaty is extended for seventy-five years or for three periods of twenty-five years each?

Bunn and Van Doren's argument drew on the treaty's negotiating history, outlined above, particularly the US engagement with the Italian proposals for Article X. In line with the Italian demands, and given that this issue was not discussed during the NPT negotiations in Geneva, Bunn and Van Doren argued that the extension for "additional fixed periods" could refer to an automatic rollover of the treaty unless a majority of the state parties at the end of each fixed period prevented that rollover from happening.

The proposed resolution was submitted by the group of nonaligned states at the 1995 NPTREC. Paragraph 1 reads:

> At the end of each fixed period a review and extension conference shall be convened to conduct an effective and comprehensive review of the operation of the Treaty. The Treaty shall be extended for the next fixed period of twenty-five years unless the majority of the parties to the Treaty decide otherwise at the review and extension conference.[51]

Yet this proposal did not gather any broader support, as the NAM opposition to indefinite extension collapsed with South Africa's decision to support it, as will be discussed in chapter 4. While Indonesia tried to rally support for the proposal during the NAM summit in Bandung during April 25–27, 1995, the NAM failed to support the Indonesian proposal and left members free to choose any option. That decision served as a death sentence for the Indonesian proposal.[52]

Green-Light Rolling Extension

The option that did not survive the preparatory process leading up to the 1995 NPTREC was the green-light rolling extension. This option is a reverse solution to the red-light rolling extension: whereas the latter required a *negative* vote to *prevent* an automatic rollover, the green-light rolling extension would require a *positive* vote to *allow* a rollover to the next fixed period.

The South African diplomats came up with the green-light rolling extension proposal in response to the Nigerian request during an earlier conference to prepare a legal overview of options related to the treaty's extension.[53] South Africa presented this proposal at the fourth preparatory committee (PrepCom), an extraordinary session held ahead of the 1995 NPTREC in late January 1995. The South Africans believed that the idea of a green-light rolling extension was most in line with that of a continuous review of the conference, articulated in Article VIII.3 of the treaty. This article mandated review conferences every five years "with the . . . objective of reviewing the operation of the Treaty." The South African position was that if the rolling extension was to be truly consistent with the idea of review, then a positive vote was necessary to roll the treaty over to the next period.[54]

It became obvious that, for the South African diplomats, the future review conferences were the suitable setting for further extensions of the treaty.[55] However, the treaty itself does not permit more than one extension conference. Bunn and Van Doren, as a solution to this problem, suggested a route via the UN General Assembly,[56] but the South African proposal did not entertain this suggestion.

The diplomatic process leading to the formulation and advocacy of this option is described in more depth in chapter 4. At this moment, suffice it to say that South African diplomats floated this idea at the fourth PrepCom, but never publicly presented it as their own preference. South African diplomats considered that if this option were to be adopted, the length of the periods would be a useful negotiating chip, and that a period of fifteen years could have been agreed upon.

While South African diplomats developed elaborate legal arguments in favor of this option, the option was killed by Vice President Thabo Mbeki at the end of the internal bureaucratic process, in favor of indefinite extension. This development is also discussed in chapter 4.

Extension with Strings Attached

The idea of an extension with strings attached was a particular articulation of a political idea that was difficult to implement given the legal constraints. For some time, Mexican representative Miguel Marin-Bosch had wanted to extend the treaty while also holding the five nuclear-weapon states' feet to the fire, especially in relation to their commitments toward nuclear disarmament, a comprehensive test ban, fissile materials cutoff, and negative security assurances.[57]

The problem with the idea of "holding feet to the fire" was that this solution was difficult to implement within the constraints of the treaty. The NPT does not permit adding additional provisions and demands without triggering the amendment procedures, articulated in Article VIII.1 and Article VIII.2.[58] These procedures are excessively onerous: they require a vote in favor as well as ratification by a majority of all state parties to the treaty, including all nuclear-weapon states and all parties that are members of the IAEA Board of Governors. That would basically make any amendment hostage to the ratification process in every single nuclear-weapon state.

This high threshold makes it almost impossible to pass any amendment.[59] Therefore, Marin-Bosch had to come up with an alternative to the conditional extension that would be, quite likely, his preferred option. The Mexican resolution, with strings attached, was that solution. The Mexican solution contained a list of steps to be undertaken, but without denoting them as legal conditions.

Seen by the supporters of indefinite extension, the Mexican resolution simply created too much uncertainty and also suggested conditionality.[60] This was less of a legal problem (though an argument had been raised that it could have become a problem at a later point), and more of a political problem. It was clearly not seen as a good solution.

Fair Solution?

The above discussion on the different options is offered not merely to indulge in history, but rather to provoke another question relevant for international relations theorists: Was the indefinite extension in 1995, adopted with the simple extension, driven by the notions of fairness and justice, as has been argued by earlier scholars?[61] One can easily see that Decision 3, pronouncing a simple indefinite extension (after all, the extension resolution contains a single line) along with Decisions 1 and 2 adopted simultaneously, was "minimally just." However, it is not impossible to argue that the other solutions—whether the green-light or red-light rolling extension—were at least equally fair, if not fairer. The green-light solution proposed by South Africa could arguably provide better and more long-term assurance of the guarantee of the different rights and commitments included in the treaty. The red-light rolling extension would do a similarly suitable job, with the added benefit of assuring future continuation of the NPT (but without giving the nuclear-weapons-states a free pass on their commitments).[62]

The decision adopted in 1995 is therefore "minimally fair" and as such its fairness cannot account for why it was adopted; there must be a different reason why this option was chosen. On this point, this book argues that the reason was because the US was able to convince the most salient members of the global diplomatic network to make it happen.

US Interest in the NPT's Indefinite Extension

"Throughout the nuclear age—this applies to later periods, too—most of the ordering ideas, and most of the desire and power to realize those ideas, came from the United States," wrote the British historian William Walker in 2000.[63] The US's interest in the NPT differentiated it the from the Soviet Union in that the US pursued nonproliferation as a serious security goal. The US was an early champion of the NPT and actively pressured its allies to sign the treaty.[64] US leadership on nonproliferation was not limited only to the NPT—it has been critical for the success of other nonproliferation cooperative initiatives as well.[65] For the US, the treaty provided an opportunity to legitimize pressure on its allies to give up their nuclear weapons aspirations (or refrain from those aspirations altogether), which was an effective way of both stemming the spread of nuclear weapons and maintaining a security edge within the alliance. Over time, the NPT and the institutional framework that arose around it became a suitable tool to confront and justify states pursuing nuclear programs. Nuclear nonproliferation became a leading foreign policy goal, one that was articulated in successive National Security Strategy reports. The pursuit of nuclear weapons became a leading "sin" of the so-called "rogue states."[66] Having a broad, internationally accepted legal norm against nuclear proliferation helped the US to justify, in the eyes of the international community, any coercive strategies against the violators of nuclear norms.[67] The continuation of the treaty was, therefore, in the US national interest.

The early process in favor of indefinite extension began in 1991, under the administration of George H. W. Bush. During this stage, however, the focus was mainly on the bureaucratic process, which was led by the ACDA. After Clinton entered into office, the process continued to be led by the ACDA, mainly as a diplomatic effort. Ambassador Thomas Graham, Jr., became the ACDA's point man tasked with indefinite extension.

The Clinton administration was more than just superficially supportive of the goal of nuclear nonproliferation. This pursuit was an important part of the fight against the alleged rogue states, one of the leading goals of the

Clinton administration.[68] Already in the first year of the administration, the National Security Council (NSC) staff prepared the Presidential Decision Directive 13 (PDD-13). This document was meant to be an articulation of the administration's nonproliferation and arms control policy. It posited that multilateral instruments, such as the NPT, should be the primary means of achieving the US's nonproliferation goals.[69] The same day the PDD-13 was released, Clinton gave his first speech to the UNGA as president. In his speech, he argued:

> I have made nonproliferation one of our Nation's highest priorities. We intend to weave it more deeply into the fabric of all of our relationships with the world's nations and institutions. We seek to build a world of increasing pressures for nonproliferation but increasingly open trade and technology for those states that live by accepted international rules.[70]

Indefinite extension of the NPT thus became an important policy objective. Furthermore, Clinton's vice president was Al Gore, who, according to one of his biographies, was "a prophetic voice on issues like . . . arms control."[71] Another biography labeled nuclear arms control as Gore's "proprietary issue."[72] From his early days in Congress, Gore decided to specialize in nuclear arms control. As a junior congressman, he followed a thirteen-week-long course of eight-hour weekly sessions on arms control, devised by his staffer Leon Fuerth (who went on to be Gore's national security adviser in the White House).[73] He became a passionate thinker about nuclear strategy: American journalist Robert Zelnick in his biography of Al Gore mentions that Gore questioned the wisdom of "nuclear theology." He cared deeply about nuclear arms control, and in his discussions would at times outshine other decision makers around the table. It is therefore not surprising that he became the administration's point man in developing numerous nuclear policies. This included working on nuclear disarmament in Ukraine and Kazakhstan (where nuclear weapons remained after the collapse of the USSR). However, it also included outreach activities ahead of the 1995 NPTREC, including outreach to South Africa and Egypt, and the delivery of the US's statement at the NPTREC itself.

By late 1994, the achievement of indefinite extension appeared more and more difficult, and the price to be exacted was increasing. Beyond the conclusion of the CTBT negotiations, however, issues related to negative security assurances, fissile material cutoff, and other topics were arising as potential conditions for extension. Clinton's administration supported these goals: the president supported the comprehensive test ban and the fissile material cut-off.[74] The moratorium on nuclear testing already applied in the US. Established through a congressional bill in the fiscal year of 1993, it was adopted by Clinton and included the goal to permanently ban all testing till 1996.[75] However, domestically, testing was a sensitive issue, and the directors of the US nuclear weapons labs—and the Republican Party—had been skeptical about the ban.[76] The administration's long-term policy was uncertain. In December 1994, McGeorge Bundy, national security adviser under both Kennedy and Johnson, wrote a long letter to Clinton, advocating foregoing nuclear testing in the US for good. "I know of no issue where a strong presidential stand is more likely to bring support at home and abroad. The American President has been the accepted leader against nuclear danger throughout the last fifty years—except when he has chosen not to play that role," Bundy wrote in the opening paragraph of his letter.[77] In his letter, Bundy explicitly tied the progress on CTBT to indefinite extension of the NPT. He also stated that he was in stark opposition to the position of National Security Advisor Anthony Lake, who advocated a more flexible position to appease the Pentagon and the nuclear establishment.[78]

ACDA's director John Holum sent Clinton a memo in December 1994, arguing that "in 1995 we face a crescendo in arms control activity—literally the biggest arms control agenda in history."[79] In addition to the NPT's extension, Holum mentioned the implementation of START and the ratification of START II as well as the Chemical Weapons Convention, ABM demarcation talks, CTBT and FMCT talks, and implementation of the treaty on Conventional Armed Forces in Europe (CFE).[80] He strongly encouraged Clinton to deliver an address on arms control, to breathe fresh air into the fledgling efforts to save the NPT's indefinite extension, but also to give attention to CTBT and START II. In January 1995, in a memorandum to President Clinton attached to Holum's letter, National Security Advisor Anthony Lake wrote that "we have no higher national security objective in 1995 than achieving the indefinite and unconditional extension of the NPT."[81]

In addition to making a statement, Holum encouraged Clinton to "seize the initiative on arms control," but also to make it clear in all presidential diplomacy how much the US cared about the NPT's extension. President Clinton's communication team also encouraged him to be active on this issue, because it was seen as bolstering the image of his decisive and proactive approach in the eyes of his domestic audience. The communications team thought that these topics not only would be politically unifying at home, but would also spur new (and supportive) academic debates.[82] The message that Clinton's team wanted him to articulate when it came to arms control was twofold:

> President Clinton is making Americans safer.
> Americans sleep better at night because President Clinton has kept his promise to reduce the threat of nuclear weapons. He is leading the world in efforts to stop the spread of weapons of mass destruction.[83]

Clinton also received letters supporting his leadership on the issue of nuclear nonproliferation from David Rockefeller and members of Congress, which helped pressure him into being more active on this issue.[84] In late February 1995, the White House communications staff prepared an elaborate schedule of numerous media opportunities, interviews, and messages to be undertaken in support of the NPT's indefinite extension.[85] The key element of the process was the big speech Clinton was meant to deliver to seize the debate. The NSC drafted the speech, which Clinton delivered at the Nixon Center on March 1, 1995. In this speech, he called for the indefinite extension of the NPT but also for ratification of START and other arms control measures.[86]

While the administration supported arms control steps, there was a reluctance to commit too much. In mid-February, the communications team met with the policy team and agreed to limit the number of initiatives undertaken by Clinton on arms control, and to focus the time with media on this issue.[87] To minimize the costs involved in the extension (for both the president and the US), the White House became involved, and the effort to extend the NPT became a "whole-of-government" approach. This approach led to the involvement of other federal departments as well as the White House itself. On February 8, 1995, a protocol was put in place in which weekly secure video calls were to be organized, co-chaired by ACDA's deputy director Ralph

Earle and Daniel Poneman, senior director for Nonproliferation and Export Controls at the NSC.[88]

Although the US tried to involve other NPT-recognized nuclear-weapon states in the rallying of support for extension, not all of them came on board. As will be discussed in chapter 3, the cooperation with France and the UK—as well as with other European countries—was quite fruitful. However, Russia was, at that time, reeling from the collapse of the Soviet Union and had very few allies to rally or influence. The Russian government could hardly exercise its effort in "its" UN regional group, since the Eastern European countries were rather reluctant to listen to Russian lobbying shortly after their respective liberations from the Soviet Union. The Chinese government was uncommitted to the indefinite extension throughout the process, and in fact shortly before the start of the NPTREC decided not to back indefinite extension but rather to be open to a red-light rolling extension (provided that the periods would be long enough).[89]

It is therefore undeniable that the US cared deeply about indefinite extension. It is also clear that indefinite extension was an unlikely prospect, and, what's more, without a vote, all but impossible. Explaining how the NPT was extended indefinitely without a vote is therefore also an important discussion of how the US utilizes its various forms of power in global governance.

2

Networked Power

THE CHIEF PUZZLE of the NPT's indefinite extension is explaining its success, knowing that only a minority of countries favored that solution. As the reader will recall, my explanation for the indefinite extension lies in the US's unique power to rally support among its partners who were uniquely well-positioned in the international system to bring other actors on board.

This argument differs from the usual accounts of great powers in international institutions. Often, power in these entities is exercised through voting. The starting point for the institutionalist school of international relations, however, is for states to establish international regimes to resolve *collective action* problems.[1]

Collective action problems may arise when states derive individual profit from noncompliance with agreements that otherwise bring about community benefit. Think about air pollution: the world would be better off if the amount of pollution decreased, but states can derive meaningful benefits (such as additional economic output, or savings on investment in ecological technology) from polluting more—therefore not complying with the rules. The nonproliferation of nuclear weapons encapsulates, similarly, a collective action problem: the world would be better off with strict control, yet states also derive meaningful benefits (economic gains from trade, political and security gains from helping friends and allies, or savings on investment in export control) from the proliferation of nuclear technologies.[2]

International institutions can persuade states to commit to carry out (or not carry out) certain practices, often in a legally binding way with some sort of monitoring. Because institutions thus bind states, great powers seek to exert some extraordinary level of control or say over institutional decision-making. Such control prevents a small minority of states from making decisions that might be contrary to the interests of great powers.[3] For this reason, the five leading powers in the United Nations Security Council (UNSC) possess veto power in the UN's only organ able to deliver legally binding decisions; Germany and France hold higher voting power within the European Council (the EU's organ representing states and able to make ultimate decisions), and the US holds more power than, say, Indonesia, in the International Monetary Fund. The unequal power of states within international organizations is often a paradigmatic example of how "informal" politics within the international politics is executed.[4]

The situation is, however, different when it comes to an international regime not only with no institutional differentiation, but with no voting as such. In some situations, the absence of voting can be understood as consensus decision-making requiring informal agreement of all participating parties.[5] Yet numerous international organizations seek a situation in which no party opposes a decision (they do not necessarily have to agree with it). The NPT regime is such a setting: traditionally, the NPT RevCons come to decisions by consensus, a practice that repeatedly has led to failure to produce outcome documents.

This situation, on paper, gives equal power to all states, although in practice this is not so. The most basic layer of inequality comes from the fact that countries are not able to devote the same amount of resources to the meetings of NPT RevCons. The result is vast inequality in the size of delegations countries send to the review conferences—it is not uncommon for the difference between a median delegation and the US delegation to be tenfold.[6] The evidence can often be observed in the meeting rooms: when the country delegates are seated, the empty desks speak volumes. Underrepresented countries are, by implication, less able to lobby for their own preferences or views. The NPT RevCons have, over time, become large and rather complex meetings, and countries sending only a handful of diplomats are naturally at a disadvantage to advance their interests in relevant committees and subsidiary bodies. If nations are unable to lobby for their preferences, or they face opposition, they might instead seek to block consensus. It is not difficult to imagine how a country with a modicum of regional status might be able to prevent consensus from materializing.[7] It is much more interesting, however, to uncover how a country is able to build a consensus and avoid having the negotiation break down, even in the face of opposition.

This book argues that the US is often able to advance its interests because it has an advantageous power position within global politics—not only materially and militarily, but principally in its connections to other actors in international politics. Its numerous connections to other powerful countries allow the US to leverage its network of allies to advance its goals. The US is able not only to build partnerships with other countries but also to leverage the connections of *US partners* to advance its preferences. This argument is not deterministic; a good strategic position enables the US to advance its foreign policy preferences if it chooses to do so.

Social Network Theory for Diplomacy

One way of thinking about the world of sovereign states is to think about it as a society. We know societies from our everyday life—our neighborhoods, towns, or even regions are examples of communities. The society of states is similar. Yet the fact that we live with our neighbors on one street does not necessarily mean we automatically live in harmony (if we did, NIMBYism would not be a thing). Similarly, thinking about the world of states as a society does not necessarily imply a harmony of interests.[8]

Think about the town where you live. Who are the people who "matter" in the town? Is that the mayor? Or perhaps the owners of the largest businesses in town? The pastor of a particularly big church congregation? Or perhaps the local football prodigy who made it in the big leagues? Similarly to any other society, in the society of states, power has different forms—it can be material power, economic power, normative power, or social power. Social power is often about juggling relationships across different subsections of the community: if you are, for example, a member of both the church choir and the local hiking club, chances are that you know a more diverse group of people than if you belonged to only one club. Within the academic discipline of international relations, the fact that states possess different forms of power is not a new finding.[9] However, what is novel in this book is leveraging our understanding of the social network power of states to explain political outcomes.

Social network theory can help us understand how powerful actors can leverage their diverse connections for policy outcomes in general. Advantageous positioning within a global network allows actors to leverage across different networks. Position within global networks does not necessarily determine outcomes, but it helps.

Sociologists have argued that the ability of actors to connect to others in the same network improves states' abilities to exercise control and influence over the whole network.[10] This ability stems from three features: the capacity to choose and activate different connections, the possibility to mobilize larger groups, and the potential to leverage one's own connections. Actors can choose *communities* in which to build relationships; states build connections to other states.[11] In the future, they can activate these relationships to advance their goals. Thinking about diplomacy as a networked activity unveils the nature of diplomatic practice as conceived by practitioners. If diplomats want to achieve a goal, they seek to build relationships with other actors.[12] Such communities enable the exchange of information and decrease the cost of organizing action. The emergence of (tightly) cooperating communities is a central concept in the study of political networks.[13]

Being a member of a diverse set of communities also has additional benefits. Networks help identify, stimulate, nurture, but also exploit overlaps in existing sets of preferences. Scholars have long considered an overlap in international organization membership as an indication of the similarity of two states' geopolitical preferences. The logic of this view is simple: as states join international organizations to achieve certain goals, the more similar their patterns of membership, the more overlap in their goals.[14] Furthermore, the more intensive contacts between states, the higher opportunities for side payments in the bargain—compensating states for concessions in other areas (this feature will be discussed further below).[15]

The argument is built on the centrality of actors in social networks.[16] In mathematical language, centrality in social networks is estimated based on the number of direct connections (shortest paths) to other nodes within the network (betweenness centrality), and also on how many direct connections (shortest paths) these other nodes have (eigenvector centrality).[17] In simple language: how well an actor (a node) connects to other actors is as important as how many connections (ties, in the language of social network theory) an actor has. Centrality—how central an actor is in a network—is another important concept of network theory.[18]

Network power is, however, different from the power exercised by "pivotal states," as recently advanced in the work of Marina Henke in her study of military coalitions.[19] Henke's argument looks at the different forms of power of the pivotal states, such as how many actors they know and how well they can compensate them. However, the present argument approaches the social network aspect more centrally by looking at the ability of a state to leverage *their networks' networks*. In other words, it takes the social network logic one step further in analyzing multilateral politics and actually takes the *social* aspect more seriously.

Again, an analogy helps here: in a town, a person who is a member of a tennis club, a wine club, and the school board has higher centrality in the town's social network than a monk who sings in a large choir. Why? Because our local socialite can draw on a broad set of connections by connecting friends from her sommelier club to those on the school board. If the school board or the tennis club wants to organize a year-end party, she can seek a discount for the wine to be served. And perhaps it will be, just by accident, naturally, her favorite sauvignon blanc. By bringing together different communities that are not otherwise connected, the socialite increases her value (social capital) in the eyes of all groups and enjoys high centrality in the town's social network through her brokerage skills.

Actors with high centrality are better able to influence policy outcomes. Scholars of international political economy recently argued that countries that are more centrally located within networks are more likely to influence outcomes of processes, because they are able to leverage their position to achieve their policy goals. Such a position is "fundamentally different from compellence power."[20] The ability to build relationships, advance the preferences, and use different networks helps well-connected actors be more effective in the advancement of their policy preferences and for inducing cooperation.[21] Such power may be related to material or military might, but its relevance stems from the power of the relationship rather than the potential to inflict material damage.

Centrality—knowing many actors and connecting many actors—matters. Actors who know many actors but connect few are less able to advance their cause or find partners for their initiatives. On the other hand, knowing and connecting many actors may help offset other, often structural, shortcomings. In the subsequent parts of this chapter, I will discuss the symbiosis between the US and other actors in the network, and also why the US was ideally suited to play the role of the leader.

Symbiosis

The relationship between the US and other countries in its network in favor of indefinite extension of the NPT was symbiotic. As much as the US benefited from the network, the network benefited from the US.

Within the diplomatic network of proponents of the NPT's indefinite extension, the US was the leader—which does not mean that it issued commands and others somehow obeyed. As networks are often formally non-hierarchical,[22] cooperation of (nominally) equal partners is a traditional part of any political network. This does not, however, necessarily translate into the absence of leadership.

In any political network, actors may agree on the goal, but their preferences may not overlap fully. Having a leader in the network is therefore helpful and brings about more successful outcomes.[23] In her study, Mette Eilstrup-Sangiovanni compares small networks of minor actors who are nonetheless successful in achieving their goals with larger networks of more powerful actors who are less committed and less successful in their efforts. As she argues, the key to the success of political networks is "facilitative leadership."[24] Facilitative leaders are, according to her, those who have trust in other actors in the network; but also, importantly, they have a high degree of structural relationships with other actors. In this setting, a structural relationship means membership in the same networks—thus, knowing and connecting many actors.

In 1995, the US was in a unique position when it came to structural relationships with other states in the world. There is no doubt that the US strategy benefited from cooperation with other policy actors or that the US leveraged its position in global diplomatic networks. However, it also benefited the group as such, by providing leadership to the effort to advance the goal of indefinite extension. Eilstrup-Sangiovanni identifies five tasks of leaders relevant here: "bringing stakeholders to the table, problem definition . . . , identifying opportunities for mutual gain, integrating the resources . . . to create synergy, [and] helping resolve conflicts."[25] The US position in this case was crucial for its ability to provide side payments and compensate other actors for their steps.

The three subsequent chapters in this book discuss at great length how the US brought stakeholders on board with the idea of indefinite extension, or at least with dropping their opposition to such extension. Where the US could not reach actors alone, it worked with other actors who could, leveraging its connections' connections. The US also provided leadership on problem definition and identification of opportunities for mutual gain by acting—in a group of disunited allies—as an entrepreneur and a provider of ideas for advancing a policy agenda. As will be shown in the chapters on the interactions with South Africa and Egypt, the creation of larger synergies and conflict resolution was key to US engagement. All in all, the relationship between the US and the network of proponents of indefinite extension was mutually symbiotic.

Structural Position of the US in the 1990s

Having explained why the social network position of states matters, and how network leadership is a symbiotic task, it remains to be explained why the US was in such a good position to advance the cause of indefinite extension.

Earlier in this chapter, I sidestepped somewhat on the discussion about what constitutes a tie. A tie is a basic connection between two actors, or nodes. In real life, a tie might be a Facebook or Instagram connection, or membership in the same choir. Within the field of international relations, scholars have conceptualized the idea of a tie in different ways: as diplomatic relations or economic ties between countries, or as membership in alliances or in international organizations.[26] The stricter the conceptualization, the further away from reality the tie risks becoming.

In the reality of international relations, ties between countries are fungible. States can exchange benefits from cooperation in one area for cooperation in another area—that is the principle of what international relations scholars refer to as package deals or side payments.[27] This gives states—particularly those with better network positions—an opportunity to tailor different forms of power (whether military alliances, trade, or other forms) in order to offer

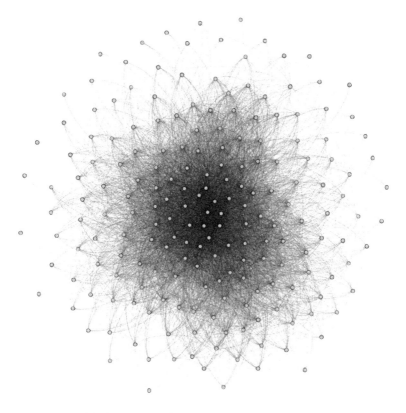

FIGURE 2   Global diplomatic network in 1995

diffuse side payments to other parties, make promises about future relationships, or draw on a shared understanding of multilateral issues.

We may therefore look broadly at how states build ties. In the following
sections, I look at how the global diplomatic, trade, and military network
looked in the mid-1990s.

Diplomatic Networks

Diplomatic ties or networks capture diplomatic relations between states:
whether State A has an embassy in State B, for example. Having such a presence in another country is a diplomatic factor in building a bilateral diplomatic
relationship between countries. Diplomatic missions help convey information
but also inject a deeper meaning into relations between states.[28] The better the
relation between countries, the better the chances for their cooperation.

Figure 2 shows the network of diplomatic connections in 1995.[29] In the center of the figure we see a group of countries—mainly the Western countries and Russia, which at that time dominated the global diplomatic network. The US had, in 1995, the broadest network of embassies, with 166 missions abroad. France had the second-highest number, with 153 missions; China was third, with 150 missions; Germany was fourth, with 149; and the UK was fifth, with 144 missions. The US also had the highest betweenness centrality in the diplomatic network, connecting actors who otherwise would not be connected; with the UK and France occupying second and third place, respectively. In terms of the diplomatic network, the US was arguably the best-connected actor and was teamed up with other well-connected actors. In terms of eigenvector centrality—measuring the connections' connections—it was third in the world, behind Germany and France (this is not entirely surprising, given that the vast US diplomatic network extends even to actors who are not themselves so well connected).

The centrality of the diplomatic network allowed the US to lobby in favor of the NPT's indefinite extension. No other country, and certainly no opponent of indefinite extension, had a comparable diplomatic network. As I will illustrate in chapter 4, the US connection with South Africa—which enjoyed broad diplomatic support on its home continent—helped advance the cause of indefinite extension among African countries.

Trade Networks

A tie can also be thought of as trade between countries, whether it causes peace or vice versa. The relationship between trade and a cooperative relationship is firmly established in international relations scholarship.[30] Social theorists dating back to the seventeenth century have theorized about the pacifying effect of trade.[31] In the mid-last century, Karl Deutsch argued that trade between countries helps build trust among partners.[32]

Figure 3 shows the trade network in 1995.[33] A tie between countries resembles trade in excess of US$5 million per year (anything smaller, and the figure would be rendered unreadable). Thicker lines denote more active relationships: the thicker the line, the more bilateral trade between the two countries. In this figure as well, we see that the US is by far the most central actor: its trade ties with other countries are nearly 1.5 times stronger when compared to number two (Germany) and almost twice as strong as those of

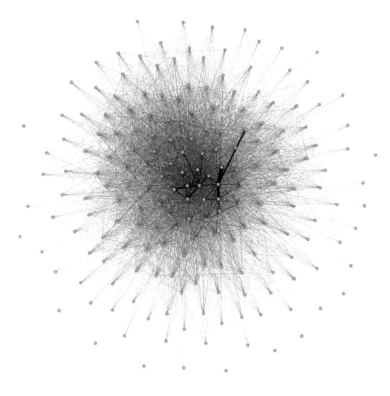

FIGURE 3   Global trade network in 1995

number three (Japan). The US also had the highest betweenness centrality in the global trade network at the time and dominated the global trade network in mid-1990. It was the largest trading partner, trading with the largest number of countries, and was therefore able to use and leverage the trade relationship to achieve goals in other areas.

It leveraged, for example, the EU trade network in the EU neighborhood. As will be demonstrated in the next chapter, the cause of indefinite extension benefited enormously from the desire of many countries in Central and Eastern Europe as well as in Central Asia for closer economic cooperation with the EU.

Alliance Networks

Finally, we can look at alliance commitments as ties between countries. Generally speaking, similarity in such commitments is also understood to mean

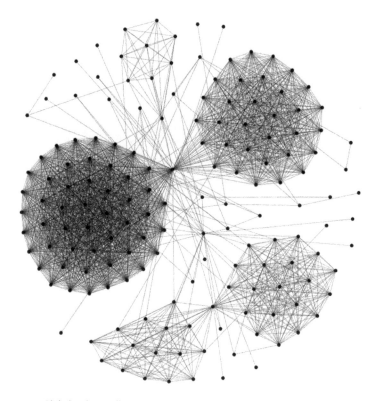

FIGURE 4   Global military alliance networks in 1994

a similarity in foreign policy preferences.[34] Allies that commit to defend and
assist one another militarily are also expressing a political commitment. Particularly in a sensitive area like nuclear politics, it is not unreasonable to think
that allies would consider each other's military interests when calibrating their
foreign policy. Furthermore, military alliances create ample opportunities to
provide side payments to allies, in exchange for political or other favors.[35]

Figure 4 shows the military alliances in 1994, one year before the NPT
Review and Extension Conference. A tie between two countries denotes a
mutual alliance commitment. In this period, the US had the highest number
of military alliance commitments among all the countries in the world,[36] with
military ties with 91 countries. The second-highest number of allies was pos-
sessed by Russia, followed by France. The US also dominated the network in
terms of being able to bridge different alliances and connect different states.

In that period, no other state had such a diverse portfolio of allies. Its military alliance with Egypt, for example, gave the US a unique ability to sway a bloc of Arab countries, as will be discussed in chapter 5.

How Does It Matter?

The fact that the US was in a structurally advantageous position in the relevant networks aided in its pursuit of its nonproliferation goals. Consider the opponents of the US, such as the countries that tabled alternative proposals discussed in chapter 1. These countries might have had the interest and necessary expertise to influence policy, but they lacked a community. The nonaligned countries talked to one another almost exclusively and seldom cooperated with other countries within the nonproliferation regime (using the terminology of social network theory, their "betweenness centrality" was extremely low).[37] Countries such as Japan or Germany have a large number of platforms to use, but compared to the US, they lack some important bilateral relationships. Therefore, the high centrality in the relevant global networks— whether diplomatic, trade, or alliances—gave the US a number of ways to build relationships with other states.

It was this centrality that made the US successful. It was able to work with Western countries that were similarly well-connected and shared the goal of indefinite extension. By doing so, it benefited from the EU's ability to leverage the power of its markets and polity in the postcommunist space in Eastern Europe and Central Asia.[38] By directly engaging South Africa, the US could engage (some) nonaligned countries and was able to prevent the formation of a unified front within the nonproliferation regime. Last but not least, the US also benefited from its ability to negotiate directly with Egypt as a leader of the Arab Group at the UN. It could therefore ensure that whatever agreements were reached would be followed by the remaining members of the Arab Group. No other country had the wherewithal to engage the global network of states in a similar fashion.

"Friends with Benefits"
US-European Cooperation

THE INITIAL TWENTY-FIVE-YEAR DURATION of the NPT was built into the treaty mainly to placate the US's European allies. Yet when the time came twenty-five years later, those were among the strongest supporters of the treaty's indefinite extension. The US enjoyed a number of diverse options for building and sustaining ties with the European countries, which all proved helpful for the pursuit of the goal of indefinite extension. Cooperation happened within the framework of the Western European and Others Group (WEOG) of the UN General Assembly. According to its historical roots, the NPT regime functions along UN regional groupings. Even today, three regional groups structure the cooperation: the Eastern European group, the Western European group, and the Non-Aligned group.

In 1995, the Eastern European group was in flux—while the group survived the collapse of the Soviet Empire at the end of the Cold War, its members were vying for close cooperation with Western European countries by seeking entry into NATO and into the EU.[1] They also became supportive of the NPT's indefinite extension. The Western European group of countries, by that time, was also supportive. Toward the end of the Cold War, Germany reversed its long-term policy and became a stronger supporter of nuclear nonproliferation.[2] France joined the NPT and became immediately one of the strongest supporters of nonproliferation norms.[3]

In January 1995, three new members joined the NPT—Sweden, Austria, and Finland. At least two of them, Sweden and Austria, have been traditional supporters of nuclear disarmament, and for these countries, the NPT's indefinite extension was as much about nuclear disarmament as it was about nuclear nonproliferation (being members of the Vienna Group of Ten informal group).[4] Sweden had good relations with the nonaligned countries, due to its Cold War support for liberation movements, whereas Austria was active in the Balkans and Eastern Europe. Through their active diplomacy at the UN, all three countries were important actors in the EU's lobbying efforts. Having three neutral countries in its midst magnified the EU's diplomatic reach but also created a sudden need to balance nonproliferation and disarmament goals. Whereas nonproliferation focused on prevention of the spread of nuclear weapons, disarmament focused on ridding the world of the existing ones. And while the EU had historically been active on the former, prior to the joining by the three neutrals, it had paid only limited attention to the latter.

Cooperation with European countries was important for the US not only because it delivered three dozen votes in favor from Europe; it was even more crucial because the EU's diplomatic network and strong economic ties meant magnifying the US lobbying reach on behalf of indefinite extension. For most European countries, indefinite extension was the preferred course of action. Teaming up with the European countries also provided the US an opportunity for an innovative cooperative activity within the EU using Joint Action, which at that time were novel diplomatic instruments.

This chapter will provide two key takeaways. First, the adoption of the indefinite extension without a vote was not an expected outcome. Not only did the European (and US) diplomats expect a vote, they were not even sure they would win such a vote. Therefore, cooperation with the EU was important for the US—it signified a potential increase in the number of parties in the meeting who could cast their vote in favor of the extension as well as a resulting momentum toward the resolution in favor. Broad support ultimately persuaded parties to acquiesce to the indefinite extension without a vote.

The second takeaway is that the European and US diplomats did not discuss potential concessions, underlining how the document on Principles and Objectives emerged right from the conference (rather than being a result of long-term negotiations). In this chapter, I will argue that the EU's support for the extension was crucial. The US benefited from numerous diplomatic platforms to build cooperation with the Europeans; and the Europeans, in turn, exercised even further influence. The EU at the time consisted almost exclusively of NATO members (before the 1995 enlargement, all EU members except Ireland were NATO members). Therefore, when NATO endorsed the goal of indefinite extension at the Gleneagles meeting of the Nuclear Planning Group in October 1992, it was easy for the members to use their various platforms to advance these goals.[5] These platforms included the Conference on Security and Cooperation in Europe (CSCE)[6] and the G-7 meeting,[7] but chiefly the WEOG at the UN and the EU.

US-European Coordination

At the outset, the US coordinated its actions with the other two treaty depositaries—the UK and the Soviet Union (later, Russia). During the first coordination meeting, the Soviets presented a paper in which they argued that only 30–35 NPT members were in favor of indefinite extension.[8] This number caused unease among the two other depositaries, who came up with three steps to promote an extension of the NPT without a limit: first, to start a campaign to highlight the benefits of the treaty, and second, to raise the issue of the NPT with the heads of states and governments during bilateral meetings. The third step agreed upon was to create an informal group, which was meant to mobilize supporters of the treaty.

The first meeting of this new group occurred in June 1992, at the sidelines of the meeting of the IAEA Board of Governors,[9] followed by the next meeting in July 1992.[10] During these meetings, the US discussed the promotion of the NPT's indefinite extension broadly with countries from across the globe. One key takeaway from the process was the need to "identify and analyze" substantive and procedural issues. Multilateral coordination was crucial.

The early meetings among the depositaries also highlighted the double-edged sword of the growing membership in the treaty: on the one hand, increasing the global nature of the treaty was positive and highlighted that the treaty served its members' goals; on the other hand, it meant that the number of parties that must be persuaded to pass an extension was also increasing.[11]

While the rest of this chapter focuses on US cooperation with European allies, one must also note that Russia was supportive of the goal of indefinite extension. Russian cooperation with the US in support of the NPT dates back to the treaty's initial negotiation and continues throughout the Cold War period well into the 1990s.[12] Yet Russian power and ability to influence other actors was limited due to its failure to attract new, even regional, supporters.[13] According to Russian expert Vladimir Orlov, Russian contributions consisted mainly of suggestions for diplomatic strategy for the conference and proposals for how to frame the agenda.[14]

US coordination with its European allies began in February 1993. In a meeting during the session of the Conference on Disarmament, US and UK diplomats met with the wider Western group to prepare for the conference.[15] Only Iceland and Luxembourg did not participate. Following organizational questions, such as discussion of the conference officials and the rules of procedure, the UK's Foreign and Commonwealth Office (FCO)'s NPT coordinator Brian Donnelly shared during this meeting that "others" have not yet realized that the indefinite extension is the best course. The message shared with the rest of the group, on behalf of the depositaries, was that the "job for the Western group was to persuade those states that indefinite extension is in their best interest."[16] After this meeting, regular meetings of the Western group indicated that the group was continuing to meet and coordinate on NPT-related issues. The early meetings focused on topics such as the rules of procedure and conference leadership or venue—seemingly rather technical issues but which had the potential to affect how the conference was run.

However, already in April 1993, during a meeting of the Western group in Geneva, an Australian representative pointed out (and the US diplomats reported) that the existing approach was "not enough." There was a need for something more—a positive persuasive action, rather than horse trading.[17] After the first preparatory committee meeting in June 1993, the US diplomats reported back, among the piles of bureaucratic dossiers, a bit of worrying information: "Eastern Europeans do not, it appears, coordinate a single position on substantive issues."[18] This was not entirely surprising: recently liberated from forty years of Soviet domination, Eastern European countries were enjoying their newly won independence and were in no mood to listen to Russia, the most powerful regional power. At a time when the Eastern European group comprised a big part of the minority in favor of indefinite extension, the lack of coordination in the group must have been worrying. The 1993 PrepCom

also revealed the hardening nonaligned position as well as a flurry of proposals related to the process and outcome of the extension conference. While
the US was on the whole satisfied with the first PrepCom, the meeting also
highlighted the need to engage broadly in favor of the extension.[19]

While the initial group of states that the US liaised with was broad, only
the European countries had what the US sought—a commitment to indefinite
extension and the ability to persuade more actors in its favor. Without it being
explicitly formulated, European countries became leading partners of the US.

EU Action

This episode of cooperation among EU members on the NPT extension
was not the first occasion in which collaboration with Europe was crucial
to advance nonproliferation goals. During the Cold War, the European
Communities—the EU's predecessor—was crucial in bringing the European
countries to the London Club, later known as the Nuclear Suppliers Group
(NSG), by virtue of having a single market (also for nuclear fuel). However,
the EU also figured in larger, political questions: by 1991, the working paper
prepared by the Soviet Union for the meeting of the three depositaries suggested that "the [European Community] has provided a useful mechanism for
bringing France closer to the NPT."[20] The initial meeting that paved the way
for cooperation between the US and numerous European countries—those
in the WEOG but also bilaterally—took place within the framework of the
WEOG and started on February 5, 1993.[21]

While the US and European countries built their relationship on the
platform of the WEOG group, the US benefited from the fact that the European countries could use the muscle of the EU and its new instrument:
the new institutional framework of the Common Foreign and Security Policy
(CFSP), created on November 1, 1993, when the Maastricht Treaty entered
into force. This gave the EU more relevance and leeway compared to other
WEOG members such as Japan or Australia.[22]

While the European Political Co-operation (EPC) and other collabora-
tive measures have been ongoing since 1970, the EU's foreign policy did not
have a firm institutional grounding. The CFSP gave the EU the capacity to
issue "Joint Actions" as an instrument to spur European actorhood in foreign
policy.[23] The EU decided to use the power for the first time to issue a Joint

Action on a foreign policy issue with a view toward the 1995 NPT Review and Extension Conference. This process culminated under the German Presidency of the European Council, and the Council adopted Decision 94/509/CFSP on July 25, 1994.[24]

Germany was also formally in the driving seat of the process. The first suggestions to use a Joint Action were raised by the German delegation already during a meeting of the political directors of the EU member states in October 1993;[25] the first strong impetus for the Joint Action emerged after the second PrepCom, which took place in January 1994. During this conference, it emerged that while a substantive number of countries (though nowhere near a majority) were in favor of indefinite extension, alternatives existed: important non-Western countries, such as Venezuela, Mexico, or Nigeria, raised objections or alternatives to indefinite extension. It also became clear that there was no agreement about the rules of procedure. That led German diplomats, for example, to be cautiously optimistic while remaining concerned about how a decision could be made and whether enough support for indefinite extension could be mustered.[26] These questions were not purely legalistic but had the potential to throw the whole conference—and its consequences—into (legal) disarray. In a meeting on February 11, 1994, the EU troika (Belgium, Greece, and Germany, as holders of the past, current, and future presidency, respectively) met with representatives of Central and Eastern Europe. During this meeting, the two sides agreed that some of the nonaligned countries created an "atmosphere of bitterness" and that there was a need to neutralize the work of the "vocal radicals."[27] During this meeting, Germany raised the possibility of issuing an EU Joint Action to rally support for the NPT's indefinite extension.

The initial reaction to the German proposal from October 1993 was mixed. While Denmark, the Netherlands, and Ireland supported Germany's proposal; France, Spain, and the UK opposed the idea. The UK, in particular, feared that issuing a Joint Action could open a can of worms, which could lead to numerous sensitive issues.[28] Yet rejecting the idea out of hand seemed impossible, and therefore Germany was tasked with formulating concrete proposals for the Joint Action. Germany's Federal Foreign Office, therefore, created a list of suggestions:

» To issue a statement beyond the framework of European Political

Cooperation (not as a statement of the twelve EU members) in order to give the decision added political weight as being issued on behalf of the EU

» To lobby states that were not yet supportive of indefinite extension, in particular the nonaligned countries, and the conference's president-designate Jayantha Dhanapala

» To avoid unanswered and sensitive political issues within the NPT setting

» To lobby countries to join the NPT

» To intensify coordination with Central European countries.

For the German diplomats, however, the Joint Action's conclusion was not at all a foregone one. In particular, they feared that France and the UK might block the decision due to considerations related to the other nonproliferation issues: "it will be particularly important to exclude every link between action and other non-proliferation 'hot topics' (CTBT, 'cut-off')."[29] The reference to CTBT and fissile material cutoff was not accidental—those were the two topics that were strongly opposed by France and the UK, the two nuclear-weapon states within the EU at that time.

Yet discussions with the EU partners were positive, since a little over a week later the Working Party on Non-Proliferation endorsed the project of Joint Action.[30] The decision was led by the "conviction . . . that joint efforts have to be made to promote the goal among critical states party to the [NPT],"[31] the desire to increase the membership in the treaty, and by limiting the power of nonmembers. The decision of the working party highlighted the relevance of Central and Eastern European countries as well as the importance of working with the moderate NAM members. Germany's diplomats shared some of these goals with the Russian diplomats during bilateral talks just a few days afterward.[32] At the end of May, the draft Joint Action was circulated by the Greek Council presidency.[33] In a few days, all EU members endorsed the Joint Action, and Germany's foreign ministry started eying a political opportunity to gain support for the Joint Action at the European Council at Corfu.[34] Seen from Bonn, the goal was to receive a political impetus in Corfu, so that the drafting action could be done early in the German Presidency (which was to begin in July 1994), and then could be swiftly followed by the démarches to the countries that were to be targeted.[35]

At the end of June at the Heads of States meeting in Corfu, the participants adopted, almost word for word, the conclusions drawn from the note that had been circulated by the Greek Presidency in early June.[36] The conclusions stipulated that the EU's action should follow four main lines:

> » To demonstrate a consensus among the EU members in favor of indefinite and unconditional NPT extension
> » To engage in joint efforts to promote the desired goal among NPT members opposed to it
> » To persuade NPT nonmembers to join the Treaty (and help them to do so if need be)
> » To send démarches (on behalf of the EU) to promote participation in the two last Preparatory Committee meetings and in favor of the unlimited extension of the Treaty.

The working group picked up the task almost immediately. In a meeting two weeks later (on July 7, 1994) under the German Presidency, the working group started to develop the wording of the Council's decision. The meeting culminated in the initial draft of the document that ultimately became Decision 94/509/CFSP.

The meeting's minutes demonstrate that Germany, as the circulated by the Greek Council presidency, identified countries that should be targeted for the démarches. Rather than enumerating the list, the document specifies the criteria according to which such a list should be composed: countries that did not participate in one or both of the earlier PrepComs, countries in the Commonwealth of Independent States, and Central and Eastern European countries.[37]

The goal of such démarches was to encourage the recipient countries to participate in the upcoming PrepCom meetings. The guidelines for the démarches' content strongly advocate the EU's insistence on continued NPT status as the cornerstone of the nonproliferation regime, and the EU's objective of achieving indefinite and unconditional extension of the treaty. The first démarches were, if need be, to be followed up by second, more tailored, ones.

This strategy clearly shows that the Council working group was aware of the EU's power in its region and among many developing countries that did not attend earlier meetings. Although nothing in the documents demonstrates direct pressure, it is not hard to imagine that the EU's enormous market power (and political weight) allowed it to be heard in the target countries. As scholars noted later, the power of the EU's market allows it to exercise numerous pressures as "power through trade."[38]

The conclusions also demonstrate Germany's importance within the group. The agreements adopted by the working party are almost identical to those pushed by Germany since early 1994. There is almost no major point promoted by Germany that was not supported by the working party of the Council.

Once the Joint Action was published, the EU's diplomatic activity in the neighborhood intensified. The European countries expanded their engagement with countries that were not yet committed to indefinite extension, as well as with those that were not yet members of the treaty (except Israel).[39]

From the Third PrepCom Till New York

With the EU Joint Action issued, the US-European cooperation focused on the preparatory committee conferences. During the third PrepCom, in September 1994 in Geneva, things took a turn for the worse. A summary from the meeting prepared by German diplomat Dr. Gabriela Guellil opened with the words, "[t]he prospects for a successful Review and Extension Conference of the NPT in New York in spring 1995 have become recently much darker. A *consensus decision* . . . about the unlimited extension does not seem feasible."[40] Germany's point person identified a number of reasons for the lack of optimism: low participation by the states that were party to the treaty (only 89 out of 165 members), lack of progress on contentious dossiers (whether procedural—such as the conference's rules of procedure—or substantive), and the perceived obstructionism by some parties (especially Iran). All three developments were worrying for a European diplomat: if a consensus decision was seen as impossible (as Guellil estimated in her opening paragraph), then a vote would have to be taken. But low participation in the conference meant that even a low number of opponents could scuttle the vote, plus the rules for such vote were unclear.[41] This all meant a lot of uncertainty for the transatlantic goal of supporting indefinite extension.

Between the third and fourth PrepComs, the US and the EU also agreed to focus on the lobbying of key NAM countries (Indonesia, Mexico, Sri Lanka,

South Africa, Nigeria, and Egypt).[42] The EU continued in the action to issue démarches to countries that were not yet party to the treaty, with the focus on the Middle East (including Israel), former Soviet states, and smaller countries in Europe, Africa, and the Pacific, using the same arguments as those in the EU Joint Action.[43] In a telegram sent to all EU missions abroad in December 1994, the German Presidency judged all of the abovementioned NAM countries as critical toward the NPT's indefinite extension.[44] The EU also lobbied Iran, which was seen as a spoiler and a potential troublemaker by German as well as US diplomats.[45] In addition to Germany's lobbying activities (both independently and under the aegis of the Council presidency), France and the UK conducted their own lobby campaign as well.

Yet, after the fourth PrepCom in late January 1995, the meeting of the Western countries estimated that about 50–60 countries firmly supported indefinite extension, and an additional 25–35 countries were considering the idea.[46] The tally did not give much reason to be positive. The meeting between a small group of European countries and the US, Japan, and Australia at the end of January 1995 was also not positive. In this meeting, the US highlighted the need to avoid any unified NAM position. Participants, however, also agreed that there was a small chance for support from major NAM countries and relied on gaining support from smaller countries within the movement. The US was particularly skeptical about any positive developments occurring in the Middle East, as US representatives Thomas Graham Jr. and Robert Einhorn highlighted difficulties working with Israel and claimed that Egypt was demanding "too much."[47]

Further meetings concentrated mainly on the exchange of information about other countries' positions; between February 1995 and the conference in July, cooperation among the Western countries hovered mostly on the discussion about who lobbied whom and how, as well as on the exchange of the tallies of support for the treaty.[48] These assessments align with the views of the diplomats, who expressed later that the Western group was almost totally focused on lobbying tactics.[49]

During the meeting in February 1995, two clusters of countries were identified as concerns: states in broader Europe that were not yet committed to indefinite extension, and the countries in the Middle East. The former group included the former Soviet countries that were not yet members of the

NPT and also Switzerland.[50] In the latter group, Egypt's position was being highlighted but the European countries remarked on its shifting attitudes (and improving relations with Israel) among the Gulf countries as a potential reason to doubt whether Arab countries would block indefinite extension.[51]

One month later, again in Geneva (this time under Canadian leadership), the US arrived at the meeting with an argument that there was now a sufficient number of countries in favor of extension. Europeans were skeptical. According to the German diplomats' observations, France was particularly cautious about the US numbers and called for continued lobbying.[52] In addition to Egypt, the position of South Africa was discussed, as European diplomats posited that "twelve other states" would follow its decision.[53]

However, by and large, these meetings focused mainly on lobbying and tactics ahead of the conference. Major discussions involved decisions about the mechanics of the voting so that the treaty review—expected to be rather negative and unfavorable—would not endanger the treaty's extension. During the March 1995 meeting, a proposal was made to collect signatures in favor of indefinite extension ahead of the conference.[54] The suggestion, made by Russia,[55] was meant to make use of the positive momentum and aimed at rallying in favor of support for indefinite extension; the goal of having many supporters was to "defang" the opponents.[56] However, the proposal was not universally well received. While the US, UK, France, Russia, and Germany thought it responded to the need created by the growing time pressure; the opponents—including Italy, Belgium, the Netherlands, Australia, Japan, and Canada—thought it might provoke a counteraction by the NAM countries. This split was also present on other issues, including nuclear disarmament, on which Australia pushed the nuclear-weapon states to come up with a "credible" plan for the conference, and which Germany rejected. The disunity within the Western group, which started to emerge shortly before the conference, bothered some countries. "The existing momentum is being weakened through the disunity in the Western group," Wolfgang Hoffmann, the German ambassador to the Conference on Disarmament, wrote in his message to headquarters.[57]

Hoffmann was also worried about the fact that this disunity went beyond simple squabbles about tactics to reveal deep differences over disarmament obligations. A few days later, his US colleagues shared with him a plan for the upcoming weeks, which clearly spelled out that "[a] simple majority is what the Treaty requires and we need to be united on this point so that other countries understand our resolve."[58] The US wanted the Germans' help with lobbying other European governments that were originally skeptical of the signature campaign, and judged that

> [The focus on disarmament] seemed to us to be designed to create fissures between the close nuclear-weapon-states, including the US, and close NATO allies . . . All of us in NATO share nuclear risks and burdens—we are in this together. As an alliance. We cannot afford to suggest that there are divisions between the US and its allies on something as crucial as NPT.[59]

In a meeting with State Department officials, the Germans were told that the previous group meeting was "a failure" and that the US was concerned about the solidarity among its allies.[60] In order to foster a single line to be toed by the European countries, the US designed a number of speaking points that the Germans were asked to share with the various European governments. These highlighted that the "Europeans and North Americans [are] the strongest and largest group of countries supporting indefinite extension and the simple majority vote."[61] Brussels, The Hague, Oslo, Ottawa, and NATO headquarters were designated as points of attention; Canberra, Helsinki, Stockholm, and Tokyo were designated as the special points where additional démarches were to be delivered. Additionally, the US asked Germany to impress upon Indonesian president Suharto (who was due to visit Germany shortly afterward) that Indonesia did not want to be associated with the likes of Iran, and to persuade him of their certainty that a vote in favor of indefinite extension would be securely won.[62]

While the Germans were keen to play along with the US and eagerly supported the goal of indefinite extension, they did not completely buy into the pressure campaign led by the US. When US ambassador to NATO Robert Hunter sent a démarche to the German delegation to NATO in Brussels, and the delegation forwarded it to the headquarters, a senior German diplomat wrote on top by hand: "We do not share the concern the Americans expressed lately also with regard to the démarche."[63] And Germans were not alone in being skeptical about the US strategy. Asked about this initiative two decades later, the Australian representative in the group, Ambassador Richard Butler, said that the US strategy "[had] a kind of religious quality to it, 'decide for Christ,'" and that the meetings of the Western group where the strategy was being decided resembled "Tammany Hall" meetings.[64] Curiously, on the same day when Germans responded to the US démarche, the German Federal Foreign Office's official tally listed over 110 countries in favor of indefinite extension, but listed South Africa, discussed in a subsequent chapter, as a "leaning no." This mischaracterization (we know that South Africans by then adopted a position in favor of indefinite extension) speaks both to South Africa's ability to hold cards close to its chest and to the flimsiness of the German assessment.

The signature action was ultimately launched in New York only at the start of the conference. The collection of signatures received the initial push once South Africa made its statement in favor of indefinite extension (as discussed in the next section). Canada was entrusted with collecting the signatures, as a way to demonstrate its support,[65] and a sufficient number of signatures was achieved just a week shy of the end of the conference.[66] Cooperation with the Europeans also delivered one of the key coups in the attempt to split the NAM—in addition to South Africa, Benin also opposed the formation of a single NAM position. Benin was persuaded to stand up to the formation of the NAM's single position by France.[67]

Driving the cooperation with the European countries via the Western group (and not via the EU) meant that the US was able to benefit from the EU's power without being constrained by the bloc's internal disagreements. As European analysts observed, the European input into the decision-making at the conference was not *European* but rather national, made by individual European countries.[68] The lack of EU participation was also visible by the fact that it submitted only one working paper to the conference, compared to much more active participation during future conferences.[69] The divides that have always existed among the EU member states—for example, on the issue of nuclear disarmament, which prevented a more forceful presence of the EU at the conference—did not preclude the EU from rallying support for indefinite extension both ahead of and at the conference.[70]

Relevance of US Cooperation with the EU

Cooperation with the European countries allowed the US to tap into the EU's powerful relations in its environs. In the first half of the 1990s, the post-Soviet countries in Eastern Europe and Central Asia worked hard to build a closer relationship with the EU's enormous market.[71] The fact that the European countries advanced the same goal as the US using the new institutional tools of the EU helped the US enormously. The US recognized this fact: after the NPT was indefinitely extended, President Clinton wrote letters to leaders in Canada, France, the Netherlands, Russia, and the UK to thank them personally for their invaluable support in the process. In his letter to the UK, Clinton highlighted the role of the Western group (chaired by Ambassador Weston of the UK), and in his letter to Paris he highlighted the EU's efforts.[72]

However, the European countries did not exclusively bear the burden of lobbying in many of these countries. The US also helped to push countries that were outside the NPT to join. Ukraine is a good example. In 1992 and 1993, Ukraine's continuous possession of nuclear weapons that it had inherited from the Soviet Union—and its absence from the NPT—was seen as a factor that could complicate any sort of NPT extension.[73] While the negotiations about Ukraine's nuclear disarmament were trilateral, involving Russia and the US, the US used the possibility of trade and aid from Europe as a negotiating tactic, exploiting the fact that Ukrainians viewed themselves as Europeans.[74] Archival documents show that fear of economic ostracism imbued the Ukrainian government's thinking on this issue at the time.[75]

Cooperation between the US and Europe highlights the strength of network ties. Although the US and the European countries worked toward the same goal, it was the EU that was able to offer certain carrots to other countries. In a way, the US efforts were bolstered by the EU's heavy lifting in Europe and Central Asia. This chapter has also underlined the network logic in US advocacy at the time. No actor besides the EU enjoyed the strength of this type of cooperation with the US. While the US pursued the efforts within the WEOG or "core group" setting, the European countries were crucial for the success of these efforts. European countries had at their disposal not only a broad diplomatic network but also economic tools associated with the EU and the ability to talk to a number of actors, and they exploited the fungibility of these resources. By teaming up with the European countries, the US gained much better access to a broad set of countries.

Furthermore, the European countries helped mitigate the heavy-handed US approach, which focused on lobbying and pressure and rubbed many European countries the wrong way. European countries (except for the nuclear-weapon states) resisted it, most notably in their resistance to the signature-collection campaign—an incident that highlights that the European countries had not adopted all US proposals word for word, but instead relied on a degree of national autonomy. Most of the European countries favored indefinite extension of the NPT, and they used all of the tools at their disposal accomplish this. The US benefited strongly from the Europeans' eagerness to achieve this goal.

"Babes in the Woods"

South Africa and the Extension

BY THE 1995 NPT Review and Extension Conference, an extraordinary new member had joined the treaty: South Africa. Under the first democratically elected government, led by the iconic Nelson Mandela, the country had just dismantled its nuclear weapons program and was joining all relevant export control arrangements. The role South Africa played in the conference is widely seen as a major contribution toward the country's budding international status.[1]

Yet there was nothing automatic about South Africa's support for indefinite extension. In fact, as this chapter illustrates, South African diplomats strongly resisted it until shortly before the conference. While South Africa was on the receiving end of US political initiatives, so were seventy other countries. Furthermore, many of the arguments highlighting the role of the US tend to overlook the fact that South Africa was a new member of the NAM, which initially had strong reservations about the NPT and the prospect for indefinite extension. The African National Congress (ANC), the ruling party newly in power in South Africa, had historically strong relations with numerous NAM countries,[2] the leading NAM countries were opposed to indefinite extension. Indeed, less than a year before the extension conference, the ANC's main nuclear "hand," Abdul Minty, declared that the NPT "is a discriminatory treaty where the nuclear-weapon states have very little pressure on them to

get rid of their weapons . . . our efforts must, of course, go to make sure that
that does not continue to operate in such a discriminatory manner."[3]

In 1995, South Africa was in a globally unique position, in which it remains
until today, as the only country that developed nuclear weapons endogenously,
only to unilaterally disarm fifteen years later. The existence of South Africa's
nuclear weapon program was officially confirmed two years after its dismantlement was complete, on March 24, 1993.[4] According to former president
Frederik W. de Klerk, the apartheid regime in Pretoria took the formal decision to design and develop a clandestine nuclear deterrent capability in 1978.
Given that the country had advanced technological capabilities, and enjoyed
technological collaboration with Western countries, it was able to reach the
nuclear threshold rather quickly. In the 1980s, the regime focused instead on
the development of its thermonuclear technology and delivery systems.[5] By the
late 1980s, driven by a combination of both domestic and regional developments, the country's security policy was at a crossroads. After President P. W.
Botha suffered a stroke, he was replaced by de Klerk, who turned out to be a
modernizer. After the end of the Cold War, South Africa's security situation
had changed. This was particularly true after the withdrawals of the Soviet
Union from regional conflicts, of Cuba from Southern Angola, and of South
Africa from Namibia. As a result of these developments, South Africa's need
for a nuclear deterrent decreased. Instead, de Klerk was more sensitive to the
international pressure on South Africa to join the NPT as he tried to bring
the country out of isolation. Combined with the precipitous political changes
at home (related to unbanning the ANC and the release of Nelson Mandela),
on February 26, 1990, de Klerk ordered the removal and dismantling of "the
Controlled Units as well as the Weapons Systems of all existing nuclear weapons, together with material and material components of incomplete weapons."[6]
After an internally organized cleanup and dismantlement process, South Africa
signed (and later ratified) the NPT in 1991, and it rejoined the International
Atomic Energy Agency (IAEA).[7] The nonproliferation push among the major
powers—and their desire to have South Africa sign on to the NPT—allowed
South Africa in turn to pressure for signature and ratification of the NPT by
other countries in the Southern African region.[8] The accession gave the country
"[a] significant moral and normative power and a unique nuclear identity as
a state that terminated its nuclear weapons program."[9]

This chapter discusses the divergence between the South African foreign policy bureaucracy and the country's political elites. It also demonstrates that even the scant attention given to the subject by South Africa's political elites did not happen until late in the process. South African diplomats, throughout the preparation process, opposed indefinite extension, favoring instead a series of conditional extensions. This course of action changed when Vice President Thabo Mbeki signaled his support for indefinite extension at a meeting on April 1, 1995, in the government guest house near Pretoria. The relationship that Mbeki developed with Gore appears to have shaped his decision to support the NPT's indefinite extension.

The South African Internal Process

Explaining South Africa's role in the extension of the NPT requires a brief explanation of the country's domestic situation. After the transition to democracy in 1994, South Africa's foreign ministry was unsettled—filled with old apartheid-era bureaucrats, but with new political masters.[10] The new political structure was supplied by the ANC, which recently had come into power but whose officials were not yet integrated into the foreign ministry. To further complicate matters, foreign affairs were handled during the transition by the Sub-Council on Foreign Affairs (SCFA) comprised of members of the major parties, whom senior officials of the apartheid-era Department of Foreign Affairs (DFA) befriended with the goal of making them familiar with the system.[11] The arrangement lent itself to significant fraternization between the senior officials and political elites.[12]

One member of the ANC who was formally excluded from the process at that moment was Abdul Minty, an ANC official active in the struggle against apartheid and against the apartheid regime's nuclear weapons program for decades prior to the transition to democracy. At the time, Minty was a senior adviser to the minister of foreign affairs, Alfred Nzo. Minty officially joined the DFA only after the 1995 NPTREC and was later associated with setting the tone of South Africa's nonproliferation policy.[13] This circumstance provided for a curious structure, in which political overlords were separated from the bureaucrats who were supposed to supply them with information. It therefore makes sense to discuss the bureaucratic process (led by the diplomats) separately from the top-level political engagement (led by Vice President

Thabo Mbeki)—because in reality, they ran separate courses until they were merged on April 1, 1995.

South African Diplomatic Efforts

South African diplomats started to think early about the position and strategy for the 1995 NPTREC, and the cabinet decided as early as 1994 that the country would play an active role at the conference[14]—the first RevCon that South Africa would attend, and one of the first multilateral conferences for the country after it emerged from apartheid. "[W]e were complete babes in the wood. And this was the first major conference for all of us. . . . to be honest, we didn't understand how the conferences worked,"[15] said Peter Goosen, director of nonproliferation at South Africa's Department of Foreign Affairs at the time. The DFA had only recently entered the multilateral forums,[16] and the subdirectorate Non-Proliferation Affairs had just five officials. Despite prior experience with handling South Africa's IAEA membership and nuclear disarmament, the manpower was thin.

For the South African diplomats, one way to update their knowledge was through participation in the meetings organized by the Programme for Promoting Nuclear Non-Proliferation (PPNN).[17] Administratively headquartered at the University of Southampton, UK, the PPNN was made up of a group of senior officials (some active and some retired), academics, and experts who organized a series of conferences in advance of the 1995 NPTREC to bring diplomats from numerous countries up to date with matters related to the conference. A former senior UN official, Ben Sanders, acted as the group's executive chairman, and John Simpson, a Southampton-based professor, as the program director. In a meeting that took place July 9–12, 1993, at Chilworth Manor, one of the thirty-eight diplomats in attendance was Peter Goosen.[18] Participants received three days of workshops focused on procedural issues, treaty interpretation, security considerations, safeguards and compliance verification, peaceful uses, export issues, and regional issues.[19] Lectures were given by either PPNN members or invited third-party experts. The program was padded with generous breaks for lunches, cocktails, and dinners, with the hope that extra time would lead to cementing personal ties between diplomats.[20]

On one of the evenings, Goosen met with Sven Jurchewsky, a Canadian diplomat, at a pool table. Jurchewsky told Goosen that for the Canadians, the ultimate goal for the 1995 NPTREC was to have an indefinite extension of the NPT, but with significant concessions from the nuclear-weapon states.[21] Goosen agreed that the NPT should be extended, and that there should be a mechanism of accountability.[22] In a meeting on the sidelines of the third PrepCom meeting in 1994, Jurchewsky continued to share some of the Canadian thoughts on the subject of accountability. The Canadian perspective at the time evolved around the adoption of the Comprehensive Test Ban Treaty (CTBT), export controls, reduction in nuclear weapons levels, and the role of tactical weapons—long-term staples of the nonproliferation agenda.[23]

The US was similarly interested in assessing South Africa's views and influencing the country's position early on. In August 1994, Thomas Graham, Jr., traveled with Susan Burk to South Africa to advocate indefinite extension. South African officials, however, explained that at that point a decision about the country's position for the conference had not been established by the fledgling Government of National Unity. Yet South African diplomats told the Americans that they considered the ideal solution to be perpetual extension of the NPT, an answer that was repeated in response to the official US démarches in early 1995.[24] The same language of perpetual extension was also used in the first meeting of the Nuclear Suppliers Group in which South Africa participated in March 1995. The South African diplomats insisted that the word "indefinite" had to be replaced with "perpetual" in relation to the NPT's extension, in the final declaration. What neither Canadian nor US interlocutors knew, however, was that for South Africans, indefinite and perpetual extension did not mean the same thing.[25]

The "Third Option"

While South Africa's official mantra—that no decision on the South African position for the conference had been taken—was technically correct, it did not mean that the country's diplomats had not developed positions. Participation in PrepCom meetings and regular interaction with diplomats from around the world required South African diplomats to pursue some sort of policy, even without blessing from the top. This bureaucratic process led to developing a private position—one argued privately, not officially. It was to be "deduced" rather than openly stated[26] and was expressly kept secret so as not to be revealed too early. While not formally approved by the Minister of Foreign Affairs, South African diplomats acted on a private-position basis until two weeks before the conference, and available documents confirm that they relied on this position when preparing their strategy for the conference.

At the fourth PrepCom in Geneva in January 1995, South Africa officially presented its legal opinion on the options for extending the treaty.[27] The legal opinion was written in reaction to UN General Assembly Resolution 49/75F, which invited "States parties to provide their legal interpretations of article X, paragraph 2, of the treaty and their views on the different options and actions available."[28] It identified three possible scenarios: an indefinite extension, extension for *an* additional fixed period, or extension for additional fixed *periods*. Indefinite extension meant an unlimited duration of the treaty until all state parties withdrew from it. An extension for a single additional fixed period meant automatic termination of the treaty after the expiry of the period. The analysis of the third option occupied most of the legal document. South Africa's legal experts explained that extension for additional fixed periods would necessitate some sort of mechanism for the transition from one fixed period to another, to distinguish it from an indefinite extension. Consistent with the idea of a periodic review of the NPT, South African lawyers argued that a RevCon toward the end of the review cycle would be a suitable moment for such a review. But would such a mechanism be negative (requiring a decision of state parties to *prevent* rollover to another period), or positive (requiring a decision of state parties to *initiate* rollover of the treaty)? The South African lawyers decided that the third option with a positive mechanism would be the one consistent with Article X.2 of the NPT and the Vienna Convention on the Law of Treaties. Given his legal background and his position at the helm of the DFA nonproliferation department, Goosen was part of the team that drafted this legal opinion.[29]

In a memorandum written after the fourth PrepCom, Goosen, who by then had been posted to the Conference for Disarmament in Geneva, explained that "South Africa has, to date, taken care not to commit itself publicly to any of the extension options."[30] This was not to let domestic debate run its course, but to "maintain a flexible position where we could act as the broker between the NAM and the developed countries."[31] Goosen's recommendation was to continue pursuing the private option. "This policy [of not officially binding toward any of the options] has proven to be successful as is evidenced by the widespread recognition which has been given to the position which we have been privately arguing."[32] The memorandum continued to explain that "an extension which has the potential of drawing support is a rolling extension of successive fixed periods which would extend the treaty in perpetuity, but where a positive vote would be required between each of the successive periods to initiate the start of the following period"[33]—effectively, from a legal perspective, a position equal to the third option with a positive mechanism. The memorandum stated that "it is strongly recommended that South Africa should maintain its current position until the start [of the conference]," but that such position "should be deduced, not openly stated."[34]

Goosen cited an invitation to a dinner organized by Canada's representative to the Conference for Disarmament in Geneva as recognition of the privately argued option. A dozen countries[35] met "to discuss possible actions which [would] ensure that the April NPT Conference [had] a successful conclusion."[36] "The primary focus of the discussion at the dinner was the South African proposal of a 'Third Option' for the extension of the NPT," wrote Goosen,[37] referring to South Africa's preferred option by its listing as third in South Africa's legal opinion. The German participant at the dinner, Ambassador Hoffmann, recalled South Africa's "interesting emphasis" on "additional fiksed [sic] periods" as bringing an interesting legal argument to the table, although he did not suggest South Africans preferred either of the options.[38]

Goosen continued to identify those advocating indefinite extension, such as Russia, the US, and US allies, as the main risk. His vision of South Africa's position was to build a bridge away from indefinite extension. In support of the third option, the memo then suggested that the DFA should lobby the South African Development Community (SADC) member countries for support as well as African countries on the IAEA's Board of Governors, along with Brazil, Colombia, Ecuador, Peru, India, Indonesia, Iran, and Pakistan. "NO ACTION" was to be taken in multilateral missions, in order not to reveal the position too soon.[39]

Jean duPreez, the desk officer at the DFA's nonproliferation desk, forwarded Goosen's memo, almost in its entirety, to Foreign Minister Nzo.[40] The memo for Minister Nzo clearly spells out that "[i]t is recommended that South Africa's [sic] should support the rolling extension of successive fixed periods which would extend the Treaty in perpetuity, but where a positive vote would be required between each of the succeeding periods to initiate the start of the following period."[41] This memo also spelled out the strategy for bridge-building.

South Africa's diplomats identified the debate about the length of the periods as the key argument against the third option. The solution was to "maintain . . . flexibility on the length of each period." The document expected that the majority of countries would favor five-year periods, whereas the US was not willing to consider anything shorter than a twenty-five-year period. The plan was for South Africa to break the deadlock with a proposal for a fifteen-year period.[42] To clarify the position, duPreez wrote on March 2, 1995, that "the Department . . . recommends that South Africa seek support for an extension option which is based on a rolling extension of successive fixed periods which would extend the Treaty."[43] This memorandum warned against a "50 percent plus one" majority vote, meaning that the decision about the eventual extension should not be taken by the smallest possible majority. The document also warned against making a decision to which countries such as Indonesia, Iran, Mexico, or Nigeria would be opposed.

The "private position" put forward by the South African diplomats, and advocated until April 1995, was a rather radical proposal. It would require a positive vote before each rollover, which would be the most demanding requirement of all proposals submitted to the conference. Such a position was likely to appeal to the NAM while alienating the Western countries and Russia, which by then had set the course on indefinite extension.[44] It was also likely to alienate the US.[45] South African diplomats were therefore technically correct to say that their policy principals had neither exercised their mind nor formulated an official policy. This, however, did not prevent the diplomats from acting according to a well-defined strategy.

Interestingly, in the absence of formal guidelines, the officials acted exactly along the lines of ANC policy—not that the ANC dictated or crafted the strategy in any way, but such strategy and policy were consistent with the ANC's. The ANC policy toward the NPT was one of skepticism based on the view that it was a double-standard treaty and—combined with the rejection of nuclear weapons as the long-standing policy—that the "private position" made complete sense.[46] For an official who did not know *exactly* what a policy principal would prefer, the green-light rolling extension was the best runner-up option that could have been made. This policy was fully consistent with ANC preferences and statements prior to South Africa's transition to democracy. At the same time, it was also superficially consistent with a strong preference for nuclear disarmament. When support for indefinite extension was uncertain (South African diplomats expected some seventy countries to support such solution, well short of 50 percent of the state parties), the option hatched by South African diplomats made sense.[47]

The secrecy and obfuscation pursued by South African diplomats allowed them to prevent their preference from being recognized. Goosen's preferred language of talking about "perpetual extension" in his interactions with foreign interlocutors might have confused them, as even most native English speakers would not see much difference between indefinite and perpetual extension. There is no reason to believe that Goosen explained what the difference was in his mind, as his memorandum exhorted the need to maintain the strictest secrecy.[48]

This is especially important when it comes to South Africa's cooperation with Canada, discussed above: Goosen's interests overlapped with Canadian views when it came to the enhanced NPT review mechanism. Both Goosen and Canada's Jurchewsky supported the idea of having a mechanism to hold the nuclear-weapon states accountable. What they differed on was whether the treaty should be held hostage to the implementation of such a mechanism. While Canada saw this mechanism as strengthening the treaty once it was extended indefinitely, Goosen's idea was to make periodic renewal conditional on the treaty's performance. South Africa's insistence on *perpetual* extension made it possible for Jurchewsky to leave the pool table meeting in Chilworth (and future meetings) with an understanding that he and Goosen would work together toward an indefinite extension with conditions.[49]

US Lobbying Attempts

While South African diplomats had dealt with the NPT's prospect for extension since 1993, the country's political elites were confronted with the topic for the first time in early 1995, when three letters from the US requested South Africa's support for NPT indefinite extension. Two were written to President Mandela—one by President Bill Clinton, and one by General Colin Powell.[50]

At that time, Colin Powell had recently retired from his position as chairman of the Joint Chiefs of Staff. He was recruited by Thomas Graham, Jr., to write to Mandela on the issue.[51] In December 1994, the ACDA director

John Holum wrote a memorandum to US deputy secretary of state Strobe
Talbott and US deputy national security advisor Sandy Berger that "South
Africa [was] not yet committed [to] NPT indefinite extension." Powell agreed
to write to Mandela only if the letter were signed off by the State Department
and the NSC (ultimately both agencies agreed to this request).[52]

Clinton also wrote a letter to Mandela less than a week later, on February
13, 1995. In his letter, Clinton highlighted that the NPT's extension was "a
matter of crucial importance to global security and of great interest to [him]
personally." He highlighted the role of the NPT as "the cornerstone of efforts
to combat the spread of nuclear weapons" and the fact that South Africa's
own entry in the NPT in 1991 "symbolized South Africa's democratic transition . . . and enhanced security in Africa and for all countries." Praising the
arms control achievements and START I and II, he highlighted US compliance with the treaty.[53] Still, determining how influential these letters were is
exceedingly difficult: they were not widely discussed within the South African
administration, and a response to Clinton's letter arrived almost a month later
written in dry, bureaucratic, noncommittal language.[54]

The third letter was sent to South African executive vice president Thabo
Mbeki by US vice president Al Gore. Mbeki's legal adviser Mojanku Gumbi
forwarded the letter to the Ministry of Foreign Affairs, where it landed on the
desk of Jean duPreez. This gave duPreez an opportunity to convene a policy
meeting on April 1, in which policy was discussed at the highest levels and
decisions to pursue indefinite extension were made.[55]

Before that meeting, however, Mbeki traveled to the US, visiting New York
and Washington, DC, from February 26 to March 3, 1995. In New York,
he spoke to the representatives of corporations, gave a talk at the Council on
Foreign Relations, and held dinners and meetings with executives at New
York's gentlemen's clubs. In DC he met politicians and media representatives.
The key item on his agenda was opening the US–South Africa Bi-National
Commission. Mbeki at that time was well known for his view that strong relations with the US were crucial for South Africa's nascent democracy.[56] The
commission, headed at the vice-presidential level, was aimed at improving
bilateral cooperation between the US and South Africa.

Mbeki met with President Clinton and held multiple meetings with Vice
President Gore (both within a group and privately). During their meeting

in the Oval Office, Clinton pressed Mbeki on the issue of indefinite extension, explaining the importance that the US attached to such an outcome.[57]
"Permanent renewal of the NPT is my top foreign policy priority, and I need
your help," Clinton told Mbeki, according to one of the participants in the
meeting.[58] Mbeki and Gore also discussed the issue extensively during their
private dinner and subsequent working meetings. Yet Mbeki's vice-presidential
office had paid scant attention to the topic of the NPT's extension in the
run-up to the trip,[59] arriving to the US with a different agenda that focused
on trade, aid, and transition assistance. Moreover, South Africans at the time
were concerned with the sanctions that had been imposed, by the Clinton
administration, on South African military giants ARMSCOR and Denel due
to a contravention of the 1977 arms embargo against South Africa.[60]

During their interactions, Gore stressed to Mbeki that indefinite extension
of the treaty would not remove the leverage that non-nuclear-weapon states
held over the nuclear-weapon states' disarmament commitments. Gore's talking points included the fact that, despite the extension, the NPT remained
open to amendments that allow the treaty to "adapt to any future situation."
Gore also assured Mbeki that indefinite extension would not endanger future
review conferences of the treaty. Lastly, Gore argued that, rather than provide
leverage, a weakening of the NPT would encourage uncertainty that would,
in turn, lessen the NWS's appetite for future arms control steps.[61]

Although Mbeki left the US on March 3, Gore's interest in pursuing Mbeki
did not diminish. He wrote Mbeki a letter on March 9 and again on March
15. On March 17, they had a phone call.[62]

It is likely that Mbeki shared the South African nonpaper from the fourth
PrepCom with Gore, because on March 24, Daniel Poneman of the NSC
drafted a letter for Gore to be sent to Mbeki, along with "a closer analysis"
of South Africa's nonpaper.[63] The analysis, prepared by the NSC, stipulated
that "a rolling fixed period extension would place the treaty in jeopardy at the
end of each fixed period, and therefore would clearly not extend the NPT in
perpetuity." The NSC postulated that instead of being a bridge-building de-
vice, South Africa's proposal was "an invitation to a divisive and contentious
Extension Conference that [would] damage the NPT."[64] The analysis ended
by reiterating that the US stands "ready to work with you to achieve the aims
you identified. The best way to promote our common goal of [a] strong and

lasting NPT is for South Africa to lend its influence and moral authority to [secure] broad international support for an indefinite and unconditional extension of the Treaty."[65] This line resembles one from the draft letter from Gore to Mbeki, which stated that indefinite extension "can be greatly and positively influenced by South African leadership, and [that he] would be prepared to work closely with [Mbeki] to that end."[66]

This elaborate work, however, never elicited a formal response because Gore's letter was never sent. On March 30, South Africa's ambassador to the US, Franklin Sonn, called US assistant secretary of state for African Affairs George Moose to request an official reaction to South Africa's nonpaper. Moose's reaction highlighted that the US had deployed a lobbying effort in "nearly every one of the 173 NPT parties" and that "many countries" were interested in supporting indefinite extension even though they had not yet committed to it publicly. Importantly though, Moose said that about a third of the states in Africa were "interested in the views of other African states, in particular South Africa . . . [and the] South African announcement [in favor of indefinite extension] would have a decisive effect in broadening support for this option." He also added that he "strongly believe[d] that South Africa's position would be mirrored by not only parties in Africa but throughout the world."[67]

The summary of that call was routinely shared with the White House, which led to a furious reaction by Daniel Poneman. "The attached non-paper was not clear[ed] with us; when I brought it to [the] attention of [Assistant Secretary of State for Political-Military Affairs Thomas E. McNamara and Deputy Assistant Secretary of State for Political-Military Affairs Robert Einhorn], neither had heard of it. . . . This is obviously a serious breakdown in the process."[68] Poneman then insisted that the work on the "VP letter [was] now more urgent." However, no letter was sent before the crucial meeting took place in Pretoria.

According to contemporaneous accounts by senior South African officials, Mbeki sympathized with Clinton's views, and likely understood the relevance that the US attached to the NPT's indefinite extension.[69] Whatever exchange occurred between Mbeki and Gore (and Clinton), however, did not trickle down to the other branches of the South African government. Foreign Minister Alfred Nzo, after attending a consultation in Cairo on the issue at the end of March 1995, stated that South Africa saw it "preferable to extend the

NPT for a limited period,"[70] although he planned to deliberate about the final position with other African countries. Abdul Minty, Nzo's principal adviser on nuclear issues, supported "a straight NAM line" in favor of a fixed-period extension (an even more restrictive option than the one advanced by the DFA bureaucrats).[71]

South Africa Supports Indefinite Extension

On April 1, 1995, a little more than two weeks before the review conference, a small number of high-level officials from the DFA, ANC, and South Africa's cabinet assembled for a meeting presided over by DFA Director-General Rusty Evans. This was the meeting convened by Jean duPreez after the original letter arrived from Gore to Mbeki in February 1995. Eight individual options as well as the expected support of each were presented. It is likely that the officials from the nonproliferation desk (Goosen flew in from Geneva to attend) proposed the course suggested in earlier memoranda.[72] After the presentations, the meeting took a surprising turn. As Goosen explained, "the most senior of our principals that was present [Mbeki; according to the list of attendees] . . . turned around and said, 'No, I think [the] position has to be that we support indefinite extension.'"[73] After a brief discussion, the point was adopted. Mbeki also suggested, and the meeting approved, that South Africa would propose a set of "Principles," meant to strengthen the treaty review process and to address criticism about performance of the treaty. Importantly, however, "it was decided that the proposal for a set of 'Principles' was not conditional for our support for indefinite extension of the Treaty."[74] With this, Mbeki's own preferences quickly trumped those of both bureaucrats and his own party (including, importantly, the preferences of Minty).

The task to prepare the list of principles was given to Goosen and duPreez. They had to come up with the first draft within twenty-four hours. As Goosen recollects, "We went to the office and we sat there sort of saying, 'Well, what are we going to ask for?'"[75] It is important to remember that neither Goosen nor duPreez had any experience from previous RevCons and thus had neither practical nor institutional knowledge to fall back on. At the same time, however, Goosen did have experience from participating in the PPNN meetings and had been informed by Jurchewsky about what the Canadians considered to be appropriate guidelines. By the afternoon of April 2, 1995, Goosen and duPreez had prepared the initial draft of the items for the principles, which was then presented to, and ultimately approved by, the senior leadership of the DFA.[76]

The meeting on April 1 also established a multipronged lobbying strategy. Mbeki decided that he should write a letter to Gore to pitch him the idea of a strengthened review process, with the goal of eliciting a diplomatic response from the US. The strategy also included regional discussions within the SADC, the Organization of African Unity (OAU), and the NAM. A recommendation was made to appoint Minty as emissary to discuss and explain the position in several countries. A call was to be made to the EU ambassadors in this regard.[77]

The memorandum from the meeting does not state what the motivation behind Mbeki's decision was, but we can guess what it was from Goosen's recollections and the letter Mbeki wrote to Gore. Goosen was struck by one of the arguments made in the meeting,

> that human beings have the right, and it's almost as if it's a human right, to have their life not to be threatened by weapons of mass destruction. And as a consequence, South Africa . . . would have to adopt the position which would support the elimination of these weapons and the non-proliferation of these weapons. . . . The argument that was made was a very interesting one, it was the first time I'd heard that sort of argument being put forward.[78]

Mbeki made a similar argument in his letter to Gore, writing: "South Africa sees its non-proliferation and arms control policy as being integral to its commitment to democracy, human rights, sustainable development, social justice and environmental protection."[79] Whether it was Mbeki's real motivation or a post hoc justification, this line placed South Africa's position within fundamental rights and values and made freedom from weapons of mass destruction part of individual rights.[80] This motivation also strikes a difference with the original memoranda referred to above, submitted by the DFA diplomats: no mention of the fundamental rights is present in them.

Interestingly, Mbeki's letter to Gore and Nzo's letter to his SADC counter-parts[81] are strikingly similar to the statement Nzo ultimately delivered to the conference. All three begin with the acknowledgment of the crucial position of the treaty. Both letters continue by reaffirming a national commitment to the NPT, underlining that the surrounding concerns are not worth weakening the NPT out of fear of future proliferation. Acknowledging the criticism of the treaty, the letters and the statement propose to establish a list of "Principles for Nuclear Non-Proliferation and Disarmament" as a guide for future evaluation of the treaty's performance. Importantly, these principles were not stipulated in the letters. While the letter to Gore invites the US to discuss the wording of such principles,[82] the letter to SADC does not extend a similar invitation. Nzo's opening statement included the list of principles, marking the key difference distinguishing its content from that of the letters. The letter to the SADC ministers was produced ten days after the Pretoria meeting of April 1, along with the letter to Gore dated April 10, and transmitted only on the opening day of the conference.[83]

Gore's reaction to Mbeki's letter was positive and welcoming. He offered to organize a meeting in New York to discuss South Africa's ideas on strengthening the review process, and suggested this could be done in a statement at the end of the conference.[84]

South Africans in New York

Between the meeting on April 1 and the tabling of the document to the Friends of President group in New York on May 1, the list of principles underwent some changes. Tracking these changes, however, is not easy. The document produced by Goosen and duPreez on April 2, "Issues to be taken into account when considering the proposal for Principles for Nuclear Non-Proliferation and Disarmament," unfortunately cannot be found in South Africa's archives. However, given that Nzo's speech is almost identical to the letters sent before the conference, we have good reason to believe that it adheres to that document. A section of Nzo's speech introducing the principles starts with the words "We believe that the following broad issues should be taken into account when formulating the set of Principles for Nuclear Non-Proliferation and Disarmament."[85]

Nzo's speech listed eight issues to be taken into account:

Restatement of commitment to nonproliferation
Strengthening and adherence to IAEA safeguards agreements
Access to nuclear energy for peaceful purposes
Progress on the Fissile Material Cut-Off Treaty (FMCT)
A reduction in arsenals

Negotiation on the Comprehensive Test Ban Treaty (CTBT)
Commitment to regional Nuclear Weapon Free Zones (NWFZ)
Enforcement of negative security assurances.[86]

As one of the diplomats who provided feedback on the early drafts remarked, the FMCT and the CTBT were the main topics of discussion at the time, so it was natural that they were in the draft.[87] These were also the topics that the Canadians considered to be most important.[88] The only aspect likely not to have been considered by the Canadians was the negative security assurances—"this was very much a NAM point—on which . . . Peter Goosen always had a very explicit position."[89]

After Nzo delivered his speech, he and Gore met on the sidelines, and Gore instructed the team of US diplomats to work together with the South Africans. "We want you to work closely together," Gore said to his diplomats, in a meeting with Nzo and both countries' delegations.[90] In addition, the South Africans were invited by conference president Dhanapala to submit a formal proposal of the "Principles." This happened on May 1, after the South African delegations undertook negotiations with a number of delegations. Curiously, the UK and France negotiated with South Africa (also on behalf of Germany, Russia, and the US) and at one point came up with their own draft of the principles document.[91] The South African diplomats, however, kept tight control of the document's content. Before submitting the list to the Friends of President group, they presented fifteen versions of the principles to various national delegations. During these negotiations in the Friends of President group, South Africans led the efforts and were instrumental in actually creating a bridge, which allowed the NPT to be extended indefinitely by consensus.

In addition to the activities in New York, the South African delegation to the NAM summit, which took place in Indonesia's Bandung in the middle of the NPT RevCon, defended its choice to support indefinite extension. By doing so, the South African delegation prevented an emergence of a NAM consensus against the treaty's indefinite extension. The lack of a NAM consensus made the nonaligned countries a set of "free agents" that could be more easily persuaded to support indefinite extension. The South African decision to support indefinite extension led to the split within the Non-Aligned

Movement, which was not able to agree on a unified front opposed to indefinite extension at the meeting in Bandung taking place during the conference.[92] Harald Müller, expert adviser to the head of the German delegation, remarked in an oral history interview that the "NAM was completely divided and therefore they played much less of a role . . . it was divided because South Africa had split them";[93] whereas Sven Jurchewsky in his interview stated that South Africa helped "kill the NAM radicals."[94]

During the conference, there were accusations of infighting within the South African delegation and reports that the "white nuclear diplomats" rode roughshod over the "black newcomers."[95] Abdul Minty at that time rejected (in an interview with a trade magazine) that characterization,[96] despite its veracity, given that the old guard did not initially support indefinite extension, as was discussed earlier in this chapter. However, tensions among the members of the South African delegation existed, and Abdul Minty returned to them later. During a critical oral history conference, Minty recalled that the turf wars persisted within South Africa's delegation.[97] These tensions were reflected both in the questions of who was to actually conduct the negotiations and in the content and substance of the negotiations. Yet the delegation did not compromise on the goal of pursuing indefinite extension.

Joseph Cirincione, at the time leading the nongovernmental Campaign for the Nonproliferation Treaty, stated that "the South Africans offered us a bridge to the non-aligned."[98] Not only did South Africa's decision split the NAM, but the decision to come up with a list of principles helped to smooth out the conference. The leader of the British delegation, Sir Michael Weston, called South Africa's role in the conference "absolutely crucial throughout," while Russian ambassador Grigory Berdennikov stated that South Africa's change of views "helped other NAM delegations to adopt the right approach."[99] Canadian ambassador Christopher Westdal, whose country was in charge of collecting signatures under the resolution in favor of indefinite extension, remarked that "those principles became vitally important because they helped the pill go down."[100]

Why Cooperation with South Africa Mattered

This chapter discussed US efforts to recruit South Africa to support indefinite extension of the NPT. South Africa was a crucial supporter for the US in its efforts to push for indefinite extension. South Africa's moral standing and the respect it commanded within Africa as well as more broadly within the NAM assured that it would "deliver" more than just its own vote.

As this chapter has shown, South Africa's diplomats were initially opposed to indefinite extension. Instead, the country promoted the idea of perpetual extension through a green-light rolling mechanism, which was in direct contrast to the idea of indefinite extension. South African diplomats were predominantly proposing, and planning for, the support of a rolling extension that would require a positive vote between each of the rollovers. The goal of such a policy was to hold the five NPT nuclear-weapon states accountable for their disarmament progress. While this idea was fully worked out by the South African diplomats who pursued it vigorously, the course was completely reversed two weeks prior to the conference.

At the time, Vice President Mbeki decided to support indefinite extension. We can assume that Mbeki, in his calculus, considered both the future relations of his country with the US and the normative commitment of the fledgling Government of National Unity to the fulfillment of human rights. Even if support for indefinite extension was related (although not fully attributed) to political pressure from the US, the decision to propose the "Principles and Objectives" document was South Africa's own idea. The adoption of principles intended to increase accountability of the nuclear-weapon states was not necessarily tied to indefinite extension, but if South Africa had not proposed such a provision, extension might well have occurred only after an acrimonious battle over the voting mechanism, leaving the treaty parties deeply divided and in turn weakening the NPT. Instead, the extension is widely viewed today as having strengthened the treaty.

South Africa's role in the *extension* should not be overstated, however, as extension probably would have occurred even without its support. But without South Africa, the decision about the Principles and Objectives would not have emerged, which suggests that even a secondary power like South Africa can influence global regimes in important ways.

Cooperation with South Africa was important to the US for two reasons. First, it obviously helped divide the NAM and persuaded a number of African countries to join the campaign for indefinite extension. The US thus helped the cause of indefinite extension by leveraging South Africa's network.

Importantly, cooperation with South Africa created the impression of "meat on the table"—the idea that something was being given in exchange for indefinite extension. This view was not entirely correct, as South Africans themselves never signed the petition in favor of indefinite extension. However, the fact that they supported it and came with a list of principles meant that the US and its allies could fudge a link. The US's cooperation with South Africa would not have been possible without the leadership of Thabo Mbeki, who clearly expected a future benefit for his country from the relationship with the US. No other state could have offered him that.

"This Is What Happens When You Become Greedy"
Egypt's Intervention

WHILE SOUTH AFRICA was widely seen as an important actor prior to the 1995 NPT Review and Extension Conference, the Middle East was considered a relevant, though not critical, topic of discussion at the review conferences.[1] Most observers agreed that the Arab countries' reservations about Israel's nuclear program made them reluctant to endorse the indefinite extension of the NPT.[2] The first resolution calling for a nuclear-weapon-free zone in the Middle East was adopted in the UN General Assembly in 1974; Iran (at the time still under the Shah) sponsored a resolution on this subject, in an attempt to bolster its regional leadership.[3] Over time, however, Egypt as the traditional leader of the Arab world assumed leadership on this issue, while Iran after the Islamic Revolution in 1979 stopped being the frontrunner on the theme (for some time, at least).[4] The theme of the Middle East without nuclear weapons thus became embedded in the broader Arab-Israeli conflict.[5] This issue also garnered wider support among the nonaligned countries.[6]

The particular position of Egypt within Arab politics, combined with its long-standing alliance with the US, gave the country a special position in the discussions ahead of the 1995 NPTREC. While US relations with Europe were mainly instrumental ahead of the conference, and relations with South Africa mattered in the early stages, the US-Egypt relationship was of crucial importance during the conference's final negotiations. During this "end game" negotiation, Egypt agreed to refrain from calling a vote on the indefinite extension of the treaty, in exchange for sponsorship of the resolution on the Middle East Weapons of Mass Destruction Free Zone (MEWMDFZ, for the aficionados) by the three depositary states. The deal paved the way for the US to pass the treaty's extension without a vote—a major goal of conference president Dhanapala, given the lack of rules on how a vote should be conducted. In exchange, the Egyptians secured global support for a rather niche concern—a much bigger coup than they expected.

In this chapter, I will show that while Egypt refused to support indefinite extension of the NPT (in spite of its close ties with the US), it was ultimately persuaded to not oppose extension without a vote in exchange for important concessions from the US. As I will show, the US extended concessions to Egypt in deference to Egypt's support among the Arab countries. For its part, Egypt accepted these concessions because they elevated its demands to a higher status than would otherwise occur given the narrow and fractured support for Egypt's own resolution on the MEWMDFZ.

The NPT as Seen from Cairo

Since the inception of the NPT, Egypt had been reluctant to sign the treaty due to concerns about Israel's nuclear weapons program.[7] While the main concern for both the nonaligned countries and the Global South was related to the lack of progress on nuclear disarmament among the nuclear-weapon states, Egypt's concern was more regional in nature—since the 1960s, Egyptian leaders have been concerned about the nuclear capabilities of their neighbor, Israel. Yet, as Hassan Elbahtimy persuasively shows, until the Six-Day War, Egyptian leaders seriously underestimated the nuclear threat from Israel.[8] After that war, however, as Israel's nuclear program reached maturity, Egypt has been calling attention to it.[9]

Egypt had been an active participant in the Eighteen-Nation Disarmament Committee (ENDC) leading the negotiations on what later became the NPT, and Egypt's representative in the committee wrote the authoritative study on the committee's deliberations.[10] Immediately in 1968, Egypt signed, but did not ratify, the treaty. Egypt's choice led to a hemorrhaging of its domestic nuclear industry, when numerous civilian nuclear experts left the country.[11] During the 1970s, Egypt toyed with the idea of matching Israel's military nuclear capability, but has been unsuccessful in gaining a partner for these efforts.[12] Toward the second half of the 1970s, Egypt began to focus on the civilian uses of nuclear energy with the goal of generating electricity.[13]

The situation changed in the late 1970s, when the US changed the terms of engagement. By that time, Egypt was a US ally and agreed under US pressure to ratify the NPT in order to benefit from access to nuclear technology for peaceful purposes.[14] To make the industrialization push possible, it seemed imperative to ratify the treaty in order to gain access to energy.[15] The needs of domestic electricity production prompted the minister of electricity, Maher Abaza, to explore nuclear sources, even at the cost of ratifying the NPT. Contrary to his predecessors, Foreign Minister Boutros Boutros-Ghali was not fundamentally opposed to this option and tasked his staff with exploring the consequences of such a step.[16] Nabil Fahmy, at that time a diplomat at the Egyptian mission to the Conference on Disarmament in Geneva, recalled that there was some support for this step among top diplomats; even though when asked about it forty years later, all senior diplomats profess their opposition to the ratification.[17] Yet, as Amr Moussa recalls in his memoirs, the fact that the treaty had limited validity till 1995 helped ease the pain among the diplomats.[18] In pushing for an NPT ratification, the US hinted that it would try persuading Israel to join the NPT; it also hinted toward support for the peaceful uses of nuclear energy in Egypt.[19] In this context, Egypt ratified the treaty in 1981.

Ironically, the country never fully developed a nuclear energy program. After the first Gulf War during which Iraq and Israel threatened the use of weapons of mass destruction, the issue of WMDs in the Middle East was again at the center of attention. World leaders recognized the challenge. In his speech to Congress, President George H. W. Bush said that "[i]t would be tragic if the nations of the Middle East and Persian Gulf were now, in the wake of war, to embark on a new arms race."[20] Egyptians seized the opportunity to develop an initiative to bring arms control discussions back to the region. The strategic calculation of Egypt's diplomats has always been primarily focused on Israel, in part due to the domestic salience of Israel's nuclear program. Particularly after the revelations by Mordechai Vanunu about the existence of Israel's nuclear weapon program, it was impossible for Arab countries— including Egypt—to pretend that Israel was not yet a nuclear power.[21] This generated potential for public pressure, which even a nondemocratic regime like Egypt cared about. These heightened risks allowed Egypt to seek a broadly acceptable reason for action.

Egypt's foreign ministry developed a plan to push for a regional zone free from all weapons of mass destruction (this was broader than an earlier focus on nuclear weapons exclusively), which was then announced by Egypt's President Hosni Mubarak (it later became known as "the Mubarak initiative"). The Mubarak initiative was endorsed by all regional countries, including Israel.[22] In 1991, former US ambassador to the Conference on Disarmament in Geneva, James Leonard, wrote, in an article for *Arms Control Today*, that he was "convinced that official support for such a zone, including that of Israel, is serious and not mere lip-service."[23] In 1992, Egypt took control of the agenda in the Committee on Arms Control and Regional Security (ACRS) working group that emerged out of the Madrid Peace Process.

While the majority of participants in the ACRS showed greater attention to the conventional weapons talks, for Egypt, the WMD issues were more important. A major problem that emerged during the ACRS discussions involved a sequence of stops that was supposed to be put into place to bring the region into the WMD-free zone. While Egypt (as the leader of the Arab Group) pushed for Israel's denuclearization as a first step toward peace in the region, the Israelis believed that any disarmament steps should be discussed after peace was achieved.[24] US diplomats saw the zone issue as a marathon—Leonard mentioned that he thought it would take "many years, perhaps decades" before the zone could be fully established.[25] Egyptians, on the other hand, saw it as a sprint, and wanted it to be established as soon as possible. As the NPT extension discussions were picking up, the ACRS process was headed toward failure, and it was becoming increasingly obvious that Israel was in no mood to sign the NPT in the foreseeable future. At the same time, relations between Israel and the Arab countries were improving, but Egyptian-Israeli political relations were dominated by the nuclear dossier, given that Egypt had already signed a peace treaty with Israel in 1979.[26] Intermittently, Egyptian diplomats even threatened to leave the NPT if Israel did not join.[27]

In 1994 and 1995, Egypt continued pushing for Israel's accession to the NPT and for the development of a regional WMD-free zone in every interaction with regional partners. This effort created considerable pressure on Israel, exacerbated by the US and Russian governments, which had asked Israel to put out a "statement of intent" that could placate the Egyptians.[28] The press in both Israel and Egypt discussed the potential for a new conflict. While Israeli leaders—such as then foreign minister Peres—endorsed the idea of a nuclear-weapon-free Middle East, they rejected the specific steps such as signing the NPT.[29] For its part, Egypt repeatedly asked Israel for specific time-bound schedules.[30] This steered Egypt's view (held primarily within the foreign ministry) away from indefinite extension of the treaty. Egypt did not hide this position—it was frequently picked up in the assessments by Western diplomats,[31] but Egypt also used its standing within the NAM to lobby governments against indefinite extension.[32]

In early 1993, ACDA Assistant Director Norman Wulf traveled to Geneva to attend the meeting of the Conference on Disarmament. On the sidelines, he met Mounir Zahran, Egypt's ambassador to that conference. During this meeting, Zahran raised the issue of Israel's nuclear program and stated that Egypt would not be in favor of the treaty's indefinite extension.[33] Soon after, Egypt formally reached out to the US with the goal of coordinating on the issue of the 1995 NPTREC and to discuss Egyptian concerns about Israel as well as issues related to the security assurances or safeguards.[34] As Egypt's opposition to indefinite extension of the treaty became obvious, US diplomats regularly visited Cairo in the attempt to persuade Egypt to drop its objections or at the very least not to make trouble. In December 1994, Secretary of State Warren Christopher met Egypt's Foreign Minister Amr Moussa on the sidelines of the Budapest Summit of the Conference on Security and Cooperation in Europe. Moussa pressured Christopher to publicly chastise Israel for its nuclear program and its nonparticipation in the NPT. However, while agreeing to the goal of a nuclear-weapon-free zone in the Middle East, Christopher rejected putting any pressure on Israel and vowed instead to continue "working quietly behind the scenes."[35] In the run-up to the conference, Vice President Gore traveled to Cairo in March 1995 in an attempt to speak to President Mubarak, and Assistant Secretary of State for Near Eastern Affairs Robert Pelletreau threatened to cut off Egypt's military aid over its vocal opposition to indefinite extension.[36] In March 1995, Secretary of State Christopher traveled to Cairo and lobbied Mubarak to drop his opposition to indefinite extension.[37]

Separately, the US put pressure on other countries in the region not to join Egypt's initiative to block indefinite extension.[38] When President Mubarak traveled to Washington, DC, two weeks ahead of the conference, he repeatedly stated that Egypt was not in favor of the extension in the absence of Israel's membership, but he also promised not to lobby other countries against the treaty's indefinite extension, a pledge that was contradicted by his own foreign ministry.[39]

Shortly before the conference, Egypt convened a meeting of the Arab League in Cairo with the goal of pushing against indefinite extension. In this meeting, Egypt aimed to discuss a draft resolution and forge a unified Arab stance on the extension, linking it to Israel's joining of the treaty.[40] The summit concluded with a general agreement on Egypt's goals[41] and issued a statement that criticized the NPT as "unjust" due to Israel's nonmember status and because of the lack of support on peaceful uses of nuclear energy.[42] Yet it did not endorse any specific action and left the final decision for the NAM summit in Bandung.[43]

A Bad Hand

Egypt came to the NPTREC with the view that the treaty could be extended for a quarter-century. In fact, in an opening statement, Foreign Minister Moussa endorsed extension for that period. His assessment at the beginning of the conference was that a majority in favor of indefinite extension did not exist.[44] Not surprisingly, given the undemocratic nature of the Mubarak regime, Moussa's view was shared by the Egyptian media: the newspaper *Al Ahram* reported on the first day of the conference that a majority of countries supported a twenty-five-year extension.[45]

Moussa believed that the NPT, which was not universal, was likely to breed resentment by putting restrictions on the non-nuclear-weapon states. Yet Egypt's position was weakened by broader developments. South Africa's announcement that it would support indefinite extension—barely three weeks after South African foreign minister Nzo and his chief nuclear adviser Minty had informed Egyptian officials otherwise[46]—undercut Egypt's position. The NAM, otherwise a force to be reckoned with, failed to adopt a single unified position. The Arab countries did not form a single front. And lastly, Vice President Gore, who was the highest-ranking official in the US delegation, met with Moussa and warned him not to lobby against indefinite extension.[47]

This situation arguably dealt Egypt a bad hand. Its traditional allies were scattered, and it was becoming obvious to Egyptian diplomats that they would not be able to block the treaty extension. "The American pressure started to produce results," Moussa stated in a later interview.[48] Most diplomats assumed that the decision would be taken by a vote and that Egypt's vote would therefore not be highly consequential.[49] Moussa stated that after his return from New York, he had realized that "the fact was that the US was going to win. *Khalas,* that's it. So forget about the others, it is the US who was going to win that thing."[50] In light of this realization, Egyptians decided to change their strategy.[51]

For this reason, Egypt tabled, three days before the end of the conference, a resolution calling for universal adherence to the NPT and against nuclear weapons in the Middle East, naming Israel as a party outside the NPT and expressing "deep concern at the continued existence . . . of unsafeguarded Israeli nuclear facilities."[52] Egypt's initial calculation was that while the Western countries had the votes to push through indefinite extension, Egypt would still be able to get its resolution passed. Then Minister of Foreign Affairs Moussa later wrote in his memoirs that his instructions were to do anything possible to prevent the NPT's indefinite extension unless Israel were to join the treaty.[53] The resolution was the epitome of the worst fear among US diplomats, since it risked pushing Israel further away from the peace process.[54]

However, the situation quickly changed when it became obvious that conference president Jayantha Dhanapala wanted the decision on the extension to be adopted without vote, i.e., by consensus. Such adoption required that no party would be opposed to extending the treaty indefinitely. This turn of events meant that Egypt's considerations had to be accommodated, otherwise it could demand a vote. The US decision to comply with Dhanapala's wish to extend the treaty without a vote opened the door for the Egyptians. "The minute they decided to try to get consensus they gave us leverage. . . . [this is what happens] when you become greedy," Fahmy said in an interview.[55]

US-Egyptian Negotiations

As opposed to South Africa, for which the biggest negotiation happened before the conference, for Egypt, the lion's share of the negotiations took place in New York in the last days of the conference. These negotiations were primarily conducted between the US and Egypt and happened at two levels—on one level, among the diplomats in New York, and on the other level, between Washington, DC, and Cairo.

It is relevant to note that the two countries negotiated Egypt's resolution directly, while each negotiated on behalf of other countries. Although the MEWMDFZ resolution was cosponsored by other Arab countries, those countries did not take part directly in negotiations with the US. Unbeknown to the Americans in New York, the Egyptian negotiating team enjoyed a great amount of latitude from the upper levels of its government.[56] Egypt's President Hosni Mubarak had been extensively briefed on the strategy for the conference about a month beforehand[57] and in turn was interpreted by the Egyptian delegation as putting substantial trust in Moussa, who for his part delegated significant power to Nabil Elaraby, the chief negotiator in New York.[58]

The initial pressure by the US was for Egypt to drop the resolution.[59] During the negotiations, in a fit of frustration, the US ambassador to the UN Madeline Albright "pinned [Elaraby] against the wall" in New York, shouting at him, "I know your new instructions. [These] are not your new instructions."[60] Elaraby's response was: "I have other instructions to follow. If you are right, it's *my* punishment that will occur and my government will expel me from service."[61] After this episode, Elaraby contacted Moussa, who instructed him to "drag them to vote, and then . . . break the consensus which they seek by rejecting the infinite extension. We will not give them what they want for free."[62]

Given the time pressure—it was three days before the end of the conference, after all, US negotiators tried to force Egypt's hand by asking the White House to engage Cairo directly, but this effort failed. President Clinton did write a letter to President Mubarak to complain about the difficulty of finding an agreement with the Egyptians in New York, but no change in the Egyptian delegation's behavior was forthcoming.[63] Moreover, Mubarak did not answer a call from Vice President Gore,[64] and Mubarak's key foreign policy adviser

Osama El Baz's call to the Egyptian delegation in New York also went unanswered. While El Baz instructed the foreign ministry to avoid confrontation with DC, the foreign ministry's senior official Mahmoud Karem instructed Elaraby to "fight against the Americans every day."[65] Toward the end of the negotiations, Cairo instructed the delegation that the "crucial final stage of the conference should be seen as a safeguard to maximize our initial position on the universality of the Treaty and the need for Israel to comply with it and place all its facilities under international supervision."[66]

The main objection by the US was related to the rejection of referring to Israel by name in the resolution.[67] The language in the US draft resolution talks of the universal adherence to the treaty and notes the presence of unsafeguarded facilities in the Middle East.[68] This seemingly simple difference exploited the fact that in addition to Israel, other countries in the region still had unsafeguarded nuclear facilities, or were outside the treaty.[69] This approach offered a way out. The two countries agreed on a resolution that did not mention any country by name and that generalized the call to rid the region of all weapons of mass destruction and their delivery systems in a verifiable manner.

The last issue raised by the negotiators was who was to sponsor the resolution. Egypt refused to sponsor it because it did not mention Israel by name.[70] "Egypt could not submit a draft resolution on the Middle East which it sponsored without specifically naming Israel, which had the only substantial nuclear program in the region and remained a non-member of the NPT,"[71] without a loss of face both regionally and domestically, observed Nabil Fahmy. The US suggested that the resolution be put up for a vote and promised not to oppose it (abstaining instead), provided that the extension was passed without a vote. Egypt, however, insisted that all decisions be afforded the same treatment—either be voted on, or not.[72]

Having the resolution cosponsored (tabled) by all three depositary states offered a way out.[73] Albeit a departure from its original plans, the US gave in to this demand as it helped to resolve the issue. The draft resolution was approved by the NSC in Washington, DC, before being tabled in New York.[74] The fact that the US agreed to this step in a bilateral setting with Egypt, without previously securing agreement from the UK or Russia,[75] highlights the diffuse nature of networks: the UK sponsored the resolution *without* seeing it; Russia agreed to sponsor it *before* seeing it.[76]

No Vote, and Yet . . .

Egyptians were still unhappy with the indefinite extension of the NPT and were not prepared to support it by consensus. Conference president Dhanapala offered a way out with the formulation that "a majority exists among States party to the Treaty for its indefinite extension,"[77] but allowed a limited number of countries to express themselves as being a part of the majority or not. Egypt was one of the countries that took the floor to indicate that it was not part of the majority.[78]

The final outcome of the negotiations between Egypt and the US ensured that indefinite extension of the treaty was carried out without a vote. Negotiating with Egypt—and getting Egypt on board—meant that the group of Arab states also would not oppose indefinite extension, whereas negotiating with any other member of the Arab caucus (or Iran) would not have brought the rest of the group on board. At the same time, Egypt could not have negotiated the resolution with anyone else: neither the UK nor Russia could have produced the same outcome as the US—that the other two state depositaries of the NPT would cosponsor the agreement.

The highest-ranking Egyptian in New York, Nabil Elaraby, stated that he thought the trade-off was "worth it" at the time.[79] Nabil Fahmy wrote in his memoirs that the conference "was not a major success" for Egyptian diplomacy.[80] Egypt's Foreign Minister Moussa, for his part, decried that Egypt spoke at the conference with multiple voices, which weakened the country's position.[81] In a later interview, he stated that the result was "not satisfying to me, but there are certain things that we have to live with."[82] Moussa's heroic attempts to single out Israel led to him being portrayed as a bare-chested pharaoh in the Egyptian newspaper *Al Akhbar*.[83]

Curiously, other experts were not as skeptical. The postmortem conference organized in Monterey, California, in July 1995 saw the resolution as a first step toward developments within the region that would make the zone possible within a framework of a more cooperative security architecture in the region.[84] Yet, tellingly, NPT experts foresaw the future of the MEWMDFZ more as a regional issue than as a topic that would capture the whole NPT regime.

While Egypt failed to prevent the NPT's indefinite extension, it succeeded in making the MEWMDFZ the cornerstone of NPT politics. Until then, discussion about nuclear weapons in the Middle East occurred primarily within the framework of regional security discussions. While the prospect of peace in the Middle East has always enjoyed global attention, nuclear weapons in the Middle East had not been a central theme of the NPT regime prior to 1995. This changed after the adoption of the MEWMDFZ resolution at the 1995 NPTREC.

Admittedly, the US diplomats quite likely did not foresee the consequences of the resolution.[85] While Egypt did not manage to get everything it wanted and was defeated in the "big picture," it succeeded in an important diplomatic coup. The resolution on the MEWMDFZ propelled a niche regional issue into a central topic of relevance for NPT politics.

6

Postextension Politics of the NPT

ONCE DHANAPALA'S HAMMER WENT DOWN, and the treaty was extended indefinitely, six opponents of indefinite extension were allowed to express that they were not part of the majority in favor of the extension. "Nigeria is of the view that the decision to extend the NPT indefinitely without applying to that decision a time-bound programme of nuclear disarmament measures poses grave security risks for present and future generations," thundered the Nigerian ambassador Ibrahim Gambari.[1] Iranian ambassador Cyrus Nasseri claimed that "[t]hose who had the perceived permanency as vital to their security concerns, national interests and political requirements now have the further obligations to fully respect . . . concerns, interests and requirements . . . of all others."[2] Egyptian ambassador Nabil Elaraby read out his government's statement that said "Egypt . . . believes that the method used to achieve [the NPT's] indefinite extension was neither the best nor the most successful and that it may have negative consequences."[3] For or against, in all of their speeches the speakers emphasized the commitment undertaken that day.

Twenty-four years later, during the 2019 session of the preparatory committee for the 2020 Review Conference of the Treaty on the Non-Proliferation of Nuclear Weapons, representatives of different states mentioned the commitments of the 1995 Non-Proliferation Treaty (NPT) Review and Extension Conference sixty-two times. In this chapter, after reviewing the agreements made in 1995, I will look at the postextension politics of the NPT, as well as the performance on the agreements made in 1995. The book will end with a look back at US social network power a quarter-century later.

Outcome of the NPTREC

Three documents resulted from the historic conference, representing the three decisions passed together without a vote (though, apparently—given the presence of the countries that stated they were not part of the majority—not by consensus). These three documents were negotiated in the Friends of President group, composed of representatives of a small number of countries. This model, originating in the 1985 NPT RevCon, allowed Dhanapala to keep the group of negotiating partners as well as the number of participants (and hence the number of demands and chances for conflict) relatively small. Decision 1 involved strengthening the review process for the NPT; Decision 2 involved the principles and objectives for nuclear nonproliferation and disarmament, and Decision 3 presented the body of the extension decision. Shortly after the conference, Ben Sanders (Dhanapala's adviser and PPNN's executive director) wrote in a paper that the first two decisions were "the price" of the extension.[4] A fourth document, passed separately, presented the resolution on the Middle East.

Decision 1

The decision on strengthening the review process was relatively brief and uncontroversial, based on the negotiating history and the memoirs of the direct participants.[5] It included provisions for the continuation of future review conferences once every five years and, in the three years preceding the review conferences, for annual convening of the PrepCom meetings. These preparatory meetings were supposed to go beyond bureaucratic and logistic issues to discuss substantive issues: "principles, objectives and ways in order to promote the full implementation of the Treaty, as well as its universality, and to make recommendation thereon to the Review Conference."[6] The decision also mandated that the review conferences should be both forward and backward looking. Overall, this decision was uncontroversial and preserved the institutional structure for the NPT review that has been in place since the start of the treaty.

After the document was passed, observers and participants alike agreed that the new review process would constitute "a powerful instrument" and a serious innovation in how the review process was run.[7] Despite clear wording in the decision that the treaty review should look both backward and forward, it was agreed at the postmortem conference, a few months later, that "the review needs to be forward looking, since looking at the past five years and finding blame is counterproductive."[8] The new process also required proper preparation. Nongovernmental organizations, such as PPNN and the Monterey-based Center for Nonproliferation Studies, saw this as a breath of fresh air in their activities and geared toward fulfilling the mandates.[9] Major funders, such as the Ford Foundation, provided funding to study the implications of Decision 1 on the future shape of the nonproliferation process.[10]

Decision 2

It was the second decision, on principles and objectives (P&O) for nuclear nonproliferation and disarmament, that received considerable attention during the conference. This document is much longer and more elaborate than Decision 1, containing five preambular paragraphs and twenty operative paragraphs. The preamble of the document speaks of the "ultimate goal of the complete elimination of nuclear weapons."[11] The operative paragraphs speak of the "principles and objectives . . . to move with determination towards the full realization and effective implementation" of the NPT. These principles and objectives are divided into a number of groups: universality of the treaty, nonproliferation, nuclear disarmament, nuclear-weapon-free zones, security assurances, safeguards, as well as the peaceful uses of nuclear energy.

The document adopted on May 11 is substantively different from its initial draft, which South Africa submitted to the Friends of President club on May 1. Following its submission, the UK—together with France, Germany, Russia, and the US—worked out an alternative paper on the evening of the same day.[12] While there are numerous small textual differences, some of the major differences illustrate the key fractures of the conflict.

The preambular paragraph cited above, which reiterates the ultimate goal of complete nuclear disarmament, was new and not included in either the South African or British drafts. Universal adherence to the NPT became "an urgent priority" in the final draft, language taken from the British proposal.

The call for universality was not seen as particularly controversial—universality is the "motherhood and apple pie" of multilateral diplomacy, as a member of the Canadian delegation, Tariq Rauf, explained later.[13]

In the section on nuclear disarmament, the reference to "efforts to achieve the elimination of nuclear weapons," present in the original South African draft, was dropped in the final version.[14] Although a seemingly technical detail, in 1995 a lively legal discussion was under way about whether the obligation to conduct negotiations on nuclear disarmament (as mandated by the NPT) should also include an obligation to bring these negotiations toward conclusion. The discussion was resolved, in legal terms, in 1996 by the International Court of Justice, which in the advisory opinion "Legality of the Threat or Use of Nuclear Weapons" clearly said that the obligation to conduct negotiations on nuclear disarmament also includes an obligation to conclude such negotiations.[15] The section on disarmament also includes a mention of the "ultimate goals of eliminating [nuclear] weapons and . . . of general and complete disarmament under strict and effective international control."[16]

In a departure from the original South African draft, which stipulated that "nothing in the Treaty shall be interpreted as affecting the inalienable right of all the Parties to develop . . . nuclear energy for peaceful purposes," and the British draft, which stipulated only that "international cooperation consistent with the non-proliferation objectives of the Treaty should be encouraged,"[17] the final version of the decision speaks of the "particular importance" attached to the inalienable right of all parties to the use of nuclear energy for peaceful purposes. The language was toned down significantly compared to South Africa's initial draft, but augmented compared to the British proposal. These drafts were quite similar, however, in terms of the completion of negotiations of the comprehensive test ban, fissile material cutoff, and systemic efforts to decrease the reliance on nuclear weapons.

The principal author of the initial South African draft of the Principles and Objectives, diplomat Peter Goosen, wrote later, "they would be a lodestar which focuses our attention on the goals which States parties [sic] would strive for."[18] Goosen wrote that the two decisions were not "a compromise to achieve indefinite extension[, but] a vehicle with which we could enter into a process towards the achievement of 'the ultimate goals of the complete elimination of nuclear weapons.'"[19] While the disarmament provisions are relatively brief—occupying only two out of twenty operative paragraphs—their importance cannot be overstated. Sanders in his postmortem observations remarked that "to a growing number of non-nuclear-weapon states, no longer only among the non-aligned, the NPT is about the elimination of all nuclear weapons. The conference has underlined the nature of the NPT as a disarmament measure."[20] A postmortem conference in Monterey underlined the same feature: "NWS will now be expected to be even more forthcoming on disarmament, since they argued for indefinite extension by claiming that it would allow for further nuclear disarmament."[21]

Goosen clearly thought of the Principles and Objectives decision as the starting point—his paper for PPNN includes six next steps for the future direction. "The point is that we should constantly be ready to identify new steps or measures which can be added to the agenda as the ones which already appear are accomplished and therefore removed," Goosen stated matter-of-factly.[22] The issues included in the discussion about disarmament—especially the comprehensive test ban and the fissile material cutoff—were seen as requiring serious attention from the nuclear-weapon states, in lieu of the adoption of measures in name only.[23]

Decision 3

Decision 3 was the barest of the three decisions adopted at the NPTREC. It announced, in one brief operative paragraph, that "a majority exists among States party to the Treaty for its indefinite extension" and hence "the Treaty shall continue in force indefinitely."[24] This formulation was chosen precisely to indicate the majority demanded by the treaty, while avoiding signaling a consensus, which would invariably lead to a vote.

Importantly, Decision 3 does not refer to the other two decisions and is designed in this way to avoid any semblance of interconnection. This choice was the reason why South Africa, as the leading country behind Decision 2, decided not to sponsor the resolution in favor of indefinite extension.[25]

Resolution on the Middle East

The resolution on the Middle East was negotiated largely between the US and Egypt, as discussed in the previous chapter. Contrary to frequent assertions, this resolution was not "part of the package" passed in 1995—it was passed separately with the goal of avoiding a vote on the extension. A memorandum by the conference's secretary-general Prvoslav Davinić spelled out that the package consisted of "altogether three" decisions alone, and its relationship to the resolution on the Middle East was deliberately left ambiguous. The resolution passed on May 11, 1995, and called for adherence to the NPT by all regional states as well as for taking "practical steps in appropriate forums aimed at making progress towards, inter alia, the establishment of an effectively verifiable Middle East zone free of weapons of mass destruction . . . and their delivery systems."[26]

Following the feat of the extension, minimal attention was given to the resolution on the Middle East by countries outside the region. Among the twelve countries speaking after the resolution on the Middle East was passed, none of the non-Arab countries spoke about the theme, and Algeria spoke about it only tangentially.[27] The postmortem conferences and events did not consider the agreement as part of the package, and did not discuss it at any length. As Tariq Rauf mentioned in a later interview, nobody expected any success on the issue. The resolution was a piece of aspirational declaration.[28] Until it wasn't.

Post-1995 History of the NPT

The documents adopted in 1995 at the NPT Review and Extension Conference extensively shaped the NPT regime in the subsequent regimes. The first postextension RevCon, in 2000, ended up with a successful outcome, despite headwinds ahead of the conference: negotiations on the FMCT were stalled within the Conference on Disarmament; the US Senate rejected the ratification of the CTBT; the new US administration, led by George W. Bush, was engaged in a dispute about missile defense with Russia; and Brazil, Egypt, Ireland, Mexico, New Zealand, Slovenia, South Africa, and Sweden formed a new group called the New Agenda Coalition (NAC), which criticized nuclear-weapon states for their slow pace on nuclear disarmament.[29] According to the leader of the US delegation, Ambassador Norman Wulf, one reason for success was that the five nuclear-weapon states were engaging in active discussions.[30] Today this format, known as the "P5 process," is a cornerstone of the NPT regime that provides a regular setting for the nuclear-weapon states to discuss sensitive issues among themselves.[31]

Various observers agree that the 2000 RevCon reached a genuinely consensual outcome document, which included in its conclusion the so-called

"Thirteen Practical Steps" to advance nuclear disarmament. The list included numerous rehashed points from the decisions of 1995 but added a new language of urgency and a new level of detail. Conspicuously, the issue of Middle East Weapons of Mass Destruction Free Zone (MEWMDFZ) was missing from the list. The Thirteen Practical Steps were proposed by the NAC, and the fact that they were adopted is widely seen as a recognition of the NAC's pivotal role in nuclear disarmament discussions at the turn of the millennium.[32]

Yet, five years later, the situation was completely different: the 2005 NPT RevCon ended in failure. Furthermore, it was set up to fail from the beginning. Throughout the preparatory process, the US and France not only presented no progress on the Thirteen Practical Steps but also refused to reaffirm past commitments.[33] Instead, the US wished to focus on nonproliferation transgressions of particular states (chiefly Iran), an approach that was almost universally rejected.[34] American nonproliferation expert William Potter in his analysis of the NPTREC said that the real winners of the conference were at the extremes—those who came with extremist agendas and those who made sure to block those agendas.[35] The EU, however, was in a position to shine as an institutional actor. While in 1995, the actorhood of the European countries was national, not *European,* by 2005 the *European* aspect was much more pronounced.[36] According to Potter, the biggest loser of the 2005 RevCon was the NPT itself, as the states appeared to see the treaty as an instrument for the pursuit of their narrow self-interests (rather than as a reflection of their national interests).[37] As Harald Müller, the nuclear policy expert who acted as a scientific adviser to the German delegation, later observed, 2005 demonstrated two things: the nuclear-weapon states had no intention of giving up their nuclear weapons, and the US appeared to be giving up on its leadership within the NPT.[38]

The situation improved substantially at the 2010 RevCon, largely thanks to the leadership of US president Barack Obama. Of 69 mentions from no fewer than 21 countries that spoke of the Obama administration's nuclear policy initiatives in their conference statements, only 3 were negative—delivered by Cuba and Iran.[39] Obama's plans for the New START, and his vision of a world without nuclear weapons, were positively received. Egypt was much more cooperative than it had been in 2005 (chiefly due to the agreement to mandate the UN secretary general to convene a conference on MEWMDFZ; more on that below) and was widely seen as the most successful actor of the conference.[40] The cooperative approach of the Obama administration led to a universally highly regarded outcome of the 2010 conference.

Iran's nuclear program was a prominent topic, and—due to that country's intransigence along with verifiable IAEA reports—the conference was ultimately critical of the steps undertaken by Iran.[41] Iran's violations notwithstanding, the 2010 conference agreed on a relatively positive outlook on the future of cooperation on nuclear matters for peaceful purposes, to the satisfaction of the nonaligned movement.[42] The crown of the conference's success was the adoption of the Action Plan—consisting of 64 concrete recommended actions related to nuclear disarmament, nonproliferation, peaceful uses of nuclear energy, and the MEWMDFZ—thus far the last large, cooperative, consensually adopted document within the NPT setting.[43]

Between the 2010 RevCon and the preparatory process for the 2015 RevCon, numerous events demonstrated that the 2010 Action Plan would not be followed: disappointment with the pace of nuclear disarmament led to the emergence of the Humanitarian Initiative; the idea of a conference on the establishment of the MEWMDFZ fell apart; and the nuclear saber-rattling between the US and Russia had increased. No wonder the 2015 NPT RevCon was a much less merry affair.

The conference ended in acrimony and without an outcome document, but even the road to that nonoutcome was a painful one. Two topics dominated the conference: the issues related to nuclear disarmament and the MEWMDFZ issue. Disarmament became an issue both because of the Humanitarian Initiative and because the activities of the nuclear-weapon states were seen as insufficient. On the Middle East, Egypt stepped up its diplomatic activity and pushed for strong wording in the Final Document, which in turn resulted in blockage of the final agreement by France, the UK, and the US.

For its part, Egypt objected to almost every other suggestion by other countries in other areas.[44] The fact that the conference fell apart on these issues underscored the lack of desire among the parties to seek and find a compromise.[45] In the RevCon's final week, conference president, Algerian diplomat Taous Feroukhi, brought together a focus group representing nineteen countries, which produced an outcome paper that was ultimately not endorsed.[46]

The Russian Federation remained rather passive throughout the negotiation. For its part, the EU became divided on the issue of nuclear disarmament and could not act strongly as a cohesive group. While the EU had an agenda on which the countries agreed—for example, on peaceful uses of nuclear energy or nuclear nonproliferation—the member states were too divided by questions surrounding disarmament.[47]

The acrimony of that conference continued well after 2015. Although the 2020 NPT RevCon was postponed due to the COVID-19 global pandemic, the preparatory committee conferences took place in 2017, 2018, and 2019 and saw an emergence of the nuclear weapon ban treaty, increased conflict between the US and Russia, but also renewed discussions about Iran's nuclear program. No cross-platform cooperation emerged. Although the US showed interest in at least paying lip service to the goal of nuclear disarmament with the announcement of the initiative on Creating an Environment for Nuclear Disarmament (CEND), it is simply too soon to gauge the impact of such initiatives. Most observers of CEND are perplexed by it, especially by the very open-ended and uncertain nature of the exercise.[48]

Commitments of 1995: A Quarter-Century Later

Measuring the progress of some of the commitments undertaken in 1995 is easy. The RevCons continue taking place every five years, and in the three years preceding each RevCon, the PrepComs are held. These sessions discuss substantive policy issues, and there is no doubt that they focus on bureaucratic and logistical issues as well as substantive topics of discussion.

The NPT has also made substantive steps toward universalization. Today, only three countries remain outside the treaty: India, Israel, and Pakistan (whether North Korea's withdrawal from the treaty was actually legally executed—and hence whether that country is still a party to the treaty—is a matter for discussion). In the aftermath of the NPT's indefinite extension, a host of smaller countries, along with some political heavyweights like Brazil and Cuba (a heavyweight within the NAM) joined the treaty.[49] The progress on nuclear-weapon-free zones has also been somewhat encouraging: the 1967 Treaty of Tlatelolco, establishing a NWFZ in Latin America and the Caribbean, entered into full force in 2002 with the accession of Cuba; the 1985 Treaty of Rarotonga, effectively making the South Pacific a NWFZ as well, was expanded in 1996 when France, the UK, and the US signed the protocol governing their territories in the region.[50] The Treaty of Bangkok, establishing a NWFZ in Southeast Asia, entered into force in 1997; the Treaty of Pelindaba, establishing a NWFZ in Africa, was open to signature shortly after the 1995 NPTREC and entered into force in 2009. The Central Asian NWFZ treaty was opened for signature in 2006 and entered into force three years later.[51]

Complaints about the slow and halting progress on access to nuclear energy for peaceful purposes among the non-nuclear-weapon states have been a matter of discussion within the NPT regime, particularly the export control regimes— such as the Nuclear Suppliers Group and the Zangger Committee—which are continuously criticized for their role in stemming the spread of nuclear technology. Some academics even see the role of export control regimes in the nuclear market as a cartel.[52] Another key element of the discussion is related to the application of nuclear safeguards, particularly those of the so-called Additional Protocol, which is a document that requires countries to grant access to any location desired by IAEA inspectors for nuclear verification.[53] More recently, the IAEA came up with a more tailored approached, called State-Level Concept, which takes into account a broad range of information from different sources to tailor the level of supervision to the level of nuclear activities and risk. This approach is meant to optimize the use of IAEA's resources. Many Western countries laud the Additional Protocol and the State-Level Concept, and the US, at least under George W. Bush, even toyed with the idea of requiring countries to sign the Additional Protocol as a condition for supplying nuclear materials to other countries.[54] Other countries—including those with sizable nuclear activities, such as Argentina, Brazil, and Iran—have been extremely critical of both ideas.[55] They see them not only as violating the inalienable right to develop peaceful uses of nuclear energy but also as a potential risk to their intellectual property in the nuclear field.

Progress is much less visible in other areas. In fact, in some areas we have actually seen the reversal of certain advancements. A number of new nonproliferation challenges arose. The mid-2000s saw a rise in concern about Iran's nuclear program and the international community's complex reaction to it, including multiple rounds of sanctions by the UN Security Council and unilateral sanctions imposed by the US and the EU. This dossier was only tentatively closed in 2015 with the conclusion of the Joint Comprehensive Plan of Action (JCPOA), which put in place an extremely detailed inspection program for Iran's facilities. However, just three years later, the Trump administration decided to withdraw from the JCPOA, throwing the whole agreement into question.

The early 2000s highlighted the risk posed by nonstate actors in the nuclear field. In 2004, the global network of nuclear smuggling, organized by the Pakistani doctor Abdul Qadir Khan, was discovered.[56] In 2003, together with a few other countries, the US established an alternative forum called the Proliferation Security Initiative (PSI), which was meant to work toward the interdiction of WMD cargo on the high seas and disruption of proliferation networks. While PSI over time attracted over one hundred supporters, it remains highly contested within the nonproliferation field.[57]

The negative security assurances, discussed in paragraph 8 of the Decision on Principles and Objectives, have not been extended and are no longer a theme for nonproliferation discussions. Already in the first postextension PrepCom, in 1997, South Africa proposed a legally binding document that would extend negative security assurances, but this was not adopted.[58] The topic fizzled out over time. This is somewhat disappointing, given that according to the statement of the US representative at the NPTREC, Thomas Graham, Jr., the legally binding negative security assurances were something that the US was willing to extend.[59] Instead, the US's most recent Nuclear Posture Review mentions its preparedness to use nuclear weapons against cyberattacks,[60] and the "Basic Principles of State Policy of the Russian Federation on Nuclear Deterrence" includes the possibility of using nuclear weapons in case of a conventional attack.[61] The progress on nuclear disarmament, the comprehensive test ban, and fissile-material cutoff has been slow, or in some cases even reversed. The Fissile Material Cut-Off Treaty has been, in practice, observed by the five nuclear-weapon states (they all stopped producing weapons-grade plutonium), but not by the three states outside the NPT possessing nuclear weapons. Negotiations are presently stuck. The lack of progress on nuclear disarmament has led to the emergence of new institutional initiatives within nuclear politics, such as the Treaty on the Prohibition of Nuclear Weapons, also popularly known as the nuclear ban treaty, which was opened for signature in 2017 and entered into force in 2021.

Comprehensive Test Ban Treaty

While the P&O decision called for the completion of the negotiation of the CTBT by the end of 1996, and called on the "utmost restraint" by the nuclear-weapon states until the treaty enters into force, shortly after the NPT's extension was approved, both France and China still conducted a small number of nuclear tests in 1995 and 1996.[62] In September 1995, the UNGA adopted the draft of the CTBT, and shortly afterward it was opened for signature. While all five nuclear-weapon states signed the treaty on September 24, 1996, it was never ratified in the US Senate and remains not in force until today.

Signing and ratifying the CTBT led to the emergence of the Preparatory Commission for the Comprehensive Nuclear-Test-Ban Treaty Organization (CTBTO), which was established in Vienna in 1996. This move also had domestic consequences: as French scholar Emmanuelle Maitre recently argued, the test ban effectively "killed" the French antinuclear movement.[63]

Yet the moratorium on nuclear tests remains today, punctuated only by India's and Pakistan's nuclear tests in 1998 and North Korea's repeated tests in 2006, 2009, 2013, 2015, 2016, and 2017; furthermore, the US recently accused both Russia and China of conducting tests.[64] According to recent media reports, in 2020 the Trump administration also apparently discussed conducting a nuclear test in the US.[65] Given the short period for conducting the test, the general level of unpreparedness for nuclear testing, as well as the recognition that nuclear testing is not necessary for the US, this announcement was largely seen as a political bargaining chip rather than an expression of military need.[66] The Trump administration's announcement, however, underscored the fact that the test ban is far from being accomplished.

Middle East WMD-Free Zone

As mentioned at the start of this chapter, the resolution on the Middle East—from the perspective of those who participated in the NPTREC—was not expected to become a major issue. Only the Arab countries expected this topic to be a major theme. The early postextension years were true to form: while resolutions on the topic were being passed in the UN General Assembly, there was little change on the ground. This shifted in 2005, when the lack of progress on the establishment of the MEWMDFZ became a key reason for the collapse of the 2005 NPT RevCon.[67] In 2010, Egypt succeeded in reinserting the topic on the RevCon agenda, and this time it got a major concession: as part of the final Action Plan, the conference endorsed that the UN secretary general, together with the three sponsors of the 1995 resolution (Russia, the

UK, and the US) and all regional states, would organize a conference on the establishment of the MEWMDFZ in 2012.[68] In October 2011, Finland was designated host of the conference, and Finnish Vice Minister of Foreign Affairs Jaakko Laajava was designated conference facilitator. Throughout the region, the lack of Middle Eastern facilitators was seen as a snub and as an obstacle to the success of the conference.[69] It was canceled in 2012, citing the disagreements among the states. This disagreement is widely seen to stem from the diverging perspective between Israel and the other regional states. The breakdown of the process led to a showdown at the 2015 NPT RevCon, during which Egypt forced through language on convening the conference within 180 days, which was unacceptable to Canada, the UK, and the US. These countries then blocked the adoption of the final declaration at the conference.[70]

As the route through the NPT RevCons appeared difficult, Egypt once again pushed the idea of the conference through the UN General Assembly. In December 2018, the UNGA passed a resolution that entrusted the UN secretary general "with the convening, no later than 2019 . . . of a conference on the establishment of a Middle East zone free of nuclear weapons and other weapons of mass destruction."[71] Convened in November 2019, that conference held session for a period of one week and was ignored by the US and Israel, ending with a political declaration and a plan to convene again in 2020.

While little progress has been made on the issue of MEWMDFZ since 1995, the topic has become the dominating theme of the NPT RevCons. It is thus likely that it will remain a relevant theme in this setting. As was already remarked at the end of chapter 5, this is surely not what the diplomats back in 1995 expected.

Nuclear Disarmament and the Ban Treaty

In the early days (and years) after the NPT's indefinite extension, progress on nuclear disarmament seemed promising. France and the UK announced that they were going to retire their tactical nuclear weapons. Moreover, arms control discussions were ongoing between the US and Russia, with the support of presidents Clinton and Yeltsin.

Nonetheless, in May 1998 both India and Pakistan tested their nuclear weapons, which was followed by a series of missile tests and smaller conflicts.[72]

In the early 2000s, the US formally withdrew from the Anti-Ballistic Missile Treaty. However, the Bush administration was also "committed to achieving a credible deterrent with the lowest-possible nuclear weapons consistent with our national security needs, including our obligations to our allies," in the words of the president.[73] President Obama, as well as leaders in the UK, spoke at length about the need for nuclear disarmament but did not take any concrete steps in that direction.[74]

Instead, the national security strategies of the nuclear-weapon states continued to rely heavily on nuclear weapons and nuclear deterrence. Modernization projects have been undertaken in all nuclear-weapon states, extending the lifetime of nuclear weapons well into the second half of the twenty-first century. The mantle of nuclear disarmament found unlikely champions: in 2007, four prominent US statesmen—three former secretaries of state and a prominent senator—coauthored an op-ed for the *Wall Street Journal* in which they argued for nuclear disarmament.[75] Their piece revitalized global attention on nuclear disarmament among the broader public.

The most prominent initiative of the last two decades to advance nuclear disarmament was the so-called Humanitarian Initiative that led to the Treaty on the Prohibition of Nuclear Weapons (TPNW). The Humanitarian Initiative—so named because it attempted to ban the use of nuclear weapons based on their humanitarian impact—has gained traction since 2012, and membership quickly increased. The first conference on the Humanitarian Impact of Nuclear Weapons, hosted in Norway in 2013, was attended by 127 countries; 146 members attended the 2014 conference in Nayarit, Mexico; and the December 2014 conference in Vienna was also attended by the US and the UK, as the first nuclear-weapon states to participate. That conference ended with the bilateral Vienna Pledge calling for a ban on the production, stockpiling, and use of nuclear weapons. The pledge was initially supported by 107 states and was adopted by the UNGA during its seventieth session as Resolution 70/48, with 139 out of 168 countries voting in favor.[76]

The proponents rallied support for the pledge using three key arguments: First, the history of close calls. As existing research has argued, nuclear history is full of "near misses" in which only a small step prevented the use of nuclear weapons.[77] Second, the potential catastrophic impact of nuclear explosions on human society. Nuclear explosions release energy in the forms of heat, blast, and radiation, bringing immediate, long-term destruction. By the calculations of the International Campaign Against Nuclear Weapons (ICAN), "a regional nuclear war involving around 100 Hiroshima-sized weapons would disrupt the global climate and agricultural production so severely that more than a billion people would be at risk of famine."[78] And third, the legal argument. Campaign leaders—the International Committee of the Red Cross (ICRC) and the Red Crescent—state that due to the indiscriminate suffering nuclear weapons bring about, their impact is incompatible with the principles of distinction, proportionality, necessity, and infliction of unnecessary suffering.[79]

In August 2016, the UN Open-Ended Working Group (OEWG) recommended convening a conference in 2017 to negotiate a legally binding instrument to ban nuclear weapons in an effort to advance multilateral nuclear disarmament negotiations. Sixty-eight participating countries voted in favor, 22 opposed, and 13 abstained. Those who voted against and abstained were mainly NATO countries, countries wanting to join NATO, and Japan.[80]

That outcome was the result of a long history, which draws ideationally on debates from the era of negotiating the NPT, but more concretely from a process that began in the early 2000s. As American scholar Rebecca Davis Gibbons illustrates in her masterful account, the original supporters of the Humanitarian Initiative had a much more complex instrument in mind that would favor a "building block" approach toward a nuclear weapons convention. Only over time did the focus among the proponents shift from a nuclear weapon convention to a "simple ban treaty," without elaborate (and difficult to negotiate) provisions for verification and disarmament.[81] Proponents of a simple ban treaty argue that the mere existence of the treaty (and associated membership thereof) would be enough to create normative pressure on the nuclear-weapon states to disarm.[82]

When the final negotiation on the TPNW started in New York in the Spring of 2017, 122 countries took part. This limited participation in the TPNW negotiations reflects the unwillingness of the countries pushing for the treaty to accept compromises and look for accommodation with countries that might be willing to support new steps toward multilateral

nuclear disarmament in principle but find major flaws in the TPNW.[83] In
July 2017, the draft treaty was adopted and in September it was opened
for signature. Following ratification primarily by small and middle powers, the TPNW entered into force in January 2021. Proponents of nuclear
disarmament laud the treaty and its transformative power to change the
way nuclear politics is being conducted by reframing the discussion in humanitarian terms.[84] However, as British scholar Laura Considine argues,
the treaty seems to fit a pattern in international politics of "rethinking the
unthinkable."[85]

While the ban treaty is probably not going to deliver nuclear disarmament, that theme is likely to remain on the NPT's agenda for years to come.
In many ways, the commitments undertaken in 1995 have not been fulfilled,
despite some numerical decreases in nuclear weapon arsenals. Yet thinking
within the NPT is stuck between those interested in persuading the nuclear-
weapon states to pursue meaningful steps (which remains difficult), and those
more interested in posturing than in progress.

What If Indefinite Extension Had Not Happened?

One may ask whether the path of the global nonproliferation regime would
be different had an alternative extension been chosen. As discussed in chapter 1, other alternative suggestions were available: red-light rolling extension,
green-light rolling extension, or extension with strings attached. The latter
was a solution that posed several difficulties; for this reason, I will focus on
the rolling-extension alternatives.

The proposal by a group of nonaligned countries for a red-light rolling
extension foresaw a process in which the subsequent 2000 RevCon would
make "concrete recommendations" for "*inter alia,* the attainment, within
specific time-frames" of a progress toward the CTBT, FMCT, legally binding negative security assurances, elimination of nuclear weapons and other
weapons of mass destruction, establishment of nuclear-weapon-free zones,
and an "unimpeded" transfer of nuclear technology for peaceful purposes.[86]

The CTBT negotiations were in fact completed by then, but the treaty's
ratification was stalled for reasons (explained earlier) that an alternate NPT
extension was unlikely to change. The FMCT negotiations were being blocked
as well, by Pakistan as an NPT nonparty.[87]

As the reader will recall, the proponents of the alternatives to indefinite extension pushed these alternatives in order to put pressure on the nuclear-weapon states to disarm. A contrasting argument was made by the nuclear-weapon states and their allies: that the risk that the NPT might disappear in fact or in effect would make states hedge against its undoing. The risk of disappearance would be lower in case of the red-light rolling extension, since a majority of states would have to vote against the extension. Nevertheless, any risk of the treaty's disappearance would lower the possible normative commitments to it.

Both nuclear-weapon states and non-nuclear-weapon states hedged against the treaty's potential collapse. Among the former, the hedge would take the form of continuous possession of nuclear weapons, hence undermining nuclear disarmament efforts. Among the latter, the hedge would take a technological form through the pursuit of nuclear latency.[88] If the risk of the treaty disappearing was real, then the ability of the US to appeal to normative commitments (a strategy frequently used in dissuading friends and foes from the pursuit of nuclear weapons) would have considerably less chance of success, and increasingly more countries would pursue latency. This hedge would most likely undermine nonproliferation efforts.

However, the uncertainty and hedging against the treaty collapse would also have a negative impact on the peaceful uses of nuclear energy, by imposing curbs on trade of nuclear technologies for peaceful purposes. Given the risk that the treaty limitations on building nuclear weapons could disappear, states might be more hesitant to provide advanced nuclear technologies to other countries, simply out of uncertainty about the future legal regime governing these technologies.[89]

In terms of regional issues, any of the alternative treaty extensions would almost certainly have led to different outcomes than the ones brought about by indefinite extension, particularly regarding the MEWMDFZ. Without indefinite extension, the resolution on MEWMDFZ sponsored by the NPT depositaries would not have occurred. A resolution passed with votes from the nonaligned states would be most likely purely declaratory, and it would be impossible for Egypt to attract broader attention to the issue that was so high on the Egyptian agenda.

In short, it is difficult to imagine a world in which either a red-light or a green-light rolling extension would lead to more progress on nuclear disarmament than has already occurred. It is unlikely that the pressure from non-nuclear-weapon states would have persuaded nuclear-weapon states to disarm.

US Social Network Power in 2020

Back in 1995, the US central position within global networks helped it advance the goal of indefinite extension. Through cooperation with the European countries, Egypt, and South Africa, the US managed to lobby and entice countries, divide the opposition, and bring opponents on board. Back in 1995, the US could draw on a large network and on its position in the global diplomatic, trade, and military networks. It was, simply stated, a hegemon.[90]

A reasonable question can be asked: How much purchase does the social network theory provide in explaining US multilateral nuclear policy in 2021 and beyond? After all, the US failed to prevent the emergence of the TPNW—the Humanitarian Initiative—a treaty that arguably creates difficulties for the US and its allies in Europe.

This book shows that even great powers need secondary powers to legitimate and advocate their preferences. The social network theory, as applied in this book, is not deterministic—it does not say what has to happen, only how an actor's position within various social networks affects that actor's exercise of power and advocacy of preferences. In the past decade and a half, the message that the world has become multipolar and that the US no longer holds the dominant position has grown. Still, in recent years, a number of American theorists and practitioners have recognized the importance of global networks for the advancement of US foreign policy. These are often contextualized as "policy networks," groups of institutions (or individuals, depending on the definition) "who share a common expertise, a common technical language to communicate that expertise, [and] normative concerns."[91] These networks are important for discussion about numerous topics of global governance—from marine protection to sanctions enforcement. Within the nonproliferation field, scholar Jeffrey Knopf has argued that both transnational networks and US leadership are crucial for successful international cooperation on WMD nonproliferation.[92] Anne-Marie Slaughter, a Princeton professor and senior policy maker, has advocated that the US must pursue a "grand strategy of network centrality," in which it must be in the center of prominent international networks.[93] In a later book, Slaughter doubled down on this argument, positing that the US must embed itself in the relevant networks if it wants to influence global governance.[94] Political scientists Alexander Cooley and Daniel Nexon seem to agree. In their recent work, *Exit from Hegemony*, they argue that as US hegemony wanes, the importance of various networks for US foreign policy increases.[95]

Intuitively, this argument makes sense. The benefits of US hegemony extended well after the lapse of the "unipolar moment."[96] As was discussed in chapter 2, an advantageous position within a global network can sometimes be used by states to counterweigh an otherwise disadvantageous position. Even if countries' material power declines compared to their competitors—a frequent measure of the decline in US power—the ability to "get things done" on the basis of a stated position within the international networks might be beneficial. One of the key insights of social network theory for international relations scholarship, after all, is that the advantageous position within international networks is helpful for actors to counterbalance material shortcomings. If that dictum applies to small and medium powers, it applies doubly to great powers, which by nature enjoy strong embedding within international networks.[97]

Furthermore, we should understand that while the case for the end of hegemony is probably clear, the US will, for the foreseeable future, be a dominant power in the global system. Its economic, military, and diplomatic might is unequaled on the world stage, and it enjoys many of the intangible benefits of hegemony. For example, because of the strength of the US dollar in the global monetary system and the centrality of US banks, US unilateral sanctions are de facto adhered to even outside US jurisdiction.[98]

Even then, if any perceived eroding of US power can be counterbalanced by continuous network centrality in theory, it remains up to the US to see whether that centrality can be leveraged in practice. And this is where current discussions about US foreign policy come into play. The Trump administration did not strengthen or nurture cooperation with its allies, such as the European countries. While the North Atlantic alliance is still alive and active, the repeated spats between Trump and the European allies severely fractured support. And while numerous European countries cautiously supported the Trump administration's final initiatives—such as the initiative on Creating an Environment for Nuclear Disarmament—many also considered the administration not to be serious about arms control, as evidenced by pulling out from the Intermediate Nuclear Forces (INF) and the Open Skies treaties, and sending out mixed signals about the extension of the New START. The Biden administration has shown, in its first months, keen interest in showing more interest in arms control and nonproliferation, for example by extending the New START. In his remarks to the Conference on Disarmament in February 2021, Secretary of State Antony J. Blinken also pledged that the US "will do [its] part to make [the upcoming RevCon] a success."[99]

In examining why the US did not prevent the emergence of the TPNW, for example, it is clear that previous US administrations—whether led by Barack Obama or Donald Trump—did not view the TPNW as a threat. The Obama administration sent a letter to NATO allies highlighting that "efforts to negotiate an immediate ban on nuclear weapons or to delegitimize nuclear deterrence are fundamentally at odds with NATO's basic policies on deterrence and our shared security interest,"[100] while exerting no effort to stop the negotiations or to use different tools of statecraft to influence other countries. By not coordinating its position with European allies early on to counteract the ban treaty movement, which US friends in the Global South (such as South Africa) were broadly supportive of, the US became less able to influence these negotiations.

The European countries' reaction to the US withdrawal from the INF—the Intermediate-Range Nuclear Forces treaty forged in 1987 between Reagan and Gorbachev—was similarly telling. On the one hand, one could observe a rally-round-the-flag effect of herding around NATO and proclaiming NATO unity in calling on Russia to comply.[101] On the other hand, shock about the decision and a sense foreboding prevailed. The EU called on the US to "consider the consequences of its possible withdrawal from the INF on its own security, on the security of its allies and of the whole world," while German foreign minister Heiko Maas stated that pulling out of the treaty would have "many negative consequences."[102] The Dutch government's Advisory Council on International Affairs' recent report on the future of nuclear weapons concluded that the "United States' current foreign policy . . . is weakening the international multilateral order."[103]

And so, while the US could, theoretically, still manage to leverage various networks to advance multilateral nonproliferation goals, the presiding administration must be willing and able to activate these networks before any of them can start bearing fruit. This applies to multilateral arms control treaties in particular and to multilateral agreements in general. The beneficial networked position enables the pursuit of certain goals, but alone it does not guarantee reaching them. The decision to involve partners is necessary to make use of America's networked power. This observation comes back to a sentence from McGeorge Bundy's letter to Bill Clinton in 1995: "The American President has been the accepted leader against nuclear danger throughout the last fifty years—except when he has chosen not to play that role."[104]

Notes

All citations of archival documents include reference to source (usually, an archive or a website). A few documents from Germany's Political Archive of the Federal Foreign Office were provided outside of their boxes (as they were, presumably, pulled from multiple boxes). They are listed as "selected documents," and their copies are available from the author.

Titles of documents are presented in their original language and also translated. Russian and Arabic titles were transliterated into the Latin script, following accepted conventions, and also translated. After a recent change to the FOIA virtual reading room of the US Department of State, direct links to individual documents cannot, unfortunately, be acquired. Readers must therefore search for document titles using the search function at https://foia.state.gov/Search/Search.aspx.

Introduction

1. United Nations, *1995 Review and Extension Conference of the Parties to the Treaty on the Non-Proliferation of Nuclear Weapons, Final Document, Part III—Summary and Verbatim Records, NPT/CONF.1995/32* (United Nations, New York, *1996*), 179, https://documents-dds-ny.un.org/doc/UNDOC/GEN/N96/328/12/IMG/N9632812.pdf?OpenElement.

2. "Decision 1: Strengthening the Review Process for the Treaty," https://unoda-web.s3-accelerate.amazonaws.com/wp-content/uploads/assets/WMD/Nuclear/1995-NPT/pdf/NPT_CONF199532.pdf; "Decision 2: Principles and Objectives for Nuclear Non-Proliferation and Disarmament," https://unoda-web.s3-accelerate.amazonaws.com/wp-content/uploads/assets/WMD/Nuclear/1995-NPT/pdf/

NPT_CONF199501.pdf; and "Decision 3: Extension of the Treaty on the Non-Proliferation of Nuclear Weapons," https://unoda-web.s3-accelerate.amazonaws.com/wp-content/uploads/assets/WMD/Nuclear/1995-NPT/pdf/NPT_CONF199503.pdf; in *1995 Review and Extension Conference of the Parties to the Treaty on the Non-Proliferation of Nuclear Weapons, Final Document, Part I—Organization and work of the Conference, NPT/CONF.1995/32, Annex* (United Nations, New York, 1995).

3. Kathleen Hart, "NPT Conference Opening Marred by Discord over Voting Rules," *Nucleonics Week* 36, no. 16 (1995): 1.

4. Joseph F. Pilat, "The NPT's Prospects," in *1995: A New Beginning for the NPT?* ed. Joseph F. Pilat and Robert E. Pendley (Boston: Springer, 1995), 47–61.

5. Hans M. Kristensen and Robert S. Norris, "Global Nuclear Weapons Inventories, 1945–2013," *Bulletin of the Atomic Scientists* 69, no. 5 (2013): 75–81.

6. Siegfried S. Hecker, ed., *Doomed to Cooperate: How American and Russian Scientists Joined Forces to Avert Some of the Greatest Post-Cold War Nuclear Dangers* (Los Alamos, NM: Bathtub Row Press, 2016).

7. "Sarnia Symposium on the International Nuclear Non-Proliferation Regime in the 1990s," *MS424 A3079/1/1/1 (Archives of the University of Southampton, Southampton, UK) 8.*

8. John Simpson and Darryl Howlett, "The NPT Renewal Conference: Stumbling toward 1995," *International Security* 19, no. 1 (1994): 41–71.

9. Joseph F. Pilat, "Future of the NPT," in *Kernwaffenverbreitung Und Internationaler Systemwandel: Neue Risiken Und Gestaltungsmöglichkeiten (Nuclear Weapons Proliferation and Change in International System: New Risks and Policy Options),* ed. Joachim Krause (Baden-Baden, Germany: Nomos Verlagsgesellschaft, 1994), 443–57.

10. Pilat, "The NPT's Prospects," 58.

11. Harald Müller, "Smoothing the Path to 1995: Amending the Nuclear Non-Proliferation Treaty and Enhancing the Regime," in *Nuclear Non-Proliferation: An Agenda for the 1990s,* ed. John Simpson (Cambridge: Cambridge University Press, 1987), 123–37; Harald Müller, David Fischer, and Wolfgang Kötter, *Nuclear Non-Proliferation and Global Order* (Oxford: Oxford University Press, 1994); Harald Müller, "Beyond 1995: The NPT and Europe," in Pilat and Pendley (1995), *1995: A New Beginning for the NPT?* 151–61. Müller's views were shared by his fellow German, Joachim Krause. See Joachim Krause, "The Future of the NPT: A German Perspective," in Pilat and Pendley (1995), *1995: A New Beginning for the NPT?* 135–50.

12. Importantly, Sanders did not think highly of the criticism. He wrote, "much of the criticism directed at the treaty is not only largely unjust, but . . . it can be clearly shown to lack a factual basis." See Ben Sanders, "1995: A Time for Optimism?" in Pilat and Pendley (1995), *1995: A New Beginning for the NPT?* 77–89.

13. For more information on the PPNN, see Michal Onderco, "The Programme for Promoting Nuclear Non-Proliferation and the NPT Extension," *International History Review* 42, no. 4 (2020): 851–68.

14. W. Alton Jones's arms control program, led by George Perkovich, published annual reports that are a magnificent source for analysis of the zeitgeist of the 1990s in the arms control area. Ford Foundation's archives are today available for study in the Rockefeller Archive Center in Sleepy Hollow, NY, and offer unique insights into numerous off-record meetings from this period.

15. George Bunn, "Statement by George Bunn (on Behalf of Lawyers Alliance for World Security) to the 1995 NPT Review/Extension Conference" (April 27, 1995); George Bunn and Roland Timerbaev, "Letter to Michael Krepon" (January 27, 1995); Roland Timerbaev, "Statement by Roland Timerbaev at the NGO Meeting During the 4th NPT Prepcom" (January 25, 1995; personal communication, 2016); George Bunn, "Lawyers Alliance for World Security (Laws) Is for a Reliable Extension of the NPT (Statement to the January 1995 NPT Prepcom" (1995). These documents are available at the Personal Archive of Roland M. Timerbaev at the PIR Center in Moscow.

16. "NVV-Überprüfungs - Und Verlängungskonferenz 1995. Treffen Der Core Group Am 10.02.1995 (NPT Review and Extension Conference 1995. Meeting of the Core Group on February 10, 1995)" (1995), *Political Archive of the German Federal Foreign Office, row 675, box 48828*, Berlin.

17. John Holum, "NPT Extension. Meeting between Sri Lankan Ambassador Jayantha Dhanapala and ACDA Director Holum and Deputy Director Earle. Friday, March 31, 1995 (Washington DC)" (1995), *NPT–March 1995, box 1, OA/ID720, Nonproliferation and Export Controls, the files of Daniel Poneman, Clinton Presidential Records/NSC, Clinton Presidential Library/NARA, Little Rock, AR)*.

18. Barbara Crossette, "Treaty Aimed at Halting Spread of Nuclear Weapons Extended," *New York Times*, May 12, 1995,1.

19. Barbara Crossette, "China Breaks Ranks with Other Nuclear Nations on Treaty," *New York Times*, April 19, 1995.

20. Or Rabinowitz and Nicholas L. Miller, "Keeping the Bombs in the Basement: U.S. Nonproliferation Policy toward Israel, South Africa, and Pakistan," *International Security* 40, no. 1 (2015): 47–86; Francis J. Gavin, "Strategies of Inhibition: US Grand Strategy, the Nuclear Revolution, and Nonproliferation," *International Security* 40, no. 1 (2015): 9–46; Tristan A. Volpe, "Atomic Inducements: The Case for 'Buying Out' Nuclear Latency," *Nonproliferation Review* 23, no. 3–4 (2016): 481–93; Gene Gerzhoy, "Alliance Coercion and Nuclear Restraint: How the United States Thwarted West Germany's Nuclear Ambitions," *International Security* 39, no. 4 (2015): 91–129; Jeffrey W. Taliaferro, *Defending Frenemies: Alliances, Politics, and Nuclear Nonproliferation in US Foreign Policy* (Oxford: Oxford University Press, 2019).

21. Gavin, "Strategies of Inhibition"; Francis J. Gavin, *Nuclear Statecraft: History and Strategy in America's Atomic Age* (Ithaca, NY: Cornell University Press, 2012).

22. The White House: *The National Security Strategy of the United States of America* (NSS report, Washington, DC, March 2006, https://nssarchive.us/wp-content/

uploads/2020/04/2006.pdf); *A National Security Strategy of Engagement and Enlargement* (NSS report, Washington, DC, July 1994, https://nssarchive.us/wp-content/ uploads/2020/04/1994.pdf); *The National Security Strategy* (NSS report, Washington, DC 2010, https://nssarchive.us/wp-content/uploads/2020/04/2010.pdf); *National Security Strategy* (NSS report, Washington, DC, 2015, https://nssarchive.us/wp-content/ uploads/2020/04/2015.pdf).

23. Deon Geldenhuys, *Deviant Conduct in World Politics* (Houndmills, Basingstoke, UK: Palgrave Macmillan, 2004); Anthony Lake, "Confronting Backlash States," *Foreign Affairs* 73, no. 2 (1994): 45–55; Miroslav Nincic, *Renegade Regimes: Confronting Deviant Behavior in World Politics* (New York: Columbia University Press, 2005).

24. William Walker, "Nuclear Enlightenment and Counter-Enlightenment," *International Affairs* 83, no. 3 (2007): 431–53.

25. For the most forceful statement, see John J. Mearsheimer, "The False Promise of International Institutions," *International Security* 19, no. 3 (1994): 5–49. For a recent restatement with a reference to nuclear nonproliferation, see John J. Mearsheimer, "Bound to Fail: The Rise and Fall of the Liberal International Order," *International Security* 43, no. 4 (2019): 7–50.

26. Daniel Verdier, "Multilateralism, Bilateralism, and Exclusion in the Nuclear Proliferation Regime," *International Organization* 62, no. 3 (2008): 439–76.

27. Andrew J. Coe and Jane Vaynman, "Collusion and the Nuclear Nonproliferation Regime," *Journal of Politics* 77, no. 4 (2015): 983–97.

28. Roland Popp, "The Long Road to the NPT: From Superpower Collusion to Global Compromise," in *Negotiating the Nuclear Non-Proliferation Treaty: Origins of the Nuclear Order*, ed. Roland Popp, Liviu Horovitz, and Andreas Wenger (Abingdon, UK: Routledge, 2017), 9–36.

29. Nick Ritchie, "A Hegemonic Nuclear Order: Understanding the Ban Treaty and the Power Politics of Nuclear Weapons," *Contemporary Security Policy* 40, no. 4 (2019): 409–34; Jan Ruzicka, "Behind the Veil of Good Intentions: Power Analysis of the Nuclear Non-Proliferation Regime," *International Politics* 55, no. 3 (2018): 369–85.

30. Thomas Graham, Jr., *Disarmament Sketches: Three Decades of Arms Control and International Law* (Seattle: Institute for Global and Regional Security Studies; University of Washington Press, 2002); Susan B. Welsh, "Delegate Perspectives on the 1995 NPT Review and Extension Conference," *Nonproliferation Review* 2, no. 3 (1995): 1–24.

31. David A. Lake, *Hierarchy in International Relations* (Ithaca, NY: Cornell University Press, 2009), p.12-13

32. "DFA Director-General Discusses US-SA Relations, Pariah States, DFA Restructuring" (June 2, 1995), US *Department of State, FOIA Virtual Reading Room, Case no. F-2016-00610.*

33. Coe and Vaynman, "Collusion and the Nuclear Nonproliferation Regime."

34. Friedrich Kratochwil, "Thrasymmachos Revisited: On the Relevance of Norms

and the Study of Law for International Relations," in *The Puzzles of Politics: Inquiries into the Genesis and Transformation of International Relations*, ed. Friedrich Kratochwil (Abingdon, UK: Routledge, 2011), 83–98.

35. Barbara Koremenos, "Loosening the Ties that Bind: A Learning Model of Agreement Flexibility," *International Organization* 55, no. 2 (2001): 289–325.

36. Note that the point to which the NPT prevented the spread of nuclear weapons is heavily problematized in the academic literature. For a paradigmatic statement of this argument, see Dong-Joon Jo and Erik Gartzke, "Determinants of Nuclear Weapons Proliferation," *Journal of Conflict Resolution* 51, no. 1 (2007): 167–94. For excellent reviews of this academic debate, see Scott D. Sagan, "The Causes of Nuclear Weapons Proliferation," *Annual Review of Political Science* 14, no. 1 (2011): 225–44; William C. Potter, "The NPT & the Sources of Nuclear Restraint," *Daedalus* 139, no. 1 (2010): 68–81.

37. Jayantha Dhanapala, "The Permanent Extension of the NPT, 1995," in *The Oxford Handbook of Modern Diplomacy*, ed. Scott Cooper, Jorge Heine, and Ramesh Thakur (Oxford: Oxford University Press, 2015), 810–25; Jayantha Dhanapala and Randy Ryddel, "Multilateral Diplomacy and the NPT: An Insider's Account," in *Reflections on the Treaty on the Non-Proliferation of Nuclear Weapons: Review Conferences and the Future of the NPT*, ed. Jayantha Dhanapala and Tariq Rauf (Stockholm: SIPRI, 2017), 5–133; Graham, *Disarmament Sketches*; Thomas Markram, *A Decade of Disarmament, Transformation and Progress: An Assessment of the Development and Implementation of Policy on Disarmament, Non-Proliferation and Arms Control in South Africa 1994–2004* (Pretoria: SaferAfrica, 2004); Tariq Rauf and Rebecca Johnson, "After the NPT's Indefinite Extension: The Future of the Global Nonproliferation Regime," *Nonproliferation Review* 3, no. 1 (1995): 28–42.

38. Cecilia Albin, *Justice and Fairness in International Negotiation* (Cambridge: Cambridge University Press, 2001).

39. Harald Müller, "Justice and the Nonproliferation Regime," in *Behavioral Economics and Nuclear Weapons*, ed. Anne Harrington and Jeffrey W. Knopf (Athens: University of Georgia Press, 2019), 135–58.

40. Albin, *Justice and Fairness*, 205; emphasis in original.

41. I am thankful to Scott Sagan for suggesting the term "minimally just solution."

42. "Decision 3."

43. This episode was recounted by Harald Müller, scientific adviser to the German delegation, in a critical oral history conference in 2017. See Michal Onderco and Leopoldo Nuti, eds., *Extending the NPT* (Washington, DC: Woodrow Wilson International Center for Scholars, 2020).

44. Joachim Blatter and Markus Haverland, *Designing Case Studies: Explanatory Approaches in Small-N Research* (Basingstoke, UK: Palgrave Macmillan, 2012).

45. Derek Beach and Rasmus Brun Pedersen, *Process-Tracing Methods: Foundations and Guidelines* (Ann Arbor: University of Michigan Press, 2013).

46. I use the term "examines" instead of "tests" because, in this book, I conduct only minimal hypothesis testing per se.

47. The transcripts of all of the interviews can be found in the Digital Archive of the Wilson Center, https://digitalarchive.wilsoncenter.org/collection/496/the-1995-npt-review-and-extension-conference.

48. Rodrigo Mallea, Matias Spektor, and Nicholas J. Wheeler, eds., *The Origins of Nuclear Cooperation: A Critical Oral History of Argentina and Brazil* (Rio de Janeiro & Washington, DC: Fundação Getúlio Vargas & Wilson Center, 2015).

49. Mallea, Spektor, and Wheeler, *The Origins of Nuclear Cooperation*; Sue Onslow and Anna-Mart van Wyk, eds., *Southern Africa in the Cold War, Post-1974*, Critical Oral History Conference Series (Washington, DC: Woodrow Wilson International Center for Scholars, 2013).

50. Chapter 4 draws on material developed in Michal Onderco and Anna-Mart Van Wyk, "Birth of a Norm Champion: How South Africa Came to Support the NPT's Indefinite Extension," *Nonproliferation Review* 26, no. 1–2 (2019): 23–41.

Chapter 1: Why Indefinite Extension?

1. "Treaty on the Non-Proliferation of Nuclear Weapons (NPT)." UN Office for Disarmament Affairs (UNODA), New York, July 1, 1968, https://www.un.org/disarmament/wmd/nuclear/npt/text/.

2. Miguel Marin-Bosch, "The 1995 NPT Review and Extension Conference," *Irish Studies in International Affairs* 6 (1995): 23–31.

3. William C. Potter and Gaukhar Mukhatzhanova, *Nuclear Politics and the Non-Aligned Movement: Principles Vs. Pragmatism* (London: Routledge, 2012).

4. Barbara Koremenos, "Contracting around International Uncertainty," *American Political Science Review* 99, no. 4 (2005): 549–65.

5. For a paradigmatic realist statement about anarchy and uncertainty, see John J. Mearsheimer, *The Tragedy of Great Power Politics* (New York: W.W. Norton, 2001). For the most advanced institutionalist theorizing about how institutions accommodate and bind uncertainty, see Barbara Koremenos: "Loosening the Ties that Bind"; "Contracting around International Uncertainty"; and *The Continent of International Law: Explaining Agreement Design* (Cambridge: Cambridge University Press, 2016).

6. Koremenos, *The Continent of International Law*, 47.

7. Christopher Way and Karthika Sasikumar, *"Leaders and Laggards: When and Why Do Countries Sign the NPT?"* (working paper, Research Group in International Security [REGIS], Montreal, 2004); Scott D. Sagan, "Why Do States Build Nuclear Weapons? Three Models in Search of a Bomb," *International Security* 21, no. 3 (1996): 54–86.

8. Mohamed Ibrahim Shaker, *The Nuclear Non-Proliferation Treaty: Origin and Implementation, 1959–1979*, vol. 2 (London & New York: Oceana, 1980), 859. Shaker

also engages in some serious exegesis about the difference between the two drafts. The difference, however, is not the central point here.

9. "ENDC Meeting; Geneva, February 21, 1967; Background Paper; Significant Legal Questions Affecting the Non-Proliferation Treaty" (February 11, 1967). US *Department of State, FOIA Virtual Reading Room, Case no. M-2020-00304*https://foia. state.gov/Search/Results.aspx?caseNumber=M-2020–00304.

10. The formulation is written in de Palma's memorandum from the meeting; see ACDA, "FRG Views on Non-Proliferation Treaty" (January 26, 1967), *US Department of State, FOIA Virtual Reading Room, Case no. M-2020-00304*.

11. Shaker, *The Nuclear Non-Proliferation Treaty*, 859.

12. Ibid., 860.

13. George Bunn and Charles Van Doren: *Options for Extension of the NPT: The Intention of the Drafters of Article X.2*, PPNN study no. 2 (Southampton, UK: Programme for Promoting Nuclear Nonproliferation, 1991) and *Two Options for the 1995 NPT Extension Conference Revisited* (Washington, DC: Lawyers Alliance for World Security, 1992); Shaker, *The Nuclear Non-Proliferation Treaty*.

14. Leopoldo Nuti, "'A Turning Point in Postwar Foreign Policy': Italy and the NPT Negotiations, 1967–1969," in *Negotiating the Nuclear Non-Proliferation Treaty: Origins of the Nuclear Order*, ed. Roland Popp, Liviu Horovitz, and Andreas Wenger (Abingdon, UK: Routledge, 2017), 77–97.

15. Shaker, *The Nuclear Non-Proliferation Treaty*, 861.

16. Bunn and Van Doren, *Two Options*.

17. Shaker, *The Nuclear Non-Proliferation Treaty*, p. 862 (vol. 2).

18. Ibid.

19. Nuti, "'A Turning Point in Postwar Foreign Policy,'" discusses the note written by Rusk to Fanfani; Shaker, *The Nuclear Non-Proliferation Treaty*, discusses the US and Canadian reactions within the ENDC.

20. Jennifer Erickson and Christopher Way, "Membership Has Its Privileges: Conventional Arms and Influence within the Nuclear Nonproliferation Treaty," in *The Causes and Consequences of Nuclear Proliferation*, ed. Matthew Kroenig, Erik Gartzke, and Robert Rauchraus (New York: Routledge, 2011), 32–60; Verdier, "Multilateralism, Bilateralism, and Exclusion."

21. Harald Müller and Wolfgang Kötter, *Germany, Europe & Nuclear Non-Proliferation, PPNN study no. 1* (Southampton, UK: Mountbatten Centre for International Studies, 1991); Harald Müller, "The Internalization of Principles, Norms and Rules by Governments: The Case of Security Regimes," in *Regime Theory and International Relations*, ed. Volker Rittberger (Oxford: Clarendon, 1993), 361–90.

22. This applied not only to NATO allies but also to other countries. See, for example, on Sweden, the work of Thomas Jonter in his *The Key to Nuclear Restraint:*

The Swedish Plans to Acquire Nuclear Weapons During the Cold War (London: Palgrave, 2016).

23. In another paper, I study participation in the NPT RevCons in more detail. See Michal Onderco, "Variation in Delegation Size in Multilateral Diplomacy," *British Journal of Politics and International Relations* 21, no. 2 (2019): 421–38.

24. Ben Sanders, *NPT Review Conferences and the Role of Consensus, Issue review no. 4* (Southampton, UK: PPNN, 1995), 1.

25. Ibid., p.1

26. On cosponsorship analysis, see Michal Onderco, "Collaboration Networks in Conference Diplomacy: The Case of Non-Proliferation Regime," *International Studies Review* 22, no. 4 (2020): 739–57.

27. Dhanapala and Ryddel, "Multilateral Diplomacy and the NPT"; Reaching Critical Will, "History of the NPT 1975–1995," *Reaching Critical Will website*, n.d., https://www.reachingcriticalwill.org/disarmament-fora/npt/history-of-the-npt-1975-1995.

28. For discussions on CTBT, see Pierce S. Corden, "Historical Context and Steps to Implement the CTBT," in *Banning the Bang or the Bomb? Negotiating the Nuclear Test Ban Regime*, ed. I. William Zartman, Mordechai Melamud, and Paul Meerts (Cambridge: Cambridge University Press, 2014), 17–31. However, the book by Or Rabinowitz remains unparalleled in its historical discussion about nuclear test limitations. See Or Rabinowitz, *Bargaining on Nuclear Tests: Washington and Its Cold War Deals* (Oxford: Oxford University Press, 2014).

29. Carlton Stoiber, "The Evolution of NPT Review Conference Final Documents, 1975–2000." *Nonproliferation Review* 10, no. 3 (2003): 126–66.

30. The definitive work on the rule of consensus within the NPT review process was written by Ben Sanders. See his *NPT Review Conferences*. For a recent criticism of this approach, see Robert Einhorn, "The NPT Review Process: The Need for a More Productive Approach," *Arms Control Today* (September 2016), https://www.armscontrol.org/act/2016-09/features/npt-review-process-need-more-productive-approach?utm_content=bufferodb18&utm_medium=social&utm_source=twitter.com&utm_campaign=buffer.

31. Dhanapala and Ryddel, "Multilateral Diplomacy and the NPT"; Reaching Critical Will, "History of the NPT."

32. Stoiber, "The Evolution of NPT Review Conference Final Documents."

33. Ibid., 136.

34. On the origins of NSG, and its activities in the early years, see Sarah Bidgood, "The Establishment of the London Club and Nuclear-Export Controls," in *Once and Future Partners: The United States, Russia and Nuclear Non-Proliferation*, ed. William C. Potter and Sarah Bidgood (Abingdon, UK: Routledge, 2018), 135–62; Isabelle Anstey, "Negotiating Nuclear Control: The Zangger Committee and the Nuclear Suppliers'

Group in the 1970s," *International History Review* 40, no. 5 (2018): 975–95; Jayita Sarkar, "U.S. Policy to Curb West European Nuclear Exports, 1974–1978," *Journal of Cold War Studies* 21, no. 2 (2019): 110–49; William Burr, "A Scheme of 'Control': The United States and the Origins of the Nuclear Suppliers' Group, 1974–1976*," *International History Review* 36, no. 2 (2014): 252–76.

35. Farzan Sabet, "The April 1977 Persepolis Conference on the Transfer of Nuclear Technology: A Third World Revolt against US Non-Proliferation Policy?" *International History Review* 40, no. 5 (2018): 1134–51.

36. See, again, the analysis in Onderco, "Collaboration Networks in Conference Diplomacy."

37. Dhanapala and Ryddel, "Multilateral Diplomacy and the NPT"; Stoiber, "The Evolution of NPT Review Conference Final Documents."

38. Reaching Critical Will, "History of the NPT."

39. Stoiber, "The Evolution of NPT Review Conference Final Documents."

40. Dhanapala and Ryddel, "Multilateral Diplomacy and the NPT"; Mohamed Ibrahim Shaker, "The Legacy of the 1985 Nuclear Non-Proliferation Treaty Review Conference: The President's Reflections," in *Nuclear Non-Proliferation: An Agenda for the 1990s*, ed. John Simpson (Cambridge: Cambridge University Press, 1987), 9–23.

41. Dhanapala and Ryddel, "Multilateral Diplomacy and the NPT"; Reaching Critical Will, "History of the NPT."

42. Stoiber, "The Evolution of NPT Review Conference Final Documents."

43. Graham, *Disarmament Sketches*, 275. On Marin-Bosch and the Mexican approach to nuclear disarmament diplomacy, Arturo Sotomayor's master's thesis remains unparalleled in breadth. See his *"Mexico en el TNP en Momentos de Cambio" (master's thesis,* Instituto Tecnologico Autonomo de Mexico, Mexico City, 1997).

44. "Sarnia Symposium."

45. Müller, "Smoothing the Path to 1995"; Müller, Fischer, and Kötter, *Nuclear Non-Proliferation and Global Order*; Joseph F. Pilat and Robert E. Pendley, eds., *Beyond 1995: The Future of the NPT Regime* (Boston, MA: Springer, 1990).

46. Koremenos, "Loosening the Ties that Bind."

47. Pilat, "The NPT's Prospects."

48. Bunn and Van Doren, *Two Options* and *Options for Extension of the NPT*.

49. For the Mexican proposal, see United Nations, "Mexico: Draft Resolution," in *1995 Review and Extension Conference of the Parties to the Treaty on the Non-Proliferation of Nuclear Weapons* (UN Office of Disarmament, New York, May 5, 1995), https://digitallibrary.un.org/record/199290/files/NPT_CONF.1995_L.1-EN. For the resolution submitted by the coalition of nonaligned states, see United Nations, "Extension of the Treaty on the Non-Proliferation of Nuclear Weapons—Democratic People's Republic of Korea, Indonesia, Iran (Islamic Republic of), Jordan, Malaysia, Mali, Myanmar, Nigeria, Papua New Guinea, Thailand and Zimbabwe: draft decision," in *1995 Review*

and Extension Conference of the Parties to the Treaty on the Non-Proliferation of Nuclear Weapons (UN Office of Disarmament, New York, 1995), L.3, 234, http://daccess-ods. un.org/access.nsf/Get?OpenAgent&DS=NPT/CONF.1995/32(PARTIII)&Lang=E.

50. Jayantha Dhanapala, the conference president, for example associated the red-light rolling extension explicitly with Bunn and Van Doren. See Dhanapala and Ryddel, "Multilateral Diplomacy and the NPT." For the working papers, see Bunn and Van Doren: *Two Options* and *Options for Extension of the NPT*.

51. United Nations, "Extension of the Treaty."

52. United Nations, "Result of the Exchange of Views on the Review and Extension Conference on the NPT (Appendix to the Communiqué from the Ministerial Meeting of the Coordinating Bureau of the Non-Aligned Countries in Bandung, Indonesia, 25–27 April 1995)," letter dated April 27, 1995, in Bandung, UNGA Security Council, New York, 36–37, https://undocs.org/A/49/920; Ben Sanders, ed., *Newsbrief 2 (1995)*, PPNN / Mountbatten Center for International Studies, Archives of the University of Southampton, *Southampton, UK*.

53. Dhanapala and Ryddel, "Multilateral Diplomacy and the NPT," mention the same request on p.26

54. Office of the Chief State Law Adviser (International Law) of the Republic of South Africa, "South African Legal Opinion on Article X.2 of the NPT" (December 27, 1994), *Archives of the Department of International Relations and Cooperation (DIRCO), Pretoria.*

55. This point was raised in the legal analysis by the NSC, prepared in January 1995 for Daniel Poneman. While this analysis did not endorse any view, it suggested that only the red-light mechanism is legally permitted under the treaty. See Alan Kreczko, "Legal Analysis of NPT Extension Options" (January 19, 1995), *NPT–January 1995, box 1, OA/ID720, Nonproliferation and Export Controls, the files of Daniel Poneman, Clinton Presidential Records/NSC, Clinton Presidential Library/NARA, Little Rock, AR.*

56. Bunn and Van Doren, *Two Options.*

57. The articulation of these preferences can be found in United Nations, "Mexico: Draft Resolution." Marin-Bosch also spoke of them earlier; see his "The 1995 NPT Review and Extension Conference.", p.27ff

58. Bunn and Van Doren, *Options for Extension of the NPT.*

59. One of Charles Van Doren's later papers has subsections labeled "Amendments Are Unachievable," "Amendments Are Undesirable," and "Amendments Are Unnecessary." See his "Avoiding Amendment of the NPT," in Pilat and Pendley (1995), *1995: A New Beginning for the NPT?* 179–91.

60. See, for example, the assessment by Canadian diplomats involved in the NPT extension—Tariq Rauf, *interview by Michal Onderco*, 2017 (1995 NPT Revcon Oral History Project/NPIHP, Washington, DC); Sven Jurchewsky, *interview by Michal Onderco*, 2017 (1995 NPT RevCon Oral History Project/NPIHP, Washington, DC).

61. Albin, *Justice and Fairness in International Negotiation*; Cecilia Albin and Daniel

Druckman, "Bargaining over Weapons: Justice and Effectiveness in Arms Control Negotiations," *International Negotiation* 19, no. 3 (2014): 426–58.

62. For a more in-depth discussion of how the considerations of fairness permeate nuclear politics, see Harald Müller's work on fairness and justice in the global nuclear regime: Harald Müller and Carmen Wunderlich, eds., *Norm Dynamics in Multilateral Arms Control: Interests, Conflicts, and Justice*, Studies in Security and International Affairs (Athens: University of Georgia Press, 2013); Harald Müller and Daniel Druckman, "Introduction Justice in Security Negotiations," *International Negotiation* 19, no. 3 (2014): 399–409; Müller, "Justice and the Nonproliferation Regime."

63. William Walker, "Nuclear Order and Disorder," *International Affairs* 76, no. 4 (2000): 703–24, p.709

64. Gavin, *Nuclear Statecraft*; Nicholas L. Miller, *Stopping the Bomb: The Sources and Effectiveness of US Nonproliferation Policy* (Ithaca, NY: Cornell University Press, 2018); Rebecca Davis Gibbons, *American Hegemony and the Politics of the Nuclear Non-Proliferation Regime (PhD diss., Georgetown University, 2016).*

65. Jeffrey W. Knopf, "International Cooperation on Nonproliferation: The Growth and Diversity of Cooperative Efforts," in *International Cooperation on WMD Nonproliferation*, ed. Jeffrey W. Knopf (Athens: University of Georgia Press, 2018), 1–22.

66. Nincic, *Renegade Regimes*; Geldenhuys, *Deviant Conduct in World Politics*.

67. For the work on nuclear norms, refer to the fantastic work of the young scholars, Michal Smetana and Carmen Wunderlich. See Michal Smetana, *Nuclear Deviance: Stigma Politics and the Rules of the Nonproliferation Game* (London: Palgrave, 2020); Carmen Wunderlich, *Rogue States as Norm Entrepreneurs: Black Sheep or Sheep in Wolves' Clothing?* (Cham, Switzerland: Springer, 2020). There have been a number of exceptions to the rule that the United States pursued nonproliferation among allies and foes alike. See Rabinowitz, *Bargaining on Nuclear Tests*; Rabia Akhtar, *The Blind Eye: U.S. Non-Proliferation Policy Towards Pakistan from Ford to Clinton* (Lahore, Pakistan: University of Lahore Press, 2018).

68. See, for example, the influential opinion piece penned by National Security Advisor Anthony Lake, "Confronting Backlash States."

69. PDD-13 is still classified today. An extended summary can be found in The White House, "President Clinton Fact Sheet on Nonproliferation and Export Control Policy" (September 27, 1993), Office of the Press Secretary. Reference Documents Concerning the RERTR Program, Nuclear Science and Engineering Division/*Argonne National Laboratory,* https://www.rertr.anl.gov/REFDOCS/PRES93NP.html. I also interviewed the principal author of the document, who confirmed these insights. For further information about the impact of the PDD-13, see Robert Litwak, *Rogue States and U.S. Foreign Policy: Containment after the Cold War* (Washington, DC: Woodrow Wilson Center Press, 2000); William M. Arkin and Michael J. Mazarr, "Clinton Defense Policy and Nuclear Weapons," in

Clinton and Post-Cold War Defense, ed. Stephen J. Cimbala (Westport, CT: Praeger, 1996), 49–70.

70. William Jefferson Clinton, "Address by President Bill Clinton to the UN General Assembly" (New York, September 27, 1993), https://2009-2017.state.gov/p/io/potusunga/207375.htm.

71. Bill Turque, *Inventing Al Gore: A Biography* (Boston: Houghton Mifflin, 2000), x.

72. Robert Zelnick, *Gore: A Political Life* (Washington, DC: Regnery Publishing, 1999), 117.

73. Zelnick, *Gore: A Political Life.*

74. "Preparing for the 1995 NPT Conference" (December 15, 1993), US *Department of State, FOIA Virtual Reading Room, Case no. F-2008-02837*); "NPT 1995—Preparing for January PrepCom Meeting" (December 30, 1993), US *Department of State, FOIA Virtual Reading Room, Case no. F-2008-02837.*

75. In his memoirs, Thomas Graham, Jr., remembers that Clinton was persuaded by the chairman of the Joint Chiefs of Staff, John Shalikashvili, who in a Principals' Committee meeting stated that he did not consider explosive testing as crucial for the maintenance of the US nuclear deterrent. See Graham, *Disarmament Sketches.*

76. For a more detailed overview, see a recent article by Frank von Hippel, "The Decision to End U.S. Nuclear Testing," *Arms Control Today 49* (December 2019), https://www.armscontrol.org/act/2019-12/features/decision-end-us-nuclear-testing.

77. McGeorge Bundy, "Letter to President Clinton" (1995), *NPT–March 1995, box 4, OA/ID720, Nonproliferation and Export Controls, the files of Daniel Poneman. Clinton Presidential Records/NSC, Clinton Presidential Library/NARA, Little Rock, AR.*

78. Clinton graciously sent a personal note to Bundy in response, to convey "my personal appreciation for providing me with your advice and counsel." See William Jefferson Clinton, "Letter to Bundy on Nuclear Arms Control" (1994), *WHORM-Subject File-General, box 02284, OA/ID720, folder FO 009, Clinton Presidential Records/ NSC, Clinton Presidential Library/NARA, Little Rock, AR.*

79. John Holum, "Holum Letter on Arms Control in 1995" (December 28, 1994), *NPT–January 1995, box 2, OA/ID 720, Nonproliferation and Export Controls, the files of Daniel Poneman, Clinton Presidential Records/NSC, Clinton Presidential Library/ NARA, Little Rock, AR.*

80. Holum, "Holum Letter on Arms Control."

81. Anthony Lake, "Holum Letter on Arms Control in 1995" (1995), *NPT–January 1995, box 2, ID720, Nonproliferation and Export Controls, the files of Daniel Poneman, Clinton Presidential Records/NSC, Clinton Presidential Library/NARA, Little Rock, AR.*

82. Bob Boorstin, "1995 Communications Initiatives" (1995), *NPT–February 1995, box 1, OA/ID720, Nonproliferation and Export Controls, the files of Daniel Poneman, Clinton Presidential Records/NSC, Clinton Presidential Library/NARA, Little Rock, AR.*

83. Ibid., p. 2

84. David Rockefeller, Jr., "Letter to President Clinton" (1993), *WHORM-Subject File-General, box 02284, OA/ID23306, folder FO 009, Clinton Presidential Records/NSC, Clinton Presidential Library/NARA, Little Rock, AR*; Richard J. Durbin and Richard A. Gephard, "Letter to President Clinton" (1995), *NPT–March 1995, box 4, OA/ID720, Nonproliferation and Export Controls, the files of Daniel Poneman, Clinton Presidential Records/NSC, Clinton Presidential Library/NARA, Little Rock, AR.*

85. "Schedule and Taskings on Engagement/Nonproliferation Roll-out" (February 24, 1995), *NPT–February 1995, box 2, OA/ID720, Nonproliferation and Export Controls, the files of Daniel Poneman. Clinton Presidential Records/NSC, Clinton Presidential Library/NARA, Little Rock, AR.*

86. William Jefferson Clinton, "Remarks to the Nixon Center for Peace and Freedom Policy Conference [March 1, 1995]," in *Public Papers of the Presidents of the United States: William J. Clinton, Book 1* (Washington, DC: US Government Printing Office, 1995), 283–89.

87. Boorstin, "1995 Communications Initiatives."

88. Daniel Poneman, "SVTS Meeting on NPT Extension" (February 8, 1995), *NPT–February 1995, box 1, OA/ID 720, Nonproliferation and Export Controls, the files of Daniel Poneman. Clinton Presidential Records/NSC, Clinton Presidential Library/ NARA, Little Rock, AR.*

89. Zukang, Sha, *interview by Katrin M. Heilmann*, 2016 (1995 NPT RevCon Oral History Project/NPIHP, Washington, DC). See also Crossette, "China Breaks Ranks."

Chapter 2: Networked Power

1. Institutions and regimes are not, in the minds of IR scholars, identical. Institutions are often given much broader meaning. However, for this book, this difference is not relevant. I therefore use the terms "regime" and "institution" interchangeably in this chapter.

2. Jeffrey Knopf provides a detailed overview of the collective action problem in nuclear nonproliferation. See his "After Diffusion: Challenges to Enforcing Nonproliferation and Disarmament Norms," *Contemporary Security Policy* 39, no. 3 (2018): 367–98.

3. This way of thinking about international institutions best fits the rationalist institutionalist way of thinking. See Robert O. Keohane, *After Hegemony: Cooperation and Discord in the World Political Economy* (Princeton, NJ: Princeton University Press, 1984); Barbara Koremenos, Charles Lipson, and Duncan Snidal, "The Rational Design of International Institutions," *International Organization* 55, no. 4 (2001): 761–99; Andreas Hasenclever, Peter Mayer, and Volker Rittberger, *Theories of International Regimes*, Cambridge Studies in International Relations (Cambridge & New York: Cambridge University Press, 1997).

4. Randall W. Stone, *Controlling Institutions: International Organizations and the Global Economy* (Cambridge: Cambridge University Press, 2011).

5. On voting in international organizations, see Eric A. Posner and Alan O. Sykes, "Voting Rules in International Organizations," *Chicago Journal of International Law* 15, no. 1 (2014): 195–228; Giovanni Maggi and Massimo Morelli, "Self-Enforcing Voting in International Organizations," *American Economic Review* 96, no. 4 (2006): 1137–58; Koremenos, Lipson, and Snidal, "The Rational Design of International Institutions."

6. Onderco, "Variation in Delegation Size."

7. Within the nonproliferation regime, Egypt's ability to block consensus at the 2015 NPT RevCon over the Middle East WMD-Free Zone may serve as an example. See William C. Potter, "The Unfulfilled Promise of the 2015 NPT Review Conference," *Survival* 58, no. 1 (2016): 151–78.

8. For further thinking about the international system as a society, see Hedley Bull, *The Anarchical Society: A Study of Order in World Politics* (London: Macmillan, 1977).

9. Michael Barnett and Raymond Duvall, *Power in Global Governance* (Cambridge: Cambridge University Press, 2005). For recent works on application within the nonproliferation regime, see Ruzicka, "Behind the Veil of Good Intentions"; Ritchie, "A Hegemonic Nuclear Order."

10. John F. Padgett and Christopher K. Ansell, "Robust Action and the Rise of the Medici, 1400–1434," *American Journal of Sociology* 98, no. 6 (1993): 1259–319; Mark S. Granovetter, "The Strength of Weak Ties," *American Journal of Sociology* 78, no. 6 (1973): 1360–80.

11. Deborah Avant and Oliver Westerwinter, eds., *The New Power Politics: Networks and Transnational Security Governance* (Oxford: Oxford University Press, 2016); Heidi Hardt, "The Goldilocks Effect: Knowledge Networks in International Organizations" (working paper, 2018).

12. Paul Meerts, *Diplomatic Negotiation: Essence and Evolution* (Den Haag, The Netherlands: Clingendael, 2015); Mette Eilstrup-Sangiovanni, "Global Governance Networks," in *The Oxford Handbook of Political Networks*, ed. Jennifer Nicoll Victor, Alexander H. Montgomery, and Mark Lubell (Oxford: Oxford University Press, 2018), 689–714.

13. John W. Patty and Elizabeth Maggie Penn, "Network Theory and Political Science," in *The Oxford Handbook of Political Networks*, ed. Jennifer Nicoll Victor, Alexander H. Montgomery, and Mark Lubell (Oxford: Oxford University Press, 2018), 147–71.

14. Jon Pevehouse and Bruce Russett, "Democratic International Governmental Organizations Promote Peace," *International Organization* 60, no. 4 (2006): 969–1000; Sara McLaughlin Mitchell and Paul R. Hensel, "International Institutions and Compliance with Agreements," *American Journal of Political Science* 51, no. 4 (2007): 721–37.

15. Alexander Cooley and Daniel H. Nexon, "'The Empire Will Compensate You': The Structural Dynamics of the U.S. Overseas Basing Network," *Perspectives on Politics* 11, no. 4 (2013): 1034–50; Lisa L. Martin, "Interests, Power, and Multilateralism," *International Organization* 46, no. 4 (1992): 765–92; Lisa L. Martin, *Coercive Cooperation: Explaining Multilateral Economic Sanctions* (Princeton, NJ: Princeton University Press, 1992); Marina E. Henke, "The Politics of Diplomacy: How the United States Builds Multilateral Military Coalitions," *International Studies Quarterly* 61, no. 2 (2017): 410–24.

16. Emilie M. Hafner-Burton, Miles Kahler, and Alexander H. Montgomery, "Network Analysis for International Relations," *International Organization* 63, no. 3 (2009): 559–92; Alexander H. Montgomery, "Centrality in Transnational Governance: How Networks of International Institutions Shape Power Processes," in *New Power Politics: Networks, Governance, Global Security*, ed. Deborah Avant and Oliver Westerwinter (Oxford: Oxford University Press, 2015); Zeev Maoz, *Networks of Nations: The Evolution, Structure, and Impact of International Networks, 1816–2001* (Cambridge & New York: Cambridge University Press, 2011).

17. Hafner-Burton, Kahler, and Montgomery, "Network Analysis for International Relations."

18. Patty and Penn, "Network Theory and Political Science."

19. Marina E. Henke, *Constructing Allied Cooperation: Diplomacy, Payments, and Power in Multilateral Military Coalitions* (Ithaca, NY: Cornell University Press, 2019); Marina E. Henke, "Networked Cooperation: How the European Union Mobilizes Peacekeeping Forces to Project Power Abroad," *Security Studies* 28, no. 5 (2019): 901–34.

20. William Kindred Winecoff, "Structural Power and the Global Financial Crisis: A Network Analytical Approach," *Business and Politics* 17, no. 3 (2015): 495.

21. Hafner-Burton, Kahler, and Montgomery, "Network Analysis for International Relations."

22. Network structures, however, give rise to hierarchical social structures. For recent work in international relations scholarship, see Marina G. Duque, "Recognizing International Status: A Relational Approach," *International Studies Quarterly* 62, no. 3 (2018): 577–92; William Kindred Winecoff, "'The Persistent Myth of Lost Hegemony,' Revisited: Structural Power as a Complex Network Phenomenon," *European Journal of International Relations* 26, no. 1, suppl. (2020): 209–52.

23. Erik Hans Klijn, et al., "The Influence of Trust on Network Performance in Taiwan, Spain, and the Netherlands: A Cross-Country Comparison," *International Public Management Journal* 19, no. 1 (2016): 111–39.

24. Eilstrup-Sangiovanni, "Global Governance Networks," 707.

25. Ibid.

26. For a conceptualization of ties as diplomatic relations, see Henke, "The Politics of Diplomacy"; as economic ties, see Winecoff, "Structural Power and the Global

Financial Crisis"; as alliance membership, see Stacie E. Goddard, "Embedded Revisionism: Networks, Institutions, and Challenges to World Order," *International Organization* 72, no. 4 (2018): 763–97; Dotan A. Haim, "Alliance Networks and Trade: The Effect of Indirect Political Alliances on Bilateral Trade Flows," *Journal of Peace Research* 53, no. 3 (2016): 472–90. And as membership in IGOs, see Han Dorussen and Hugh Ward, "Intergovernmental Organizations and the Kantian Peace: A Network Perspective," *Journal of Conflict Resolution* 52, no. 2 (2008): 189–212.

27. Robert Jervis, "Cooperation under the Security Dilemma," *World Politics* 30, no. 2 (1978): 167–214; Kenneth A. Oye, "Explaining Cooperation under Anarchy: Hypotheses and Strategies," *World Politics* 38, no. 1 (1985): 1–24; Martin, "Interests, Power, and Multilateralism."

28. Vincent Pouliot, *International Security in Practice: The Politics of NATO-Russia Diplomacy* (Cambridge: Cambridge University Press, 2010).

29. The data used in this analysis originates from Jonathan D. Moyer, David K. Bohl, and Sara Turner, "Diplomatic Representation Data Codebook [Diplometrics]" (Frederick S. Pardee Center for International Futures, Josef Korbel School of International Studies, University of Denver, CO, 2016), https://pardee.du.edu/diplomatic-representation-data-codebook.

30. John R. Oneal, et al., "The Liberal Peace: Interdependence, Democracy, and International Conflict, 1950–85," *Journal of Peace Research* 33, no. 1 (1996): 11–28; John R. Oneal and Bruce Russett, "Assessing the Liberal Peace with Alternative Specifications: Trade Still Reduces Conflict," *Journal of Peace Research* 36, no. 4 (1999): 423–42; Bruce Russett and John R. Oneal, *Triangulating Peace: Democracy, Interdependence, and International Organizations* (New York: Norton, 2001); Joanne Gowa and Edward D. Mansfield, "Power Politics and International Trade," *American Political Science Review* 87, no. 2 (1993): 408–20; Brian M. Pollins, "Conflict, Cooperation, and Commerce: The Effect of International Political Interactions on Bilateral Trade Flows," *American Journal of Political Science* 33, no. 3 (1989): 737–61. For an argument that political relations cause trade, see Dale C. Copeland, *Economic Interdependence and War* (Princeton, NJ: Princeton University Press, 2014).

31. Jaap de Wilde, *Saved from Oblivion: Interdependence Theory in the First Half of the 20th Century; A Study on the Causality between War and Complex Interdependence* (Aldershot, UK & Brookfield, VT: Dartmouth, 1991).

32. Karl W. Deutsch, et al., *Political Community and the North Atlantic Area: International Organization in the Light of Historical Experience* (Princeton, NJ: Princeton University Press, 1957).

33. Kristian Skrede Gleditsch, "Expanded Trade and GDP Data," *Journal of Conflict Resolution* 46, no. 5 (2002): 712–24.

34. Curtis S. Signorino and Jeffrey M. Ritter, "Tau-B or Not Tau-B: Measuring the Similarity of Foreign Policy Positions," *International Studies Quarterly* 43, no. 1

(1999): 115–44; D. Scott Bennett and Matthew C. Rupert, "Comparing Measures of Political Similarity: An Empirical Comparison of S Versus Tau-B in the Study of International Conflict," *Journal of Conflict Resolution* 47, no. 3 (2003): 367–93.

35. Marina E. Henke, "Buying Allies: Payment Practices in Multilateral Military Coalition-Building," *International Security* 43, no. 4 (2019): 128–62.

36. Data from Douglas M. Gibler, *International Military Alliances, 1648–2008* (Washington, DC: CQ Press, 2008).

37. Onderco, "Collaboration Networks in Conference Diplomacy."

38. Tanja A. Börzel and Thomas Risse: "When Europe Hits Home: Europeaniza-tion and Domestic Change," *European Integration Online Papers* 4, no. 15 (2000) and "From Europeanisation to Diffusion: Introduction," *West European Politics* 35, no. 1 (2012): 1–19; Maria Green Cowles, James A. Caporaso, and Thomas Risse-Kappen, *Transforming Europe: Europeanization and Domestic Change* (Ithaca, NY: Cornell University Press, 2001); Sophie Meunier and Kalypso Nicolaïdis, "The European Union as a Trade Power," in *International Relations and the European Union*, ed. Christopher Hill and Michael Smith (Oxford & New York: Oxford University Press, 2005); Sophie Meunier and Kalypso Nicolaïdis, "The European Union as a Conflicted Trade Power," *Journal of European Public Policy* 13, no. 6 (2006): 906–25.

Chapter 3: "Friends with Benefits": US-European Cooperation

1. Kimberly Marten, "Reconsidering NATO Expansion: A Counterfactual Analysis of Russia and the West in the 1990s." *European Journal of International Security* 3, no. 2 (2018): 135–61; Andrew Cottey, *East-Central Europe after the Cold War: Poland, the Czech Republic, Slovakia and Hungary in Search of Security* (Basingstoke, UK: Macmillan Press, 1995).

2. Müller and Kötter, *Germany, Europe & Nuclear Non-Proliferation*; Müller, "The Internalization of Principles, Norms and Rules by Governments"; Harald Müller, "Arguing, Bargaining and all that: Communicative Action, Rationalist Theory and the Logic of Appropriateness in International Relations," *European Journal of International Relations* 10, no. 3 (2004): 395–435.

3. Florent Pouponneau and Frédéric Mérand, "Diplomatic Practices, Domestic Fields, and the International System: Explaining France's Shift on Nuclear Nonpro-liferation," *International Studies Quarterly* 61, no. 1 (2017): 123–35; Nicolas Jabko and Steven Weber, "A Certain Idea of Nuclear Weapons: France's Nuclear Nonpro-liferation Policy in Theoretical Perspective," *Security Studies* 8, no. 1 (1998): 108–50.

4. Una Becker-Jakob, et al., "Good International Citizens: Canada, Germany, and Sweden," in Müller and Wunderlich (2013), *Norm Dynamics in Multilateral Arms Control*; Emmanuelle Maitre and Pauline Lévy, "Becoming a Disarmament Champion: The Austrian Crusade against Nuclear Weapons," *Nonproliferation Review* 26, no. 5–6 (2019): 537–57.

5. NATO, "Final Communique" (*October 21–22, 1992), Nuclear Planning Group (NPG) of the North Atlantic Alliance, Gleneagles, Scotland,* https://www.nato.int/cps/en/natohq/official_texts_23977.htm?selectedLocale=en.

6. Commission on Security and Cooperation in Europe, *Third Meeting of the Council. Summary of Conclusions: Decision on Peaceful Settlement of Disputes (CSCE, Stockholm, December 15, 1992),* https://www.osce.org/mc/40342?download=true.

7. Alan Heyes, Wyn Q. Bowen, and Hugh Chalmers, *The Global Partnership against WMD: Success and Shortcomings of G8 Threat Reduction since 9/11,* Whitehall Paper no. 76 (London: RUSI, 2011).

8. "NPT Depositaries Meeting—Soviet Paper on Possible Non-Proliferation Cooperation" (June 6, 1991), US *Department of State, FOIA Virtual Reading Room,* Case no. M-2008-02837.

9. "NPT Consultations on the Margins of the June IAEA Board of Governors Meeting" (June 29, 1992), US *Department of State, FOIA Virtual Reading Room, Case no. F-2008-02837.*

10. "July 8 Meeting of the Friends of NPT" (July 3, 1992), US *Department of State, FOIA Virtual Reading Room, Case no. F-2008-02837.*

11. "NPT Depositaries Meeting—September 22 and 23, 1992" (September 28, 1992); "1995 NPT Conference—Depositaries Meeting with France (September 19, 1992); and "NPT Depositaries Meeting" (August 4, 1992), US *Department of State, FOIA Virtual Reading Room, Case no. F-2008-02837.*

12. Lewis A. Dunn, "Negotiating and Sustaining the Non-Proliferation Treaty: Challenges and Lessons for US–Russia Cooperation," in *Once and Future Partners: The United States, Russia and Nuclear Non-Proliferation,* ed. William C. Potter and Sarah Bidgood (Abingdon, UK: Routledge, 2018), 117–34.

13. Grigory Berdennikov, *interview by Michal Onderco,* 2016 (1995 NPT RevCon Oral History Project/NPIHP, Washington, DC.

14. Vladimir A. Orlov, *Konferenciya 1995 Goda Po Rassmotreniyu I Prodleniyu Sroka Deystviya Dogovora O Nerasprostranenii Yadernogo Oruzhiya: Osobennosti, Rezul'taty, Uroki (1995 Review and Extension Conference of the Treaty on the Non-Proliferation of Nuclear Weapons: Features, Results, Lessons)* (1999), Scientific Notes no. 11, PIR Center, Moscow.

15. "Conference on Disarmament (CD): NPT-95 NPT Consultations with Wider Western Group, Geneva, Feb 5, 1993" (February 16, 1993), US *Department of State, FOIA Virtual Reading Room,* Case no. M-2008-02837 https://foia.state.gov/Search/Results.aspx?searchText=&beginDate=19930216&endDate=19930216&publishedBeginDate=&publishedEndDate=&caseNumber=.

16. Ibid, p.5.

17. "NPT 95—Western Group Meeting in Geneva, April 2, 1993" (April 28, 1993), US *Department of State, FOIA Virtual Reading Room, Case no. M-2008-02837.*

18. "NPT 95—First Session of the NPT Preparatory Committee (PrepCom):

Wrap-Up" (June 3, 1993), US *Department of State, FOIA Virtual Reading Room, Case no. F-2008-02837.*

19. "NPT Depositaries Meeting—Points on Agenda" (June 7, 1993), US *Department of State, FOIA Virtual Reading Room, Case no. F-2008-02837.*

20. "NPT Depositaries Meeting—Soviet Paper on Possible Non-Proliferation Cooperation."

21. "Conference on Disarmament (CD): NPT-95 NPT Consultations."

22. For an overview of the European actions in the field of nonproliferation and arms control, see Harald Müller, ed., *European Non-Proliferation Policy 1993–1995* (Brussels: European Interuniversity Press, 1993); Harald Müller and Lars van Dassen, "From Cacophony to Joint Action: Successes and Shortcomings of the European Nuclear Non-Proliferation Policy," in *Common Foreign and Security Policy: The Record and Reforms*, ed. Martin Holland (London: Pinter, 1997), 52–72.

23. Federiga Bindi, "European Union Foreign Policy: A Historical Overview," in *The Foreign Policy of the European Union: Assessing Europe's Role in the World*, ed. Federiga Bindi (Washington, DC: Brookings Institution Press, 2010), 13–40; Stephan Keukeleire and Tom Delreux, *The Foreign Policy of the European Union* (Basingstoke, UK: Palgrave Macmillan, 2014); John Peterson and Elizabeth E. Bomberg, *Decision-Making in the European Union*, European Union Series (New York: St. Martin's, 1999).

24. Council of the European Union, "Council Decision of 25 July 1994 Concerning the Joint Action Adopted by the Council on the Basis of Article J.3 of the Treaty on European Union Regarding Preparation for the 1995 Conference of the States Parties to the Treaty on the Non-Proliferation of Nuclear Weapons," *Official Journal of the European Communities*, no. L 205/1 (August 8, 1994), https://eur-lex.europa.eu/legal-content/EN/TXT/PDF/?uri=CELEX:31994D0509&from=EN.

25. Reference to this effort can be found in "Telefonat Brengelmann/Guellil Am 6.4.94 (Telephone call Brengelmann/Guellil on April 6, 1994)" (April 7, 1994), *Political Archive of the German Federal Foreign Office, row 242, box 37116/40*, Berlin.

26. "Schlussbericht Des 2.VA (Final report of the 2nd PrepCom)" (January 21, 1994), *Political Archive of the German Federal Foreign Office, row 242, box 37116/40*; "Sachbestand: Ergebnisse Der 2. Sitzung Des Verbeitungsauschusses (State of play: Results of the 2nd meeting of the Preparatory Committee)" (January 27, 1994), *Political Archive of the German Federal Foreign Office, row 242, box 37116/40*, Berlin.

27. "CONUC—Troika Meeting with the Countries of Central and Eastern Europe" (February 11, 1994), *Political Archive of the German Federal Foreign Office, row 242, box 37116/40*, Berlin.

28. "Telefonat Brengelmann/Guellil."

29. Ibid.

30. "Joint Action 'Preparation of NPT-Conference 1995'" (April 20, 1994), *Political Archive of the German Federal Foreign Office, row 242, box 37116/40*, Berlin.

31. Ibid.

32. "9. Deutsch-Russische NV-Konsultationen, Moskau, 03–06.05.1994 (9th German-Russian NPT consultations, Moscow, May 3–6, 1994)" (April 26, 1994), *Political Archive of the German Federal Foreign Office, row 242, box 37116/40*, Berlin.

33. "CONUC—Joint Action on Disarmament Non-Proliferation" (May 20, 1994), *Political Archive of the German Federal Foreign Office, row 242, box 37116/40*, Berlin; European Council, "Projet D'orientations Pour Une Action Commune En Matiere De Nonproliferation Nucleaire (Draft Guidelines for Joint Action on Nuclear Nonproliferation)" (1994). *Digital Archive Cold War History Project*, Wilson Center, Washington, DC, https://digitalarchive.wilsoncenter.org/document/175913.

34. "Gemeinsame Aktion Zur Vorbereitung Der NVV-Konferenz (Joint action in preparation for the NPT conference)" (June 10, 1994), *Political Archive of the German Federal Foreign Office (selected documents)*, Berlin.

35. "CONUC—Joint Action on the Preparation of the NPT-Conference 1995" (June 21,1994), *Political Archive of the German Federal Foreign Office, row 242, box 37116/40*, Berlin.

36. European Council: "Draft guidelines" and "European Council at Corfu. 24–25 June 1994. Presidency Conclusions" (European Parliament, 1994), https://www.consilium.europa.eu/media/21207/corfu-european-council.pdf.

37. European Council, "Resultats Des Travaux Du Groupe 'Non-Proliferation Nucleaire' (Results of the work of the 'Nuclear Non-Proliferation' Group" (1994). *Digital Archive Cold War History Project*, Wilson Center, Washington, DC, https://digitalarchive.wilsoncenter.org/document/175914.

38. Meunier and Nicolaïdis, "The European Union as a Trade Power" and "The European Union as a Conflicted Trade Power."

39. Camille Grand, *The European Union and the Non-Proliferation of Nuclear Weapons*, Chaillot Paper no. 37 (Paris: European Union Institute for Security Studies, 2000).

40. "NVV Vertrag: Stand Der Vorbereitungen Ein Halbes Jahr Vor Der Konferenz (NPT Treaty: Status of Preparations Half a Year Before the Conference)" (November 17, 1994), *Political Archive of the German Federal Foreign Office, row 675, box 48828*, Berlin Berlin5.Federal Foreign OfficeEmphasis in original.

41. One of the reasons why some of the countries were considering staying out of the conference was financial; some countries were simply unable to pay their share. During the third PrepCom, Belarussian diplomats informed Germany that cost might prevent Belarus from joining. See "NPT 1995—Follow-up on Issues Raised at November US-EU Troika Consultations" (n.d.), *Political Archive of the German Federal Foreign Office, row 537, box 37781*, Berlin. The solution to this problem was to require states to contribute to the costs of the conference whether they attend or not, which would mean that cost would cease to be a good reason to skip the conference. See "CONUC—Joint Action for the Preparation of the 1995 NPT Conference" (December 8, 1994), *Political Archive of the German Federal Foreign Office, row 537, box 37781*, Berlin.

42. "NPT 1995—Follow-up."

43. "Invitation to the Six Associated Countries about Troika Demarches" (December 1, 1994), *Political Archive of the German Federal Foreign Office, row 537, box 37781* Berlin.

44. "CONUC—Joint Action for the Preparation of the 1995 NPT-Conference." The only exception to this list was South Africa, judged by German diplomats to be "much in line with EU goals." Why they considered this to be so is uncertain.

45. German diplomats judged that much of Iran's behavior was owed to the US-Iranian relationship. See "Bilaterale Konsultationen Mit Schluessellaendern Der Blockfreien Im Vorfeld Der Konferenz (Bilateral consultations with key nonaligned countries ahead of the conference)" (January 11, 1995), *Political Archive of the German Federal Foreign Office, row 675, box 48828*, Berlin.

46. Wolfgang Hoffmann: "4.Sitzung Des Vorbereitungsausschusses Fuer Die NVV-Konferenz, New York, 23–27.1.1995 (Meeting of the Preparatory Committee for the NPT Conference, New York, January 23–27, 1995)" and "Koordinierungstreffen Der Eu Und Der Westlichen Gruppe Sowie 'Treffen in Engerem Kreis' Am 20.01.1995 (Coordination meeting of the EU and the Western group as well as 'Close circle meeting' on January 20, 1995)" (1995), *Political Archive of the German Federal Foreign Office, row 675, box 48828*, Berlin.

47. "NVV: Core-Group Zur Vorbereitung Der Verlängerungsentscheidung (NPT: Core-Group on the preparation of the extension decision)" (January 28, 1995), *Political Archive of the German Federal Foreign Office, row 675, box 48828*, Berlin.

48. See, e.g., "NVV-Überprüfungs- Und Verlängungskonferenz 1995, Treffen Der Core Group Am 10.02.1995 (NPT Review and Extension Conference 1995, Core Group meeting on February 10, 1995)" and "NVV-Konferenz: Treffen Der Core Group (NPT Conference: Meeting of the Core Group)" (February 10, 1995), both in *Political Archive of the German Federal Foreign Office, row 675, box 48828*, Berlin.

49. Onderco and Nuti, *Extending the NPT*.

50. Switzerland was the target of the first EU démarche action after the adoption of the EU's Joint Action in July 1994, upon pressure from France and Belgium. Germany argued that it would look bad if Switzerland were the first target of the démarches; however, France ultimately prevailed. See "Preparation of NPT Conference of 1995. Swiss Position/Joint Action" (June 22, 1994), *Political Archive of the German Federal Foreign Office (selected documents)*, Berlin; "Preparation of the NPT Conference 1995 (Joint Action/Swiss Position)" (June 21, 1994), *Political Archive of the German Federal Foreign Office, row 242, box 37116/40*, Berlin; "Preparation De La Conference De Prorogation Du TNP En 1995" (June 24, 1994), *Political Archive of the German Federal Foreign Office (selected documents)*, Berlin; "Secretary's Meeting with French Foreign Minister Alain Juppe, March 22, 1995, Paris" (March 23, 1995), US *Department of State, FOIA Virtual Reading Room, Case no. M-2017-11622.*

51. "NVV Konferenz: Treffen Der Core-Group Am 10.02.1995 in Genf (NPT Conference: Meeting of the Core Group on February 10, 1995, in Geneva)" (February 13, 1995), *Political Archive of the German Federal Foreign Office, row 675, box 48828*, Berlin.

52. "NVV: Treffen Der Core Group NVV Am 20/21.03.95 in Genf (NPT: Meeting of the NPT Core Group on March 20/21, 1995, in Geneva)" (March 22, 1995), *Political Archive of the German Federal Foreign Office, row 675, box 48828*, Berlin.

53. Ibid.

54. "NVV: Treffen Der Core Group Und Treffen Der Westlichen Gruppe (NPT: Meetings of the Core Group and Meetings of the Western Group)" (March 22, 1995), *Political Archive of the German Federal Foreign Office, row 675, box 48828*, Berlin.

55. Rauf and Johnson, "After the NPT's Indefinite Extension."

56. "NVV: Treffen Der Core Group Und Treffen Der Westlichen Gruppe."

57. Ibid.

58. "NVV: Überprüfungs- Und Verlängerungskonferenz (NPT: Review and Extension Conference)" (March 24, 1995), *Political Archive of the German Federal Foreign Office, row 675, box 48828*, Berlin.

59. Ibid.

60. "NVV Verlängerungskonferenz: Treffen Der Core Group Und Westlicher Gruppe (NPT Extension Conference: Meeting of the Core Group and Western Group) (March 25, 1995), *Political Archive of the German Federal Foreign Office, row 675, box 48828*, Berlin.

61. "NVV: Überprüfungs-Und Verlängerungskonferenz."

62. "NVV Verlängerungskonferenz."

63. "Verlängerung Des NVV: Amerikanische Demarche Durch Botschafter Hunter (Extension of the NPT: American Démarche through Ambassador Hunter)" (April 6, 1995), *Political Archive of the German Federal Foreign Office, row 675, box 48828*, Berlin.

64. Richard Butler, *interview by Michal Onderco*, 2018 (1995 NPT RevCon Oral History Project/NPIHP, Washington, DC. Tammany Hall was a meeting place of the Tammany Society in New York City, which governed city politics in favor of the Democratic Party through a mix of collusion, corruption, and violence between the second half of the nineteenth century and the interbellum period.

65. Jurchewsky, *interview*; Rauf, *interview*; Christopher Westdal, *interview by Michal Onderco*, 2017 (1995 NPT RevCon Oral History Project/NPIHP, Washington, DC).

66. Jurchewsky, *interview*; Thomas Graham, *interview by Michal Onderco*, 2017 (1995 NPT RevCon Oral History Project/NPIHP, Washington, DC). The process of collecting signatures was initially slow. Canada struggled to collect a sufficient number, and it was only in the third week of the conference that the required number was achieved. Australian ambassador at the conference Richard Butler labeled the Canadian diplomat in charge of the collection of signatures (Tariq Rauf) a "poor man." See Butler, *interview*.

67. Graham, *Disarmament Sketches and interview.*

68. Grand, *The European Union*; David Fischer and Harald Müller, *United Divided: The European at the NPT Extension Conference* (Frankfurt: Peace Research Institute Frankfurt, 1995).

69. Megan Dee, "Standing Together or Doing the Splits: Evaluating European Union Performance in the Nuclear Non-Proliferation Treaty Review Negotiations," *European Foreign Affairs Review* 17, no. 2 (2012): 189–212.

70. Grand, *The European Union*; Clara Portela, *The Role of the EU in the Non-Proliferation of Nuclear Weapons: The Way to Thessaloniki and Beyond, PRIF Report no. 65* (Frankfurt: Peace Research Institute Frankfurt, 2004).

71. As senior Russian diplomat Grigory Berdennikov admitted later in an oral history interview, Russian power was limited even among the former Soviet countries. See Berdennikov, *interview.*

72. "Presidential Thank-You for NPT Extension Effort" (May 23, 1995), US *Department of State, FOIA Virtual Reading Room, Case no. M-2017-11533.*

73. Programme for Promoting Nuclear Non-Proliferation, "The New Europe and Nuclear Non-Proliferation: A Seminar for Senior Government Officials" (1992), *MS424 A3079/1/1/13 f1, Archives of the University of Southampton, Southampton, UK*; Programme for Promoting Nuclear Non-Proliferation, "'Issues at the 1995 NPT Conference: An International Seminar for Government Officials. General Report" (July 9–12, 1993), *reel 7448, Ford Foundation Grants—U to Z, Rockefeller Archive Center*, Sleepy Hollow, NY.

74. Mariana Budjeryn, "The Power of the NPT: International Norms and Ukraine's Nuclear Disarmament," *Nonproliferation Review* 22, no. 2 (2015): 203–37 and *Inheriting the Bomb: Soviet Collapse and Nuclear Disarmament of Ukraine* (Baltimore, MD: Johns Hopkins University Press, forthcoming).

75. Ministry of Foreign Affairs of Ukraine, "Possible Consequences of Alternative Approaches to Implementation of Ukraine's Nuclear Policy (Analytical Report)" (February 3, 1993), *Nuclear Proliferation International History Project (NPIHP)/CCNY*, https://digitalarchive.wilsoncenter.org/document/144983.

Chapter 4: "Babes in the Woods": South Africa and the Extension

1. See Zondi Masiza and Chris Landsberg, "Fission for Compliments? South Africa and the 1995 Extension of Nuclear Non-Proliferation," *Policy: Issues and Actors* 9, no. 3 (1996); Frederick A. Van Der Merwe, "Arms Control and Disarmament in South Africa after the Cold War," *Strategic Review for Southern Africa/ Strategiese Oorsig vir Suider-Afrika* 25, no. 1 (2003): 53–87; Jo-Ansie Van Wyk, "Nuclear Diplomacy as Niche Diplomacy: South Africa's Post-Apartheid Relations with the International Atomic Energy Agency," *South African Journal of International Affairs* 19, no. 2 (2012): 179–200; Jean duPreez and Thomas Maettig, "From Pariah to Nuclear Poster Boy," in

Forecasting Nuclear Proliferation in the 21st Century, vol. 2, A Comparative Perspective, ed. William C. Potter and Gaukhar Mukhatzhanova (Redwood City, CA: Stanford University Press, 2010), 302–35.

2. Stephen Ellis, *External Mission: The ANC in Exile, 1960–1990* (London: C. Hurst & Co., 2012).

3. Abdul Samad Minty, "Keynote Address," in *The Nuclear Debate: Policy for a Democratic South Africa, proceedings of a conference sponsored by ANC Western Cape Science and Technology Group / The Environmental Monitoring Group* (Cape Town, South Africa, 1994), 7–15.

4. "De Klerk: South Africa Had the Bomb," *Africa Report 38* (May–June, 1993).

5. Bill Keller, "Building (and Dismantling) a Threat," *New York Times,* March 28, 1993, D1; Magnus Malan, *My Life with the SA Defence Force* (Pretoria: Protea Book House, 2006); Hilton Hamann, *Days of the Generals: The Untold Story of South Africa's Apartheid-Era Military Generals* (Cape Town: Zebra, 2001); Frank V. Pabian, "South Africa's Nuclear Weapon Program: Lessons for U.S. Nonproliferation Policy," *Nonproliferation Review* 3, no. 1 (1995): 1–19; Anna-Mart van Wyk, "South African Nuclear Development in the 1970s: A Non-Proliferation Conundrum?" *International History Review* 40, no. 5 (2018): 1152–73.

6. Frederik W. de Klerk, "Dismantling of Nuclear Weapons (Memorandum to the Minister of Defence)," in *The Bomb: South Africa's Nuclear Weapons Programme,* ed. Nic von Wiellig and Lydia von Wielligh-Steyn (Pretoria: Litera, 1990), 512.

7. On South Africa's joining the NPT, see Robin Möser, "'The Major Prize': Apartheid South Africa's Accession to the Treaty on the Non-Proliferation of Nuclear Weapons, 1988–91," *Nonproliferation Review* 26, no. 5–6 (2019): 559–73. On the history of South Africa's nuclear program and disarmament, see Anna-Mart van Wyk, "South African Nuclear Development in the 1970s"; Jo-Ansie van Wyk and Anna-Mart van Wyk, "From the Nuclear Laager to the Non-Proliferation Club: South Africa and the NPT," *South African Historical Journal* 67, no. 1 (2015): 32–46; Martha van Wyk, "Sunset over Atomic Apartheid: United States–South African Nuclear Relations, 1981–93." *Cold War History* 10, no. 1 (2009): 51–79.

8. Möser, "'The Major Prize.'"

9. Jo-Ansie Karina Van Wyk, *South Africa's Nuclear Diplomacy, 1990–2010: Securing a Niche Role through Norm Construction and State Identity* (PhD diss., University of Pretoria, 2013), 221.

10. Vineet Thakur, "Foreign Policy and Its People: Transforming the Apartheid Department of Foreign Affairs," *Diplomacy & Statecraft* 26, no. 3 (2015): 514–33; Jo-Ansie van Wyk, "From Apartheid to Ubuntu: Transition, Transaction and Transformation in South Africa's Post-Apartheid Foreign Ministry," *South African Journal of International Affairs* 26, no. 3 (2019): 413–34.

11. Matthew Graham, *The Crisis of South African Foreign Policy: Diplomacy, Leadership and the Role of the African National Congress* (London & New York: IB Tauris, 2015).

12. To the best of my knowledge, SCFA has never dealt with any issues related to nuclear proliferation or nuclear weapons. Not only was this confirmed by a number of interviewees, but also there appear to be no references to these themes in the papers of Thomas Wheeler, a DFA senior official responsible for liaison with SCFA.

13. See Abdul Samad Minty, interview by Sue Onslow, 2017, *Commonwealth Oral History Project*, Institute of Commonwealth Studies, https://sas-space.sas.ac.uk/6531/1/abdul_minty_transcript.pdf.

14. Nic von Wielligh and Lydia von Wielligh-Steyn, *The Bomb: South Africa's Nuclear Weapons Programme* (Pretoria: Litera, 2015).

15. Peter Goosen, *interview by Michal Onderco*, 2017 (1995 NPT RevCon Oral History Project/NPIHP, Washington, DC).

16. South Africa started joining multilateral forums only after readmission to the UN GA in 1993, although the multilateral department within the DFA had functioned since the mid-1980s. See Thakur, "Foreign Policy and Its People."

17. For a more detailed discussion of PPNN's activities, see Onderco, "The Programme."

18. Programme for Promoting Nuclear Non-Proliferation, "Issues at the 1995 NPT Conference: An International Seminar for Government Officials. List of Participants" (July 9–12, 1993), *Special Collections, box MS 424 A3079/1/1/15*, Archives of the *University of Southampton, Southampton, UK*.

19. Ibid.

20. Ben Sanders, *interview by Michal Onderco*, 2017 (1995 NPT RevCon Oral History Project/NPIHP, Washington, DC).

21. Jurchewsky first shared this story immediately after the 1995 NPT RevCon with Darryl Howlett, one of the PPNN affiliates. Howlett noted it in writing afterward; see "Darryl's Meeting with Sven Jurchewsky" (April 17, 1995), *Special Collections, box MS 424 A3079/1/1/19f1*, Archives of the *University of Southampton, Southampton, UK*.

22. Jurchewsky, *interview*.

23. Rauf, *interview*. Canada shared similar ideas with Mexico around the same time.

24. Graham, *Disarmament Sketches*; Graham, *interview*.

25. In contemporaneous memoranda, Goosen contrasted perpetual extension "as opposed to" an indefinite one. See Peter Goosen, "Nuclear Non-Proliferation Treaty (NPT): South African Position and Preparations for the NPT Review and Extension Conference" (February 24, 1995), *Archives of the Department of International Relations and Cooperation (DIRCO), Pretoria*, para. 3.2.

26. Goosen, "Nuclear Non-Proliferation Treaty."

27. Office of the Chief State Law Adviser, "South African Legal Opinion.

28. United Nations General Assembly, *Resolutions Adopted by the General Assembly,* 49/75F, *General and complete disarmament* (UNGA, New York, January 9, 1995), https://undocs.org/en/A/RES/49/75.

29. Goosen, *interview.* In his oral history interview, Jean duPreez recalled that the first version of the legal opinion was not contextualized, and had to be reworked.

30. Goosen, "Nuclear Non-Proliferation Treaty," para. 2.2.

31. Ibid., para. 2.5.

32. Ibid., para. 2.6.

33. Ibid.

34. Both citations are from Goosen, "Nuclear Non-Proliferation Treaty," para. 3.1 and 3.2, respectively.

35. Canada, Australia, Germany, Colombia, Ethiopia, Japan, Argentina, Hungary, Peru, Philippines, the Republic of Korea, and South Africa, according to the memorandum.

36. Goosen, "Nuclear Non-Proliferation Treaty," para. 2.8.

37. Ibid.

38. Wolfgang Hoffmann, "4.Prepcom Ueberpruefungs- Un Verlaengungskonferenzenz Vom 23.1. Bis 27.1.1995: Allgemeine Aussprache (4.Prepcom Review and Extension Conference from January 23 until 27, 1995: General discussion)" (1995), *Political Archive of the German Federal Foreign Office, row 675, box 48828*, Berlin.

39. Goosen, "Nuclear Non-Proliferation Treaty," para. 3.2.

40. Jean duPreez, "Nuclear Non-Proliferation Treaty (NPT): South African Position and Preparations for the NPT Review and Extension Conference" (February 27, 1995), *Archives of the Department of International Relations and Cooperation (DIRCO), Pretoria.*

41. Ibid., para. 2.1.3.

42. Ibid.,para. 2.3.4.

43. Jean duPreez, "Nuclear Non-Proliferation Treaty (NPT): South African Position and Preparations for the NPT Review and Extension Conference (March 2, 1995), *Archives of the Department of International Relations and Cooperation (DIRCO), Pretoria*, para. 6.

44. Rauf and Johnson, "After the NPT's Indefinite Extension."

45. A similar conclusion was reached by Taylor, though with some confusion on the empirical matter. See Ian Taylor, "South Africa and the Nuclear Non-Proliferation Treaty," in *The New Multilateralism in South African Diplomacy*, ed. Donna Lee, Ian Taylor, and Paul Williams (Houndmills, Basingstoke, UK: Palgrave Macmillan, 2006), 159–81.

46. ANC activist David Goldberg demonstrated this stance at a national dialogue on nuclear policy in 1993, when he argued for a shorter rather than longer NPT extension. See Van Wyk, *South Africa's Nuclear Diplomacy.*

47. South African expectations on this issue were similar to those of Germany. Wolfgang Hoffmann, Germany's ambassador to the Conference on Disarmament,

predicted around the same time that "only about 50–60 states could be thus far identified that could be certain to vote for an indefinite extension, an additional 25–35 lean toward this option." See Hoffmann, "4.Sitzung Des Vorbereitungsausschusses."

48. Goosen, "Nuclear Non-Proliferation Treaty."

49. Although Germany provides an exception, until very late in the process it had continued to classify South Africa as opposed to indefinite extension "NVV-Verlängungskonferenz. Positionen Der Vertragstaaten (NPT extension conference. Positions of the States Parties)" (April 6, 1995), *Political Archive of the German Federal Foreign Office, row 675, box 48828*, Berlin.

50. Colin Powell, "Letter to Nelson Mandela" (February 8, 1995), *folder South Africa–1995, box 9, Clinton Presidential Records/NSC, Clinton Presidential Library/ NARA*; William Jefferson Clinton, "Letter from President Clinton to President Mandela" (February 13, 1995), *folder US-South Africa Binational Commission, The Visit of Deputy President Mbeki, February 28–March 3, 1995, binder 2, box 144, Clinton Presidential Records/NSC, Clinton Presidential Library/NARA*.

51. Powell, "Letter to Nelson Mandela." In his memoirs, Thomas Graham recalled that the South African desk at the State Department identified Powell as one of two people in the United States who Nelson Mandela "might listen to" (the other being Henry Kissinger). See Graham, *Disarmament Sketches*.

52. John Holum, "South Africa NPT Extension Vote" (1994), *South Africa–1995, box 8, OA/ID872, African Affairs, the files of Donald Steinberg, Susan Rice, MacArthur DeShazer, Clinton Presidential Records/NSC, Clinton Presidential Library/NARA, Little Rock, AR*.

53. For all quotes, see Clinton, "Letter from President Clinton to President Mandela."

54. Jean duPreez, *interview by Michal Onderco*, 2018 (1995 NPT RevCon Oral History Project/NPIHP, Washington, DC). For the letter from Mandela to Clinton, see "South Africa: Response to Letter from President Clinton to President Mandela" (1995), *South Africa–1995, box 9, OA/ID872, African Affairs, the files of Donald Steinberg, Susan Rice, MacArthur DeShazer, Clinton Presidential Records/NSC, Clinton Presidential Library/NARA, Little Rock, AR*.

55. duPreez, *interview*.

56. Graham, *Crisis of South African Foreign Policy*. This view was shared by the highest civil servant in the DFA, Director-General Leo "Rusty" Evans; see Thakur, "Foreign Policy and Its People."

57. Princeton N. Lyman, *Partner to History: The U.S. Role in South Africa's Transition to Democracy* (Washington, DC: US Institute of Peace Press, 2002).

58. Princeton N. Lyman, *interview by Michal Onderco*, 2017 (1995 NPT RevCon Oral History Project/NPIHP, Washington, DC).

59. duPreez, *interview*.

60. Lyman, *Partner to History*. See also Chapter 7 of Martha van Wyk, "*The 1977 United States Arms Embargo against South Africa: Institution and Implementation to*

1997" (*PhD diss.*, University of Pretoria, 2006). The sanctions against Denel remained in place till 1997.

61. Steven Aoki, "NPT Extension: Additional Points for Mbeki" (1995), *South Africa–1995, box 9, OA/ID872, African Affairs, the files of Donald Steinberg, Susan Rice, MacArthur DeShazer. Clinton Presidential Records/NSC, Clinton Presidential Library/NARA, Little Rock, AR.*

62. We unfortunately do not know the content of these interactions, but we know they took place thanks to the NARA withdrawal/redaction sheets.

63. Daniel Poneman, "Thabo Cover Note" (1995), *South Africa–1995, box 8, OA/ID872, African Affairs, the files of Donald Steinberg, Susan Rice, MacArthur DeShazer. Clinton Presidential Records/NSC, Clinton Presidential Library/NARA, Little Rock, AR.*

64. Steven Aoki, "Mbeki Nonpaper on NPT" (1995), *South Africa–1995, box 6, OA/ID872, African Affairs, the files of Donald Steinberg, Susan Rice, MacArthur DeShazer. Clinton Presidential Records/NSC, Clinton Presidential Library/NARA, Little Rock, AR.*

65. Ibid.

66. Poneman, "Thabo Cover Note."

67. "Non-Paper for SAG on NPT" (1995), *South Africa–1995, box 6, OA/ID872, African Affairs, the files of Donald Steinberg, Susan Rice, MacArthur DeShazer, Clinton Presidential Records/NSC, Clinton Presidential Library/NARA, Little Rock, AR.*

68. Daniel Poneman, "South Africa and NPT" (1995), *South Africa–1995, box 6, OA/ID872, African Affairs, the files of Donald Steinberg, Susan Rice, MacArthur DeShazer, Clinton Presidential Records/NSC, Clinton Presidential Library/NARA, Little Rock, AR.*

69. "DFA Director-General Discusses US-SA Relations."

70. AFP, "South Africa Wants Limited Extension of Nuke Treaty," *Lexis Nexis,* March 29, 1995.

71. "DFA Director-General Discusses US-SA Relations."

72. duPreez in his oral history interview suggested that Abdul Minty suggested a one-time short extension, the position supported by DFA Director-General Evans's remarks in a meeting with the US ambassador. Abdul Minty maintains that he promoted the idea of indefinite extension. Unfortunately, there are no written minutes of the meeting available. However, Minty accompanied Nzo to Cairo (as confirmed by both Minty and Nabil Fahmy, one of their Egyptian interlocutors), after which Nzo proposed the "limited period" extension mentioned above. Sizwe Mpofu-Walsh in his doctoral dissertation argues that Minty's position "only relies on the language of 'Southern' solidarity" (p. 199). See Sizwe Mpofu-Walsh, "*Obedient Rebellion: Nuclear-Weapon-Free Zones and Global Nuclear Order, 1967–2017*" (*PhD diss.*, Oxford University, 2020).

73. Goosen, *interview*. This position is also consistent with the account presented (with much less detail) by another likely attendee, Thomas Markram. See his *A Decade of Disarmament, Transformation and Progress.*

74. "South Africa's Position on the Extension of the Nuclear Non-Proliferation Treaty (NPT)" (April 3, 1995), *Archives of the Department of International Relations and Cooperation (DIRCO), Pretoria.*

75. Goosen, *interview.*

76. Ibid.

77. "South Africa's Position on the Extension."

78. Goosen, *interview.* Two other diplomats, of whom at least one was present in the room, remembered a similar argument in their memoirs. See von Wielligh and von Wielligh-Steyn, *The Bomb*; Markram, *A Decade of Disarmament, Transformation and Progress.*

79. Thabo Mbeki, "Letter to Vice-President Al Gore" (April 10, 1995), *Archives of the Department of International Relations and Cooperation (DIRCO), Pretoria.* Interestingly, the notion of democracy is also strongly tied to South Africa's commitment in Nzo's speech to the conference, in which he draws a stark distinction between apartheid and "democratic" South Africa. See Alfred Nzo, "The Statement by the Foreign Minister of the Republic of South Africa, Mr. Alfred Nzo. The 1995 Review and Extension Conference of the Parties to the Treaty on the Non-Proliferation of Nuclear Weapons" (April 19, 1995), *Archives of the Department of International Relations and Cooperation (DIRCO), Pretoria.*

80. Readers should note that I do not evaluate whether indefinite extension of the NPT has actually been good for the goal of achieving a world without nuclear weapons, of which some academics have been critical. I simply note that Mbeki made this argument explicitly. For an example of the criticism of such linkage, see Benoît Pelopidas, "Nuclear Weapons Scholarship as a Case of Self-Censorship in Security Studies," *Journal of Global Security Studies* 1, no. 4 (2016): 326–36.

81. For example, Alfred Nzo, "Letter to Edward Bwanali, Minister of External Affairs of Malawi" (April 13, 1995). *Archives of the Department of International Relations and Cooperation (DIRCO), Pretoria.*

82. Gore's response to the letter welcomes such an invitation, and Gore recommends that the diplomats of the two countries discuss the principles at the conference. See Al Gore, "Letter to Thabo Mbeki" (April 13, 1995), *Archives of the Department of International Relations and Cooperation (DIRCO), Pretoria.*

83. Fax (or telex) headers show that the letter to Malawi's FM, although dated earlier, was transmitted just a few hours before the start of the conference.

84. Gore, "Letter to Thabo Mbeki."

85. Nzo, "The Statement by the Foreign Minister."

86. Ibid.

87. Personal email of said diplomat to the author, 2017.

88. Jurchewsky, *interview*; Rauf, *interview.* Incidentally, as Thomas Graham revealed during a critical oral history conference in Rotterdam, the demand for (and provision

of) negative security assurances was something the US government considered as one of the possible bargaining chips in exchange for indefinite extension already in winter 1994.

89. Personal email to the author, 2017.

90. Graham, *interview*. Both Graham and Goosen independently confirmed that the US delegation was supportive of the aims of the South African delegation. It is relevant to note that Gore met only two delegations in New York during his visit—South Africa's and Egypt's. See Office of the Vice President, "Trip of the Vice President to New York, NY April 19, 1995" (1995), *box 010, Vice President's trip to New York City to attend NPT Conference, NARA, Washington, DC.*

91. Michael Weston, "Principles: Discussion with South Africans: 1 May" (1995), *NPT–March 1995, box 2, OA/ID720, Nonproliferation and Export Controls, the files of Daniel Poneman Clinton Presidential Records/NSC, Clinton Presidential Library/ NARA, Little Rock, AR.*

92. Graham, *Disarmament Sketches*.

93. Harald Müller, *interview by Michal Onderco*, 2017 (1995 NPT RevCon Oral History Project/NPIHP, Washington, DC).

94. Jurchewsky, *interview*.

95. These labels were used in the contemporaneous account of Mark Hibbs; see his "South Africa 'Moved Beyond NAM' in Support of Firm NPT Extension," *Nucleonics Week* 36, no. 19 (1995): 13.

96. Ibid.

97. Onderco and Nuti, *Extending the NPT*.

98. Barbara Crossette, "South Africa Emerges as a Force for Extending Nuclear Arms Pact," *New York Times*, April 23, 1995.

99. Berdennikov, *interview*; Onderco and Nuti, *Extending the NPT*.

100. Westdal, *interview*.

Chapter 5: "This Is What Happens When You Become Greedy": Egypt's Intervention

1. In their overview of regional issues affecting the prospects for the NPT extension, Simpson and Howlett, "The NPT Renewal Conference," mention the Middle East only in the context of Iraq's nuclear program.

2. Sanders, *NPT Review Conferences and the Role of Consensus*.

3. Roham Alvandi, *Nixon, Kissinger, and the Shah: The United States and Iran in the Cold War* (Oxford & New York: Oxford University Press, 2014).

4. Mahmoud Karem, *A Nuclear-Weapon-Free Zone in the Middle East: Problems and Prospects* (New York: Greenwood, 1988).

5. Bernd W. Kubbig and Christian Weidlich, *A WMD/DVs Free Zone for the Middle East: Taking Stock, Moving Forward towards Regional Security* (Frankfurt: Peace

Research Institute Frankfurt, 2015). Etel Solingen argues that embedding the discussions of the Middle East free of nuclear weapons within the broader Arab-Israeli debate was in line with the strategy among Arab political moderates to embrace political negotiations with Israel, e.g., in the form of the Oslo and Madrid Peace Processes, rejected by more radical states. See her "The Domestic Sources of Regional Regimes: The Evolution of Nuclear Ambiguity in the Middle East," *International Studies Quarterly* 38, no. 2 (1994): 305–37.

6. Carmen Wunderlich, et al., "Non-Aligned Reformers and Revolutionaries: Egypt, South Africa, Iran and North Korea," in Müller and Wunderlich (2013), *Norm Dynamics in Multilateral Arms Control.*

7. Nabil Fahmy, *Egypt's Diplomacy in War, Peace and Transition* (London: Palgrave, 2020).

8. Hassan Elbahtimy, "Missing the Mark: Dimona and Egypt's Slide into the 1967 Arab-Israeli War," *Nonproliferation Review* 25, no. 5–6 (2018): 385–97.

9. On Israel's nuclear program, see Avner Cohen: *Israel and the Bomb* (New York: Columbia University Press, 1998) and *Worst-Kept Secret: Israel's Bargain with the Bomb* (New York: Columbia University Press, 2010).

10. Shaker, *The Nuclear Non-Proliferation Treaty.*

11. Federation of American Scientists, "Egypt: Nuclear Weapons Program," WMD around the World Commission report, updated May 30, 2012, https://fas.org/nuke/guide/egypt/nuke/.

12. As Etel Solingen explains, the nuclear abstention was a requirement for domestic industrial development. See her works, "The Political Economy of Nuclear Restraint," *International Security* 19, no. 2 (1994): 126–69 and "The Domestic Sources of Regional Regimes."

13. Barbara M. Gregory, "Egypt's Nuclear Program: Assessing Supplier-Based and Other Developmental Constraints," *Nonproliferation Review* 3, no. 1 (1995): 20–27; Maria Rost Rublee, "Egypt's Nuclear Weapons Program: Lessons Learned," *Nonproliferation Review* 13, no. 3 (2006): 555–67.

14. Federation of American Scientists, "Egypt: Nuclear Weapons Program." This decision overlapped the period when the United States embraced export control in its nonproliferation policy. Joseph Nye was the chief architect of this policy during the Carter administration.

15. Solingen, "The Domestic Sources of Regional Regimes."

16. Fahmy, *Egypt's Diplomacy*; Amr Moussa, *Kitābiyah (My Testimony)* (Cairo: Dār al-Shurūq, 2017).

17. See Fahmy's statements in his book, *Egypt's Diplomacy*, and Moussa's in his memoirs, *My Testimony*. Similar statements appear in oral history interviews; see Amr Moussa, *interview by Michal Onderco*, 2019 (1995 NPT RevCon Oral History Project/NPIHP, Washington, DC); Elaraby in oral history interview Nabil Elaraby,

interview by Michal Onderco, 2019 (1995 NPT RevCon Oral History Project/NPIHP, Washington, DC).

18. Moussa, *My Testimony*.

19. On the latter, see Moussa, *interview*.

20. George H. W. Bush, "Address before a Joint Session of the Congress on the Cessation of the Persian Gulf Conflict" (March 6, 1991), George H. W. Bush Presidential Library, College Station, TX, https://bush41library.tamu.edu/archives/public-papers/2767.

21. Karem, *A Nuclear-Weapon-Free Zone*; Solingen, "The Domestic Sources of Regional Regimes."

22. Grégoire Mallard and Paolo Foradori, "The Middle East at a Crossroads: How to Face the Perils of Nuclear Development in a Volatile Region," *Global Governance: A Review of Multilateralism and International Organizations* 20, no. 4 (2014): 499–515.

23. James Leonard, "Steps toward a Middle East Free of Nuclear Weapons," *Arms Control Today* 21, no. 3 (1991): 10–14. It is questionable how realistic this persuasion of Leonard's is. Every single scholar who provided feedback on this chapter commented with disbelief on this citation.

24. Gerald M. Steinberg, "Middle East Peace and the NPT Extension Decision," *Nonproliferation Review* 4, no. 1 (1996): 17–29.

25. Leonard, "Steps toward a Middle East Free of Nuclear Weapons," 10.

26. Steinberg, "Middle East Peace."

27. Shai Feldman, "President Mubarak's Visit and the Middle East Nuclear Debate," *Washington Institute for Near East Policy, PolicyWatch, no. 146* (April 5, 1995), https://www.washingtoninstitute.org/policy-analysis/president-mubaraks-visit-and-middle-east-nuclear-debate.

28. Feldman, "President Mubarak's Visit." On the Russian attempts to mediate, see "Rūsiyā Tuṭālibu Min Isrāʾīl Al-Indimam Li-Muʿāhada Manʿ Al-Intishār Al-Nawawī (Russia Asks Israel to Join the NPT)," *Al Ahram* (April 4, 1995).

29. Steinberg, "Middle East Peace." Similar notes can be found in the memoirs of Amr Moussa and Nabil Fahmy; see Moussa, *My Testimony*; Fahmy, *Egypt's Diplomacy*.

30. See, for example, "Miṣr Wa Isrāʾīl Tatabādalāni Al-Muqtaraḥāt Li-Taswiyya Al-Khilāf Ḥawla Al-Barnāmij Al-Nawawī Al-Isrāʾīlī (Egypt and Israel Exchange Suggestions to Resolve the Dispute around the Israeli Nuclear Program)," *Al Ahram*, March 25, 1995.

31. "Vertrag Ueber Die Nichtverbreitung Von Kernwaffen (NVV). Britische Haltung (Treaty on the Non-Proliferation of Nuclear Weapons (NPT). British position)" (1995), *Political Archive of the German Federal Foreign Office, row 675, box 48828*, Berlin; "TNP/Position De Certains Pays Arabes Et Maghrebins (NPT/Position of Certain Arab and Maghreb Countries)" (1995), *Political Archive of the German Federal Foreign Office, row 675, box 48828*, Berlin.

32. Moussa, *interview.*

33. "Conference on Disarmament (CD): NPT Bilateral Consultations, February 3–5." February 12, 1993, US *Department of State, FOIA Virtual Reading Room, Case no. F-2008-02837.*

34. "NPT 95—PrepCom 1: Egypt Wants to Consult with US on Security Assurances in Advance of the 1995 NPT Conference" (May 17, 1993), US *Department of State, FOIA Virtual Reading Room, Case no. M-2008-02837.*

35. "The Secretary's Meeting with Egyptian Foreign Minister Moussa, Budapest, December 4, 1994" (December 5, 1994), US *Department of State, FOIA Virtual Reading Room, Case no. M-2017-11694.*

36. Steinberg, "Middle East Peace."

37. US Department of State, "Press Conference with President Hosni Mubarak and Secretary of State Warren Christopher" (1995), *NPT–March 1995, box 2, OA/ID720, Nonproliferation and Export Controls, the files of Daniel Poneman, Clinton Presidential Records/NSC, Clinton Presidential Library/NARA, Little Rock, AR.*

38. Feldman, "President Mubarak's Visit."

39. Steinberg, "Middle East Peace." Shortly before the conference, the French Foreign Minister Alain Juppé met with his US counterpart Christopher, and the two agreed that most of the Arab countries were in favor of indefinite extension, but Arab countries would be "reluctant to embarrass Egypt" and be openly in favor of indefinite extension. See "Secretary's Meeting with French Foreign Minister."

40. "'A. M. Amin, "Wizarā' Al-Khārijiyya Al-'arab Yunāqishūna Ba'da Ghad Mashrū' Qarār Bi-Taṭwīr Mu'āhada Man' Intishār Al-Asliḥa Al-Nawawiyya (Arab Foreign Ministers Will Discuss a Draft Resolution on the Development of the NPT the Day after Tomorrow)," *Al Ahram*, March 20, 1995, 6.

41. "Tansīq Al-Mawāqif Al-'arabiyya Ḥawla Al-Mu'āhada Al-Nawawiyya (Coordination of Arab Positions on NPT)," *Al Ahram*, March 23, 1995; "Majlis Al-Jāmi'a Al-Arabiyya Yakhtatimu Dawratahu Al-'ādiya Al-Yawm (The Arab League Council Concludes Its Regular Meeting Today)," *Al Ahram*, March 23, 1995.

42. "Istithnā' Isrā'īl Min Tawqī' Al-Mu'āhada Al-Nawawiyya Yuhaddidu Amn Wa Salām Al-Sharq Al-Awsaṭ Wa Ghayr Maqbūl (The League's Council Decides in Its Conclusion: Exclusion of Israel from the NPT Threatens Security and Peace in the Middle East and Is Unacceptable)," *Al Ahram* March 24, 1995.

43. Mariam Sami, "Egypt Loses Bid for Arab League Support on Nuclear Treaty" (1995), https://advance.lexis.com/api/permalink/b0efcbec-21de-4f16-9ae2–045846fd9dcf/?context=1516831; BBC, "Arab League Passes Resolution on NPT" (1995). In a later interview, Egypt's then foreign minister Amr Moussa blamed US lobbying for the failure of the Arab League to come to an agreement. See Moussa, *interview.*

44. Moussa, *interview.*

45. "Miṣr Wa 107 Duwal Ghayr Munḥāza Tunāqishu Qaḍiyya Al-Muʿāhada Al-Nawawiyya Fī Bāndūnj Al-Usbūʿ Al-Qādim (Egypt and 107 Non-Aligned Countries Discuss the NPT in Bandung Next Week)," *Al Ahram*, April 16, 1995.

46. AFP, "South Africa Wants Limited Extension of Nuke Treaty."

47. Fahmy, *Egypt's Diplomacy*; Moussa, *My Testimony*.

48. Moussa, *interview*.

49. By that time, the Canadian resolution was being opened for signatures.

50. Moussa, *interview*.

51. Nabil Fahmy, *interview by Hassan Elbahtimy*, 2017 (1995 NPT RevCon Oral History Project/NPIHP, Washington, DC).

52. United Nations, "Draft Resolution Submitted by Algeria, Bahrain, Egypt, Iraq, Jordan, Kuwait, the Libyan Arab Jamahiriya, Mauritania, Morocco, Qatar, Saudi Arabia, the Sudan, Tunisia and Yemen,"in *1995 Review and Extension Conference of the Parties to the Treaty on the Non-Proliferation of Nuclear Weapons, Final Document, Part II—Documents issued at the Conference,* NPT/CONF.1995/L.7 (United Nations, New York, 1995).

53. Moussa, *My Testimony*.

54. Steinberg, "Middle East Peace."

55. Fahmy, *interview*.

56. Fahmy, *Egypt's Diplomacy*.

57. Fahmy, *interview* and *Egypt's Diplomacy*.

58. US and Israeli observers interpreted the latitude that the Egyptian delegation enjoyed as a lack of coordination between Mubarak and Egypt's foreign ministry. See, for example, Steinberg, "Middle East Peace" or Robert Robert Einhorn, *interview by Michal Onderco*, 2017 (1995 NPT RevCon Oral History Project/NPIHP, Washington, DC). Amr Moussa, Egypt's minister of Foreign Affairs from 1991 to 2001, told me in an interview that Mubarak told him to "find a way out." See Moussa, *interview*.

59. Fahmy, *Egypt's Diplomacy*.

60. Einhorn, *interview*. In less colorful terms, the episode was recalled by all Egyptian diplomats interviewed by the author who were in the room at the time.

61. Elaraby's memoir is quoted in Moussa, *My Testimony*, 436.

62. Ibid., 437.

63. Robert Einhorn argued that Mubarak was incredulous that his delegation was the sticking point of the conference, see Einhorn, *interview*; Fahmy, *Egypt's Diplomacy*. Nabil Fahmy and Amr Moussa argue that Clinton's intervention reinforced Egypt's resolve; see Fahmy, *Egypt's Diplomacy*; Moussa, *My Testimony*.

64. While the contents of the calls between the White House and Cairo are still classified, the withdrawal and redaction sheets indicate numerous points of communication between the United States and Cairo, especially with Osama El Baz. Fahmy

in his memoirs recounts that Mubarak was "not particularly fond of the American vice president," Fahmy, *Egypt's Diplomacy*, 123.

65. Moussa, *My Testimony*, 437.

66. Ibid., 441.

67. Moussa, *My Testimony*.

68. Libby Ward, "US Text (Fax to Daniel Poneman)" (1995), *NPT–May 1995, box 2, OA/ID721, Nonproliferation and Export Controls, the files of Daniel Poneman, Clinton Presidential Records/NSC, Clinton Presidential Library/NARA, Little Rock, AR*. This language found its way into the final resolution as well.

69. Graham, *Disarmament Sketches*.

70. Fahmy, *interview*.

71. Fahmy, *Egypt's Diplomacy*, 123.

72. Fahmy, *interview*; Fahmy, *Egypt's Diplomacy*.

73. Ibid.

74. Libby Ward and Robert Einhorn, "Draft (Fax to Daniel Poneman)" (1995), *NPT–May 1995, box 2, OA/ID721, Nonproliferation and Export Controls, the files of Daniel Poneman, Clinton Presidential Records/NSC, Clinton Presidential Library/NARA, Little Rock, AR*.

75. See the statements of British ambassador Sir Michael Weston and Russian ambassador Grigory Berdennikov in Onderco and Nuti, *Extending the NPT*. Andrew Barlow, a senior diplomat in the British delegation, tellingly devoted one brief paragraph to the whole discussion on the Middle East in a conference paper. See Andrew Barlow, "Personal Recollections of the 1995 NPT Review and Extension Conference" (presentation at *Charterhouse Nuclear History Conference [July 5–7, 2018]*, Charterhouse School, Godalming, UK, July 6, 2018).

76. Graham, *Disarmament Sketches*.

77. "Decision 3."

78. Elaraby, *interview*; Fahmy, *Egypt's Diplomacy*; Moussa, *My Testimony*.

79. Elaraby, *interview*.

80. Fahmy, *Egypt's Diplomacy*, 125.

81. Moussa, *My Testimony*.

82. Moussa, *interview*.

83. Eric Trager, "The Throwback: Meet the Anti-Israel Demagogue Who Will Likely Be Egypt's Next President," *New Republic*, April 29, 2011, https://newrepublic.com/article/87607/moussa-biography-egypt-arab-league-mubarak.

84. Monterey Institute of International Studies, "The 1995 Review and Extension Conference of Parties to the Non-Proliferation Treaty: Assessment and Implications for the Future. A Workshop Conducted on 27–29 July 1995" (1995), *reel 9159, Ford Foundation Grants—U to Z, Rockefeller Archive Center*, Sleepy Hollow, NY.

85. Steinberg, "Middle East Peace."

Chapter 6: Postextension Politics of the NPT

1. United Nations, *1995 Review and Extension Conference of the Parties to the Treaty on the Non-Proliferation of Nuclear Weapons, Final Document, Part III—Summary and Verbatim Records, NPT/CONF.1995/32* (United Nations, New York, *1996)*, 184, https://documents-dds-ny.un.org/doc/UNDOC/GEN/N96/216/75/IMG/N9621675.pdf?OpenElement.

2. Ibid., 186.

3. Ibid., 191.

4. Ben Sanders, "*The Nuclear Non-Proliferation Regime after the NPT Conference,*" PPNN paper Cg18/8, Programme for Promoting Nuclear Nonproliferation, Southampton, UK, 1995: 3.

5. Onderco and Nuti, *Extending the NPT.*

6. "Decision 1," para. 4.

7. Monterey Institute of International Studies, "The 1995 Review and Extension Conference," 7.

8. Ibid., 8.

9. See Onderco, "The Programme."

10. Shepard Forman, "Recommendation for Grant/FAP Action. Partial Support for the 1997 Preparatory Session of the Review Conference of the Nuclear Nonproliferation Treaty" (1996), internal memo, *reel 7448, Ford Foundation Grants—U to Z, Rockefeller Archive Center.*

11. "Decision 2."

12. South Africa's original draft as well as the UK alternative can be found in Stephen Ledogar, "Keeping up with the 'Principles' 2 May (Memorandum for Norman Wulf)" (1995), *NPT–March 1995, box 2, OA/ID720, Nonproliferation and Export Controls, the files of Daniel Poneman, Clinton Presidential Records/NSC, Clinton Presidential Library/NARA, Little Rock, AR.*

13. Rauf, *interview.*

14. Ledogar, "Keeping up with the 'Principles.'"

15. *International Court of Justice,* "Legality of the Threat or Use of Nuclear Weapons" (1996), Advisory Opinion of July 8, 1996, ICJ, http://www.icj-cij.org/docket/files/95/7495.pdf?PHPSESSID=ba2089ec29fb1f030262d9c91b131440. For a legal analytical take on this double obligation, see Monique Cormier, "Running Out of (Legal) Excuses: Extended Nuclear Deterrence in the Era of the Prohibition Treaty," in *Nuclear Non-Proliferation in International Law, vol. 5, Legal Challenges for Nuclear Security and Deterrence,* ed. Jonathan L. Black-Branch and Dieter Fleck (The Hague: T.M.C. Asser Press, 2020), 269–90.

16. "Decision 2," para. 4c.

17. Both citations can be found in Ledogar, "Keeping up with the 'Principles.'"

18. Peter Goosen, "*The Consequences of the 1995 Conference for the NPT: The*

Yardsticks for Non-Proliferation and Disarmament," PPNN paper Cg18/7, Programme for Promoting Nuclear Nonproliferation, Southampton, UK, 1995: 5.

19. Ibid.

20. Sanders, *Nuclear Non-Proliferation Regime*, 4.

21. Monterey Institute of International Studies, "The 1995 Review and Extension Conference."

22. Goosen, *Consequences of the 1995 Conference*, 6.

23. Monterey Institute of International Studies, "The 1995 Review and Extension Conference."

24. "Decision 3: Extension of the Treaty on the Non-Proliferation of Nuclear Weapons." NPT/CONF.1995/32 (Part I), Annex, 1995, https://unoda-web.s3-accelerate.amazonaws.com/wp-content/uploads/assets/WMD/Nuclear/1995-NPT/pdf/NPT_CONF199503.pdf.

25. duPreez, Jean. interview by Michal Onderco, 2018. 1995 NPT RevCon Oral History Project, NPIHP, Washington, DC.

26. "Resolution on the Middle East," in *1995 Review and Extension Conference of the Parties to the Treaty on the Non-Proliferation of Nuclear Weapons. Final Document, Part I—Organization and work of the Conference, NPT/CONF.1995/32*, Annex (United Nations, New York, 1995), https://unoda-web.s3-accelerate.amazonaws.com/wp-content/uploads/assets/WMD/Nuclear/1995-NPT/pdf/Resolution_MiddleEast.pdf. For Davinić's note, see Davinić, Prvoslav. "1995 NPT Review and Extension Conference. Assessment of the Fourth and Last Week of Work (8-12 May 1995)." In *United Nations Archives. Folder S-1082-0019-0001-00002 "Office of Disarmament Affairs (ODA) - Non-Proliferation Treaties (NPT)," 1995*.

27. United Nations, *1995 Review and Extension Conference*.

28. Rauf, *interview*.

29. Norman A. Wulf, "Observations from the 2000 NPT Review Conference," *Arms Control Today* 30, no. 9 (2000): 3–9; Tariq Rauf, "The 2000 NPT Review Conference," *Nonproliferation Review* 7, no. 1 (2000): 146–61. Slovenia later left NAC after joining NATO.

30. Wulf, "Observations."

31. For a recent analysis of the P5 process, see Shatabhisha Shetty and Heather Williams, "The P5 Process: Opportunities for Success in the NPT Review Conference," *European Leadership Network,* June 30, 2020, https://www.europeanleadershipnetwork.org/report/the-p5-process-opportunities-for-success/.

32. Tariq Rauf, "An Unequivocal Success? Implications of the NPT Review Conference," *Arms Control Today* 30, no. 6 (2000): 9; Rauf, "The 2000 NPT Review Conference."

33. Harald Müller, "A Treaty in Troubled Waters: Reflections on the Failed NPT Review Conference," *International Spectator* 40, no. 3 (2005): 33–44.

34. Claire Applegarth, "Divisions Foil NPT Review Conference," *Arms Control Today* 35, no. 5 (2005): 39.

35. William C. Potter, "The NPT Review Conference: 188 States in Search of Consensus," *International Spectator* 40, no. 3 (2005): 19–31.

36. Dee, "Standing Together or Doing the Splits."

37. Potter, "NPT Review Conference."

38. Müller, "A Treaty in Troubled Waters."

39. Harald Müller, "A Nuclear Nonproliferation Test: Obama's Nuclear Policy and the 2010 NPT Review Conference," *Nonproliferation Review* 18, no. 1 (2011): 219–36.

40. Rebecca Johnson, "Assessing the 2010 NPT Review Conference," *Bulletin of the Atomic Scientists* 66, no. 4 (2010): 1–10; Müller, "A Nuclear Nonproliferation Test."

41. Harald Müller, "The 2010 NPT Review Conference: Some Breathing Space Gained, but No Breakthrough," *International Spectator* 45, no. 3 (2010): 5–18; Johnson, "Assessing the 2010 NPT Review Conference."

42. Jeffrey S. Lantis, "Irrational Exuberance? The 2010 NPT Review Conference, Nuclear Assistance, and Norm Change," *Nonproliferation Review* 18, no. 2 (2011): 389–409.

43. United Nations, *2010 Review Conference of the Parties to the Treaty on the Non-Proliferation of Nuclear Weapons, Final Document, Part I—Review of the operation of the treaty, as provided for in its Article VIII (3), taking into account the decisions and the resolution adopted by the 1995 Review and Extension Conference and the Final Document of the 2000 Review Conference and the Final Document of the 2000 Review Conference. Conclusions and Recommendations for follow-on actions, NPT/CONF.2010/50, vol. 1* (New York: United Nations, 2010).

44. Potter, "The Unfulfilled Promise."

45. Andrey Baklitskiy, "The 2015 NPT Review Conference and the Future of the Nonproliferation Regime," *Arms Control Today* 45, no. 6 (2015): 15–18.

46. Potter, "The Unfulfilled Promise."

47. Megan Dee, "The EU's Performance in the 2015 NPT Review Conference: What Went Wrong," *European Foreign Affairs Review* 20, no. 4 (2015): 591–608; Michal Smetana, "Stuck on Disarmament: The European Union and the 2015 NPT Review Conference," *International Affairs* 92, no. 1 (2016): 137–52.

48. Rebecca Davis Gibbons, "Can This New Approach to Nuclear Disarmament Work?" *War on the Rocks* (January 23, 2019), https://warontherocks.com/2019/01/can-this-new-approach-to-nuclear-disarmament-work/; Heather Williams, "CEND and a Changing Global Nuclear Order," *European Leadership Network*, 2020, https://www.europeanleadershipnetwork.org/commentary/cend-and-a-changing-global-nuclear-order/.

49. On Brazil's signature of the NPT, see Sergio de Queiroz Duarte, "Brazil and the Nonproliferation Regime: A Historical Perspective," *Nonproliferation Review* 23, no.

NOTES TO CHAPTER 6

5–6 (2016): 545–58; Togzhan Kassenova, *Brazil's Nuclear Kaleidoscope: An Evolving Identity* (Washington, DC: Carnegie Endowment for International Peace, 2014).

50. Ben Sanders, ed., *Newsbrief 4 (1995)*, PPNN / Mountbatten Center for International Studies, University of Southampton.

51. For a recent overview of the academic scholarship on nuclear-weapon-free zones, see the recent dissertation by Mpofu-Walsh, *"Obedient Rebellion."*

52. Eliza Gheorghe, "Proliferation and the Logic of the Nuclear Market," *International Security* 43, no. 4 (2019): 88–127.

53. This is a notably nontechnical description. For more information on the Additional Protocol, see the work of Laura Rockwood, one of the Additional Protocol's key architects. Laura Rockwood, "The IAEA's Strengthened Safeguards System," *Journal of Conflict and Security Law* 7, no. 1 (2002): 123–36; Laura Rockwood and Larry Johnson, "Verification of Correctness and Completeness in the Implementation of IAEA Safeguards: The Law and Practice," in *Nuclear Non-Proliferation in International Law, vol. 2, Verification and Compliance*, ed. Jonathan L. Black-Branch and Dieter Fleck (The Hague: T.M.C. Asser Press, 2016), 57–94; Laura Rockwood, "How the IAEA Verifies if a Country's Nuclear Program Is Peaceful or Not: The Legal Basis," *Bulletin of the Atomic Scientists* 74, no. 5 (2018): 317–25.

54. Daniel Joyner, *Interpreting the Nuclear Non-Proliferation Treaty* (Oxford & New York: Oxford University Press, 2011); Ian Anthony, Christer Ahlström, and Vitaly Fedchenko, *Reforming Nuclear Export Controls: The Future of the Nuclear Suppliers Group, SIPRI Research Report no. 22* (Oxford: Oxford University Press & SIPRI, 2007).

55. Tom Coppen, "Developing IAEA Safeguards: An Institutional Perspective on the State-Level Concept," *Journal of Conflict and Security Law* 20, no. 2 (2015): 169–93.

56. Gordon Corera, *Shopping for Bombs: Nuclear Proliferation, Global Insecurity, and the Rise and Fall of the A.Q. Khan Network* (London: Hurst & Co., 2006); Mark Fitzpatrick, *Nuclear Black Markets: Pakistan, A.Q. Khan and the Rise of Proliferation Networks; A Net Assessment* (London: International Institute for Strategic Studies, 2007).

57. On PSI, see Michal Onderco and Paul van Hooft, "Why Is the Proliferation Security Initiative a Problematic Solution?" *Chinese Journal of International Politics* 9, no. 1 (2016): 81–108.

58. Ben Sanders, ed., *Newsbrief 2 (1997)*, PPNN / Mountbatten Center for International Studies, University of Southampton.

59. Onderco and Nuti, *Extending the NPT*.

60. Department of Defense, *Nuclear Posture Review* (Washington, DC: Office of the Secretary of Defense, 2018).

61. Ankit Panda, "What's in Russia's New Nuclear Deterrence 'Basic Principles'? A New Document Sheds Insight on Old Debates," *Diplomat* (June 9, 2020), https://thediplomat.com/2020/06/whats-in-russias-new-nuclear-deterrence-basic

-principles/; Cynthia Roberts, "Revelations About Russia's Nuclear Deterrence Policy," *War on the Rocks* (June 19, 2020), https://warontherocks.com/2020/06/revelations-about-russias-nuclear-deterrence-policy/.

62. In August 1995, President Clinton stated that the US would follow "zero yield" CTBT, meaning permitting no explosions with a nuclear yield.

63. Emmanuelle Maitre, "French Perspectives on Disarmament and Deterrence," in *Europe's Evolving Deterrence Discourse*, ed. Amelia Morgan and Anna Péczeli (Livermore, CA: Center for Global Security Research, Lawrence Livermore National Laboratory, 2021), 51–65.

64. Daryl G. Kimball, "US Questions Russian CTBT Compliance," *Arms Control Today* 49, no. 6 (2019): 20–22 and "US Makes Noncompliance Charges," *Arms Control Today* 50, no. 4 (2020): 29–30.

65. John Hudson and Paul Sonne, "Trump Administration Discussed Conducting First U.S. Nuclear Test in Decades," *Washington Post,* May 22, 2020, https://www.washingtonpost.com/national-security/trump-administration-discussed-conducting-first-us-nuclear-test-in-decades/2020/05/22/a805c904-9c5b-11ea-b60c-3be06oa4f8e1_story.html.

66. David Axe, "Donald Trump's Nuke-Testing Idea Is 'Catastrophically Stupid,'" *Forbes,* May 29, 2020, https://www.forbes.com/sites/davidaxe/2020/05/29/donald-trumps-nuke-testing-idea-is-catastrophically-stupid/#60f68115c116; Sarah Bidgood, "A Nuclear Test Would Blow Up in Trump's Face," *Foreign Policy* (June 11, 2020), https://foreignpolicy.com/2020/06/11/nuclear-test-arms-control-trump-united-states-brinkmanship/.

67. Patricia M. Lewis, "A Middle East Free of Nuclear Weapons: Possible, Probable or Pipe-Dream?" *International Affairs* 89, no. 2 (2013): 433–50.

68. United Nations, *2010 Review Conference.*

69. Mallard and Foradori, "The Middle East at a Crossroads."

70. Tytti Erästö, "The Lack of Disarmament in the Middle East: A Thorn in the Side of the NPT, *SIPRI Insights on Peace and Security, no. 2019/1* (January 2019), https://www.sipri.org/sites/default/files/2019-01/sipriinsight1901.pdf.

71. United Nations General Assembly. Resolution 73/546, *Convening a Conference on the establishment of a Middle East zone free of nuclear weapons and other weapons of mass destruction* (UNGA, New York, December 23, 2018), https://www.un.org/disarmament/wp-content/uploads/2019/10/Decision-A_73_546.pdf.

72. For an in-depth look into the nuclear dynamic in South Asia, see Scott D. Sagan, ed., *Inside Nuclear South Asia* (Redwood City, CA: Stanford University Press, 2009); George Perkovich, *India's Nuclear Bomb: The Impact on Global Proliferation* (Berkeley: University of California Press, 1999).

73. George W. Bush, "President Bush Speech on Missile Defence" (National Defense University, Washington, DC, May 1, 2001), http://www.fas.org/nuke/control/abmt/news/010501bush.html.

74. For an overview, see Mark Smith, "Disarmament in the Anglo-American Context," in *Nuclear Weapons after the 2010 NPT Review Conference, Chaillot Paper no. 2010*, ed. Jean Pascal Zanders (Paris: European Union Institute of Security Studies, 2010), 71–86.

75. George P. Shultz, et al., "A World Free of Nuclear Weapons," *Wall Street Journal*, January 4, 2007, https://www.wsj.com/articles/SB116787515251566636.

76. United Nations, "Humanitarian Pledge for the Prohibition and Elimination of Nuclear Weapons," in *Resolution adopted by the General Assembly on 7 December*, A/Res/70/48 (New York: UNGA, December 11, 2015), http://www.un.org/ga/search/view_doc.asp?symbol=a/res/70/48.

77. Patricia Lewis et al., "Too Close for Comfort: Cases of Near Nuclear Use and Options for Policy," *Chatham House Report* (London: Chatham House, April 2014), https://www.chathamhouse.org/sites/default/files/field/field_document/20140428TooCloseforComfortNuclearUseLewisWilliamsPelopidasAghlani.pdf; Eric Schlosser, *Command and Control: Nuclear Weapons, the Damascus Accident, and the Illusion of Safety* (London: Penguin, 2014). The argument about close calls was also at that time popularized by the 2014 movie *The Man Who Saved the World* by Danish director Peter Anthony.

78. *International Campaign to Abolish Nuclear Weapons*, "Catastrophic Harm," former text on ICAN website, 2013, http://www.icanw.org/the-facts/catastrophic-harm/.

79. For a legal analysis of the nuclear weapon ban treaty, see Newell Highsmith and Mallory Stewart, "The Nuclear Ban Treaty: A Legal Analysis," *Survival* 60, no. 1 (2018): 129–52.

80. ICAN, "ICAN Statements to the Negotiating Conference." ICAN, 2016. https://www.icanw.org/ican_statements_to_the_negotiating_conference.

81. Rebecca Davis Gibbons, "The Humanitarian Turn in Nuclear Disarmament and the Treaty on the Prohibition of Nuclear Weapons," *Nonproliferation Review* 25, no. 1–2 (2018): 11–36.

82. Tom Sauer, "It's Time to Outlaw Nuclear Weapons," *National Interest*, April 18, 2016, http://nationalinterest.org/feature/its-time-outlaw-nuclear-weapons-15814?page=show; Nick Ritchie, "Pathways to Nuclear Disarmament: Delegitimising Nuclear Violence" (paper presented at the UNGA Open-ended Working Group on "Taking forward multilateral nuclear disarmament negotiations, Palais de Nations, Geneva, May 11, 2016); Ritchie, "A Hegemonic Nuclear Order."

83. Heather Williams, "A Nuclear Babel: Narratives around the Treaty on the Prohibition of Nuclear Weapons," *Nonproliferation Review* 25, no. 1–2 (2018): 51–63.

84. Yasmin Afina, et al., *Negotiation of a Nuclear Weapons Prohibition Treaty: Nuts and Bolts of the Ban; The New Treaty: Taking Stock* (New York: UN Institute for Disarmament Research, 2017); Kjølv Egeland, "How I Learned to Stop Worrying and Embrace Diplomatic 'Polarization,'" *Peace Review* 29, no. 4 (2017): 482–88; Kjølv Egeland, "Banning the Bomb: Inconsequential Posturing or Meaningful

Stigmatization?" *Global Governance: A Review of Multilateralism and International Organizations* 24, no. 1 (2018): 11–20; Ritchie, "Pathways to Nuclear Disarmament"; Ritchie, "A Hegemonic Nuclear Order."

85. Laura Considine, "The 'Standardization of Catastrophe': Nuclear Disarmament, the Humanitarian Initiative and the Politics of the Unthinkable," *European Journal of International Relations* 23, no. 3 (2016): 681–702; Laura Considine "Contests of Legitimacy and Value: The Treaty on the Prohibition of Nuclear Weapons and the Logic of Prohibition," *International Affairs* 95, no. 5 (2019): 1075–92.

86. "Decision 3."

87. Gaukhar Mukhatzhanova, et al., "Fissile Material Cut-off Treaty: History and Status," October 2010, Report no. OSRD 20011 030 (*Defense Threat Reduction Agency, Advanced Systems and Concepts Office*, Fort Belvoir, VA), https://www.hsdl.org/?view&did=716221; Zia Mian and AH Nayyar, "Playing the Nuclear Game: Pakistan and the Fissile Material Cutoff Treaty," *Arms Control Today* 40, no. 3 (2010): 17–24.

88. On nuclear latency, see Tristan A. Volpe, "Atomic Leverage: Compellence with Nuclear Latency," *Security Studies* 26, no. 3 (2017): 517–44; Rupal N. Mehta and Rachel Elizabeth Whitlark, "The Benefits and Burdens of Nuclear Latency," *International Studies Quarterly* 61, no. 3 (2017): 517–28; Rachel Elizabeth Whitlark and Rupal N. Mehta, "Hedging Our Bets: Why Does Nuclear Latency Matter?" *Washington Quarterly* 42, no. 1 (2019): 41–52.

89. For a similar argument put forward by Joseph Pilat, see his *A World without the NPT Redux,* Geneva: UNIDIR, 2020.

90. William C. Wohlforth, "The Stability of a Unipolar World," *International Security* 24, no. 1 (1999): 5–41.

91. Thomas Biersteker, "Participating in Transnational Policy Networks: Targeted Sanctions," in *Scholars, Policymakers, and International Affairs*, ed. Abraham F. Lowenthal and Mariano E. Bertucci (Baltimore: Johns Hopkins University Press, 2014), 137–54, p. 147. Biersteker holds that such networks are composed of individuals. See also Thomas Biersteker, "Transnational Policy Networks as a Form of Informal International Governance" (paper presented at "Politics of Informal Governance," Graduate Institute/IHEID, Geneva, May 19–20, 2017). For a view that policy networks are composed of state or nonstate institutions, see Diane Stone, "Global Public Policy, Transnational Policy Communities, and Their Networks," *Policy Studies Journal* 36, no. 1 (2008): 19–38.

92. Knopf, "International Cooperation on Nonproliferation."

93. Anne-Marie Slaughter, "A Grand Strategy of Network Centrality," in *America's Path: Grand Strategy for the Next Administration*, ed. Richard Fontaine and Kristin M. Lord (Washington, DC: Center for New American Security, 2012), 43–56.

94. Anne-Marie Slaughter, *The Chessboard & the Web: Strategies of Connection in a Networked World* (New Haven, CT: Yale University Press, 2017).

95. Alexander Cooley and Daniel H. Nexon, *Exit from Hegemony: The Unraveling of the American Global Order* (Oxford: Oxford University Press, 2020).

96. Daniel W. Drezner, *The System Worked: How the World Stopped Another Great Depression* (Oxford: Oxford University Press, 2014).

97. Winecoff, "Structural Power and the Global Financial Crisis"; Goddard, "Embedded Revisionism."

98. Henry Farrell and Abraham L. Newman, "Weaponized Interdependence: How Global Economic Networks Shape State Coercion," *International Security* 44, no. 1 (2019): 42–79.

99. US Department of State, "Secretary Blinken's Remarks to the Conference on Disarmament," remarks at the High-Level Segment of the Conference on Disarmament, virtual presentation (February 22, 2021), https://www.state.gov/video-remarks-to-the-conference-on-disarmament/.

100. Kingston Reif, "UN Approves Start of Nuclear Ban Talks," *Arms Control Today* (November 2016), https://www.armscontrol.org/ACT/2016_11/News/UN-Approves-Start-of-Nuclear-Ban-Talks.

101. NATO, "Statement on Russia's Failure to Comply with the Intermediate-Range Nuclear Forces (INF) Treaty," North Atlantic Council (Brussels, February 1, 2019), https://www.nato.int/cps/en/natohq/news_162996.htm. Similar statements were issued in other forums, such as at the 2019 NPT Preparatory Committee in New York.

102. Both citations are from Kingston Reif, "Trump to Withdraw U.S. from INF Treaty," *Arms Control Today* (November 2018), https://www.armscontrol.org/act/2018-11/news/trump-withdraw-us-inf-treaty. John Bolton, national security adviser at the time, is very critical of Europe's reactions in his memoir. See his *The Room Where It Happened: A White House Memoir* (New York: Simon & Schuster, 2020).

103. Advisory Council on International Affairs, *Nuclear Weapons in a New Geopolitical Reality: An Urgent Need for New Arms Control Initiatives,* AIV Advisory Report no. 109, January 19, 2019, https://www.advisorycouncilinternationalaffairs.nl/documents/publications/2019/01/29/nuclear-weapons-in-a-new-geopolitical-reality.

104. Bundy, "Letter to President Clinton."

References

ACDA. *FRG Views on Non-Proliferation Treaty* (January 26, 1967). US Department of State, FOIA Virtual Reading Room, Case no. M-2020-00304. https://foia.state. gov/Search/Results.aspx?searchText=FRG%20Views&beginDate=&endDate=&p ublishedBeginDate=&publishedEndDate=&caseNumber=.

Advisory Council on International Affairs. *Nuclear Weapons in a New Geopolitical Reality: An Urgent Need for New Arms Control Initiatives.* AIV Advisory Report no. 109. January 19, 2019. https://www.advisorycouncilinternationalaffairs.nl/docu-ments/publications/2019/01/29/nuclear-weapons-in-a-new-geopolitical-reality.

Afina ,Yasmin, John Borrie, Tim Caughley, Nick Ritchie, and Wilfred Wan. *Negotia-tion of a Nuclear Weapons Prohibition Treaty: Nuts and Bolts of the Ban; The New Treaty: Taking Stock.* New York: UN Institute for Disarmament Research, 2017.

AFP. "South Africa Wants Limited Extension of Nuke Treaty." *Lexis Nexis*, March 29, 1995.

Akhtar, Rabia. *The Blind Eye: U.S. Non-Proliferation Policy Towards Pakistan from Ford to Clinton.* Lahore, Pakistan: University of Lahore Press, 2018.

Albin, Cecilia. *Justice and Fairness in International Negotiation.* Cambridge: Cambridge University Press, 2001.

Albin, Cecilia, and Daniel Druckman. "Bargaining over Weapons: Justice and Ef-fectiveness in Arms Control Negotiations." *International Negotiation* 19, no. 3 (2014): 426–58.

Alvandi, Roham. *Nixon, Kissinger, and the Shah: The United States and Iran in the Cold War.* Oxford & New York: Oxford University Press, 2014.

Amin, 'A. M. "Wizarāʾ Al-Khārijiyya Al-ʿarab Yunāqishūna Baʿda Ghad Mashrūʿ

Qarār Bi-Taṭwīr Muʿāhada Manʿ Intishār Al-Asliḥa Al-Nawawiyya (Arab Foreign Ministers Will Discuss a Draft Resolution on the Development of the NPT the Day after Tomorrow)." *Al Ahram*, March 20, 1995, 6.

Anstey, Isabelle. "Negotiating Nuclear Control: The Zangger Committee and the Nuclear Suppliers' Group in the 1970s." *International History Review* 40, no. 5: 975–95.

Anthony, Ian, Christer Ahlström, and Vitaly Fedchenko. *Reforming Nuclear Export Controls: The Future of the Nuclear Suppliers Group. SIPRI Research Report no. 22.* Oxford: Oxford University Press & SIPRI, 2007.

Aoki, Steven. "Mbeki Nonpaper on NPT" (1995). *South Africa–1995, box 6, OA/ID872. African Affairs, the files of Donald Steinberg, Susan Rice, MacArthur DeShazer. Clinton Presidential Records/NSC, Clinton Presidential Library/NARA, Little Rock, AR.*

———. "NPT Extension: Additional Points for Mbeki" (1995). *South Africa–1995, box 9, OA/ID872, African Affairs, the files of Donald Steinberg, Susan Rice, MacArthur DeShazer. Clinton Presidential Records/NSC, Clinton Presidential Library/NARA, Little Rock, AR.*

Applegarth, Claire. "Divisions Foil NPT Review Conference." *Arms Control Today* 35, no. 5 (2005): 39.

Arkin, William M., and Michael J. Mazarr. "Clinton Defense Policy and Nuclear Weapons." In *Clinton and Post-Cold War Defense*, edited by Stephen J. Cimbala, 49–70. Westport, CT: Praeger, 1996.

Avant, Deborah, and Oliver Westerwinter, eds. *The New Power Politics: Networks and Transnational Security Governance.* Oxford: Oxford University Press, 2016.

Axe, David. "Donald Trump's Nuke-Testing Idea Is 'Catastrophically Stupid.'" *Forbes*, May 29, 2020. https://www.forbes.com/sites/davidaxe/2020/05/29/donald-trumps-nuke-testing-idea-is-catastrophically-stupid/#60f68115c116.

Baklitskiy, Andrey. "The 2015 NPT Review Conference and the Future of the Non-proliferation Regime." *Arms Control Today* 45, no. 6 (2015): 15–18.

Barlow, Andrew. "Personal Recollections of the 1995 NPT Review and Extension Conference." Presentation at *Charterhouse Nuclear History Conference (July 5–7, 2018)*. Charterhouse School, Godalming, UK, July 6, 2018.

Barnett, Michael, and Raymond Duvall. *Power in Global Governance.* Cambridge: Cambridge University Press, 2005.

BBC. "Arab League Passes Resolution on NPT" (March 25, 1995). .

Beach, Derek, and Rasmus Brun Pedersen. *Process-Tracing Methods: Foundations and Guidelines.* Ann Arbor: University of Michigan Press, 2013.

Becker-Jakob, Una, Gregor Hofmann, Harald Müller, and Carmen Wunderlich. "Good International Citizens: Canada, Germany, and Sweden." In Müller and Wunderlich (2013), *Norm Dynamics in Multilateral Arms Control.*

Bennett, D. Scott, and Matthew C. Rupert. "Comparing Measures of Political

Similarity: An Empirical Comparison of S Versus Tau-B in the Study of International Conflict." *Journal of Conflict Resolution* 47, no. 3 (2003): 367–93.

Berdennikov, Grigory. *Interview by Michal Onderco*, 2016. 1995 NPT RevCon Oral History Project, NPIHP, Washington, DC.

Bidgood, Sarah. "The Establishment of the London Club and Nuclear-Export Controls." In *Once and Future Partners: The United States, Russia and Nuclear Non-Proliferation*, edited by William C. Potter and Sarah Bidgood, 135–62. Abingdon, UK: Routledge, 2018.

———. "A Nuclear Test Would Blow Up in Trump's Face." *Foreign Policy* (June 11, 2020). https://foreignpolicy.com/2020/06/11/nuclear-test-arms-control-trump-united-states-brinkmanship/.

Biersteker, Thomas. "Participating in Transnational Policy Networks: Targeted Sanctions." In *Scholars, Policymakers, and International Affairs*, edited by Abraham F. Lowenthal and Mariano E. Bertucci, 137–54. Baltimore: Johns Hopkins University Press, 2014.

———. "Transnational Policy Networks as a Form of Informal International Governance." Paper presented at "Politics of Informal Governance," Graduate Institute/IHEID, Geneva, May 19–20, 2017.

"Bilaterale Konsultationen Mit Schluessellaendern Der Blockfreien Im Vorfeld Der Konferenz (Bilateral consultations with key non-aligned countries ahead of the conference)" (January 11, 1995). *Political Archive of the German Federal Foreign Office, row 675, box 48828, Berlin*.

Bindi, Federiga. "European Union Foreign Policy: A Historical Overview." In *The Foreign Policy of the European Union: Assessing Europe's Role in the World*, edited by Federiga Bindi, 13–40. Washington, DC: Brookings Institution Press, 2010.

Blatter, Joachim, and Markus Haverland. *Designing Case Studies: Explanatory Approaches in Small-N Research*. Basingstoke, UK: Palgrave Macmillan, 2012.

Bolton, John. *The Room Where It Happened: A White House Memoir*. New York: Simon & Schuster, 2020.

Boorstin, Bob. "1995 Communications Initiatives" (1995). *NPT–February 1995, box 1, OA/ID720, Nonproliferation and Export Controls, the files of Daniel Poneman. Clinton Presidential Records/NSC, Clinton Presidential Library/NARA, Little Rock, AR*.

Börzel, Tanja A., and Thomas Risse. "When Europe Hits Home: Europeanization and Domestic Change." *European Integration Online Papers* 4, no. 15 (2000).

———. "From Europeanisation to Diffusion: Introduction." *West European Politics* 35, no. 1 (2012): 1–19.

Budjeryn, Mariana. *Inheriting the Bomb: Soviet Collapse and Nuclear Disarmament of Ukraine*. Baltimore, MD: Johns Hopkins University Press, forthcoming.

———. "The Power of the NPT: International Norms and Ukraine's Nuclear Disarmament." *Nonproliferation Review* 22, no. 2 (2015): 203–37.

Bull, Hedley. *The Anarchical Society: A Study of Order in World Politics*. London: Macmillan, 1977.

Bundy, McGeorge. "Letter to President Clinton" (1995). *NPT–March 1995, box 4, OA/ID720, Nonproliferation and Export Controls, the files of Daniel Poneman. Clinton Presidential Records/NSC. Clinton Presidential Library/NARA, Little Rock, AR.*

Bunn, George. "Lawyers Alliance for World Security (Laws) Is for a Reliable Extension of the NPT (Statement to the January 1995 NPT Prepcom)" (1995). Roland M. Timerbaev personal archive, PIR Center, Moscow.

———. "Statement by George Bunn (on Behalf of Lawyers Alliance for World Security) to the 1995 NPT Review/Extension Conference" (April 27, 1995). Roland M. Timerbaev personal archive, PIR Center, Moscow.

Bunn, George, and Roland Timerbaev. "Letter to Michael Krepon" (January 27, 1995). Roland M. Timerbaev personal archive, PIR Center, Moscow.

Bunn, George, and Charles Van Doren. *Options for Extension of the NPT: The Intention of the Drafters of Article X.2*. PPNN study no. 2. Southampton, UK: Programme for Promoting Nuclear Nonproliferation, 1991.

———. *Two Options for the 1995 NPT Extension Conference Revisited*. Washington, DC: Lawyers Alliance for World Security, 1992.

Burr, William. "A Scheme of 'Control': The United States and the Origins of the Nuclear Suppliers' Group, 1974–1976*." *International History Review* 36, no. 2 (2014): 252–76.

Bush, George H. W. "Address before a Joint Session of the Congress on the Cessation of the Persian Gulf Conflict" (March 6, 1991). George H. W. Bush Presidential Library/NARA, College Station, TX. https://bush41library.tamu.edu/archives/public-papers/2767.

Bush, George W. "President Bush Speech on Missile Defence." National Defense University, Washington, DC, May 1, 2001. http://www.fas.org/nuke/control/abmt/news/010501bush.html.

Butler, Richard. *Interview by Michal Onderco*, 2018. 1995 NPT RevCon Oral History Project/NPIHP, Washington, DC.

Clinton, William Jefferson. "Address by President Bill Clinton to the UN General Assembly." New York, September 27, 1993. https://2009-2017.state.gov/p/io/potusunga/207375.htm.

———. "Letter to Bundy on Nuclear Arms Control" (1994). *WHORM-Subject File-General, box 02284, OA/ID720, folder FO 009. Clinton Presidential Records/NSC, Clinton Presidential Library/NARA, Little Rock, AR.*

———. "Letter from President Clinton to President Mandela" (February 13, 1995). *Folder US–South Africa Binational Commission, The Visit of Deputy President Mbeki, February 28–March 3, 1995, binder 2, box 144, 1995. Clinton Presidential Library/NARA, Little Rock, AR.*

———. "Remarks to the Nixon Center for Peace and Freedom Policy Conference [March 1, 1995]." In *Public Papers of the Presidents of the United States: William J. Clinton, Book 1*, 283–89. Washington, DC: US Government Printing Office, 1995.

Coe, Andrew J., and Jane Vaynman. "Collusion and the Nuclear Nonproliferation Regime." *Journal of Politics* 77, no. 4 (2015): 983–97.

Cohen, Avner. *Israel and the Bomb.* New York: Columbia University Press, 1998.

———. *Worst-Kept Secret: Israel's Bargain with the Bomb.* New York: Columbia University Press, 2010.

Commission on Security and Cooperation in Europe. "Third Meeting of the Council; Summary of Conclusions: Decision on Peaceful Settlement of Disputes." CSCE, Stockholm, December 15, 1992. https://www.osce.org/mc/40342?download=true.

"Conference on Disarmament (CD): NPT-95 NPT Consultations with Wider Western Group, Geneva, Feb 5, 1993" (February 16, 1993). US Department of State, FOIA Virtual Reading Room, Case no. M-2008-02837 https://foia.state.gov/Search/Results.aspx?searchText=&beginDate=19930216&endDate=19930216&publishedBeginDate=&publishedEndDate=&caseNumber=.

"Conference on Disarmament (CD): NPT Bilateral Consultations, February 3–5" (February 12, 1993). US Department of State, FOIA Virtual Reading Room, Case no. F-2008-02837.

Considine, Laura. "The 'Standardization of Catastrophe': Nuclear Disarmament, the Humanitarian Initiative and the Politics of the Unthinkable." *European Journal of International Relations* 23, no. 3 (2016): 681–702.

———. "Contests of Legitimacy and Value: The Treaty on the Prohibition of Nuclear Weapons and the Logic of Prohibition." *International Affairs* 95, no. 5 (2019): 1075–92.

"CONUC—Joint Action for the Preparation of the 1995 NPT-Conference" (December 8, 1994). *Political Archive of the German Federal Foreign Office, row 537, box 37781*, Berlin.

"CONUC—Joint Action on Disarmament Non-Proliferation" (May 20, 1994). *Political Archive of the German Federal Foreign Office, row 242, box 37116/40*, Berlin.

"CONUC—Joint Action on the Preparation of the NPT-Conference 1995" (June 21, 1994). *Political Archive of the German Federal Foreign Office, row 242, box 37116/40*, Berlin.

"CONUC—Troika Meeting with the Countries of Central and Eastern Europe" (February 11, 1994). *Political Archive of the German Federal Foreign Office, row 242, box 37116/40, Berlin.*

Cooley, Alexander, and Daniel H. Nexon. "'The Empire Will Compensate You': The Structural Dynamics of the U.S. Overseas Basing Network." *Perspectives on Politics* 11, no. 4 (2013): 1034–50.

———. *Exit from Hegemony: The Unraveling of the American Global Order.* Oxford: Oxford University Press, 2020.

Copeland, Dale C. *Economic Interdependence and War.* Princeton, NJ: Princeton University Press, 2014.

Coppen, Tom. "Developing IAEA Safeguards: An Institutional Perspective on the State-Level Concept." *Journal of Conflict and Security Law* 20, no. 2 (2015): 169–93.

Corden, Pierce S. "Historical Context and Steps to Implement the CTBT." In *Banning the Bang or the Bomb? Negotiating the Nuclear Test Ban Regime*, edited by I. William Zartman, Mordechai Melamud, and Paul Meerts, 17–31. Cambridge: Cambridge University Press, 2014.

Corera, Gordon. *Shopping for Bombs: Nuclear Proliferation, Global Insecurity, and the Rise and Fall of the A.Q. Khan Network.* London: Hurst & Co., 2006.

Cormier, Monique. "Running Out of (Legal) Excuses: Extended Nuclear Deterrence in the Era of the Prohibition Treaty." In *Nuclear Non-Proliferation in International Law. Vol. 5, Legal Challenges for Nuclear Security and Deterrence*, edited by Jonathan L. Black-Branch and Dieter Fleck, 269–90. The Hague: T.M.C. Asser Press, 2020.

Cottey, Andrew. *East-Central Europe after the Cold War: Poland, the Czech Republic, Slovakia and Hungary in Search of Security.* Basingstoke, UK: Macmillan Press, 1995.

Council of the European Union. "Council Decision of 25 July 1994 Concerning the Joint Action Adopted by the Council on the Basis of Article J.3 of the Treaty on European Union Regarding Preparation for the 1995 Conference of the States Parties to the Treaty on the Non-Proliferation of Nuclear Weapons." *Official Journal of the European Communities,* no. L 205/1 (August 8, 1994). https://eur-lex.europa.eu/legal-content/EN/TXT/PDF/?uri=CELEX:31994D0509&from=EN.

Cowles, Maria Green, James A. Caporaso, and Thomas Risse-Kappen. *Transforming Europe: Europeanization and Domestic Change.* Ithaca, NY: Cornell University Press, 2001.

Crossette, Barbara. "China Breaks Ranks with Other Nuclear Nations on Treaty." *New York Times,* April 19, 1995, 16.

———. "South Africa Emerges as a Force for Extending Nuclear Arms Pact." *New York Times,* April 23, 1995, 16.

———. "Treaty Aimed at Halting Spread of Nuclear Weapons Extended." *New York Times,* May 12, 1995, 1.

"Darryl's Meeting with Sven Jurchewsky" (April 17, 1995). *Special Collections, box MS 424 A3079/1/1/19f1.* Archives of the University of Southampton, *Southampton,* UK. https://digitalarchive.wilsoncenter.org/document/176511.pdf?v=5625e94ca30e32d77e68316ee7c85623.

Davinić, Prvoslav. "1995 NPT Review and Extension Conference. Assessment of the Fourth and Last Week of Work (8-12 May 1995)." In *United Nations Archives. Folder S-1082-0019-0001-00002 "Office of Disarmament Affairs (ODA) - Non-Proliferation Treaties (NPT),"* 1995.

"Decision 1: Strengthening the Review Process for the Treaty." In *1995 Review and Extension Conference of the Parties to the Treaty on the Non-Proliferation of Nuclear Weapons. Final Document, Part I—Organization and work of the Conference.* NPT/CONF.1995/32, Annex. New York: United Nations, 1995. https://unoda-web.s3-accelerate.amazonaws.com/wp-content/uploads/assets/WMD/Nuclear/1995-NPT/pdf/NPT_CONF199532.pdf.

"Decision 2: Principles and Objectives for Nuclear Non-Proliferation and Disarmament." In *1995 Review and Extension Conference of the Parties to the Treaty on the Non-Proliferation of Nuclear Weapons. Final Document, Part I—Organization and work of the Conference.* NPT/CONF.1995/32, Annex. New York: United Nations, 1995. https://unoda-web.s3-accelerate.amazonaws.com/wp-content/uploads/assets/WMD/Nuclear/1995-NPT/pdf/NPT_CONF199501.pdf.

"Decision 3: Extension of the Treaty on the Non-Proliferation of Nuclear Weapons." In *1995 Review and Extension Conference of the Parties to the Treaty on the Non-Proliferation of Nuclear Weapons. Final Document, Part I—Organization and work of the Conference.* NPT/CONF.1995/32, Annex. New York: United Nations, 1995. https://unoda-web.s3-accelerate.amazonaws.com/wp-content/uploads/assets/WMD/Nuclear/1995-NPT/pdf/NPT_CONF199503.pdf.

Dee, Megan. "Standing Together or Doing the Splits: Evaluating European Union Performance in the Nuclear Non-Proliferation Treaty Review Negotiations." *European Foreign Affairs Review* 17, no. 2 (2012): 189–212.

———. "The EU's Performance in the 2015 NPT Review Conference: What Went Wrong." *European Foreign Affairs Review* 20, no. 4 (2015): 591–608.

de Klerk, Frederik W. "Dismantling of Nuclear Weapons (Memorandum to the Minister of Defence)." In *The Bomb: South Africa's Nuclear Weapons Programme*, edited by Nic von Wielligh and Lydia von Wielligh-Steyn, 512. Pretoria: Litera, 1990.

"de Klerk: South Africa Had the Bomb." *Africa Report 38* (May–June 1993): 6.

Department of Defense. *Nuclear Posture Review.* Washington, DC: Office of the Secretary of Defense, 2018.

de Queiroz Duarte, Sergio. "Brazil and the Nonproliferation Regime: A Historical Perspective." *Nonproliferation Review* 23, no. 5–6 (2016): 545–58.

Deutsch, Karl W., Sidney A. Burrell, Robert A. Kann, Maurice J. Lee, Martin Lichterman, Raymond E. Lindgren, Francis L. Loewenheim, and Richard W. von Wagenen. *Political Community and the North Atlantic Area: International Organization in the Light of Historical Experience.* Princeton, NJ: Princeton University Press, 1957.

de Wilde, Jaap. *Saved from Oblivion: Interdependence Theory in the First Half of the 20th Century; A Study on the Causality between War and Complex Interdependence.* Aldershot, UK & Brookfield, VT: Dartmouth, 1991.

"DFA Director-General Discusses US-SA Relations, Pariah States, DFA Restructuring"

(June 2, 1995). US Department of State, FOIA Virtual Reading Room, *Case no. F-2016-00610.*

Dhanapala, Jayantha. "The Permanent Extension of the NPT, 1995." In *The Oxford Handbook of Modern Diplomacy*, edited by Scott Cooper, Jorge Heine, and Ramesh Thakur, 810–25. Oxford: Oxford University Press, 2015.

Dhanapala, Jayantha, and Randy Ryddel. "Multilateral Diplomacy and the NPT: An Insider's Account." In *Reflections on the Treaty on the Non-Proliferation of Nuclear Weapons: Review Conferences and the Future of the NPT*, edited by Jayantha Dhanapala and Tariq Rauf, 5–133. Stockholm: SIPRI, 2017.

Dorussen, Han, and Hugh Ward. "Intergovernmental Organizations and the Kantian Peace: A Network Perspective." *Journal of Conflict Resolution* 52, no. 2 (2008): 189–212.

Drezner, Daniel W. *The System Worked: How the World Stopped Another Great Depression.* Oxford: Oxford University Press, 2014.

Dunn, Lewis A. "Negotiating and Sustaining the Non-Proliferation Treaty: Challenges and Lessons for US–Russia Cooperation." In *Once and Future Partners: The United States, Russia and Nuclear Non-Proliferation*, edited by William C. Potter and Sarah Bidgood, 117–34. Abingdon: Routledge, 2018.

duPreez, Jean. "Nuclear Non-Proliferation Treaty (NPT): South African Position and Preparations for the NPT Review and Extension Conference" (February 27, 1995). *Archives of the Department of International Relations and Cooperation (DIRCO), Pretoria.*

———. "Nuclear Non-Proliferation Treaty (NPT): South African Position and Preparations for the NPT Review and Extension Conference" (March 2, 1995). *Archives of the Department of International Relations and Cooperation Archives (DIRCO), Pretoria).*

———. *Interview by Michal Onderco*, 2018. 1995 NPT RevCon Oral History Project, Washington, DC: NPIHP, 2018.

duPreez, Jean, and Thomas Maettig. "From Pariah to Nuclear Poster Boy." In *Forecasting Nuclear Proliferation in the 21st Century. Vol. 2, A Comparative Perspective*, edited by William C. Potter and Gaukhar Mukhatzhanova, 302–35. Redwood City, CA: Stanford University Press, 2010.

Duque, Marina G. "Recognizing International Status: A Relational Approach." *International Studies Quarterly* 62, no. 3 (2018): 577–92.

Durbin, Richard J., and Richard A. Gephard. "Letter to President Clinton" (1995). *NPT–March 1995, box 4, OA/ID720. Nonproliferation and Export Controls, the files of Daniel Poneman. Clinton Presidential Records/NSC. Clinton Presidential Library/ NARA, Little Rock, AR.*

Egeland, Kjølv. "How I Learned to Stop Worrying and Embrace Diplomatic 'Polarization.'" *Peace Review* 29, no. 4 (2017): 482–88.

———. "Banning the Bomb: Inconsequential Posturing or Meaningful

Stigmatization?" *Global Governance: A Review of Multilateralism and International Organizations* 24, no. 1 (2018): 11–20.

Eilstrup-Sangiovanni, Mette. "Global Governance Networks." In *The Oxford Handbook of Political Networks*, edited by Jennifer Nicoll Victor, Alexander H. Montgomery and Mark Lubell, 689–714. Oxford: Oxford University Press, 2018.

Einhorn, Robert. "The NPT Review Process: The Need for a More Productive Approach." *Arms Control Today* (September 2016). https://www.armscontrol.org/act/2016-09/features/npt-review-process-need-more-productive-approach?utm_content=bufferodb18&utm_medium=social&utm_source=twitter.com&utm_campaign=buffer.

———. *Interview by Michal Onderco*, 2017. 1995 NPT RevCon Oral History Project, NPIHP, Washington, DC.

Elaraby, Nabil. *Interview by Michal Onderco*, 2019. 1995 NPT RevCon Oral History Project, NPIHP, Washington, DC.

Elbahtimy, Hassan. "Missing the Mark: Dimona and Egypt's Slide into the 1967 Arab-Israeli War." *Nonproliferation Review* 25, no. 5–6 (2018): 385–97.

Ellis, Stephen. *External Mission: The ANC in Exile, 1960–1990.* London: C. Hurst & Co., 2012.

"ENDC Meeting; Geneva, February 21, 1967; Background Paper; Significant Legal Questions Affecting the Non-proliferation Treaty" (February 11, 1967). US Department of State, FOIA Virtual Reading Room, Case no. M-2020-00304. https://foia.state.gov/Search/Results.aspx?searchText=&beginDate=19670211&endDate=19670211&publishedBeginDate=&publishedEndDate=&caseNumber=.

Erästö, Tytti. "The Lack of Disarmament in the Middle East: A Thorn in the Side of the NPT." *SIPRI Insights on Peace and Security*, no. 2019/1 (January 2019). https://www.sipri.org/sites/default/files/2019-01/sipriinsight1901.pdf.

Erickson, Jennifer, and Christopher Way. "Membership Has Its Privileges: Conventional Arms and Influence within the Nuclear Nonproliferation Treaty." In *The Causes and Consequences of Nuclear Proliferation*, edited by Matthew Kroenig, Erik Gartzke and Robert Rauchraus, 32–60. New York: Routledge, 2011.

European Council. "European Council at Corfu. 24–25 June 1994. Presidency Conclusions." (European Parliament, 1994). https://www.consilium.europa.eu/media/21207/corfu-european-council.pdf.

———. "Projet D'orientations Pour Une Action Commune En Matiere De Non-proliferation Nucleaire (Draft Guidelines for Joint Action on Nuclear Nonproliferation)" (1994). Digital Archive Cold War History Project, Wilson Center, Washington, DC. https://digitalarchive.wilsoncenter.org/document/175913.

———. "Resultats Des Travaux Du Groupe 'Non-Proliferation Nucleaire' (Results of the Work of the 'Nuclear Non-Proliferation' Group" (1994). Digital Archive Cold War History Project, Wilson Center, Washington, DC. https://digitalarchive.wilsoncenter.org/document/175914.

Fahmy, Nabil. *Interview by Hassan Elbahtimy*, 2017. 1995 NPT RevCon Oral History Project, NPIHP, Washington, DC.

———. *Egypt's Diplomacy in War, Peace and Transition.* London: Palgrave, 2020.

Farrell, Henry, and Abraham L. Newman. "Weaponized Interdependence: How Global Economic Networks Shape State Coercion." *International Security* 44, no. 1 (2019): 42–79.

Federation of American Scientists. "Egypt: Nuclear Weapons Program." WMD around the World Commission report, updated May 30, 2012. https://fas.org/nuke/guide/egypt/nuke/.

Feldman, Shai. "President Mubarak's Visit and the Middle East Nuclear Debate." The Washington Institute for Near East Policy, *PolicyWatch,* no. 146 (April 5, 1995). https://www.washingtoninstitute.org/policy-analysis/president-mubaraks-visit-and-middle-east-nuclear-debate.

Fischer, David, and Harald Müller. *United Divided: The European at the NPT Extension Conference.* Frankfurt: Peace Research Institute Frankfurt, 1995.

Fitzpatrick, Mark. *Nuclear Black Markets: Pakistan, A.Q. Khan and the Rise of Proliferation Networks; A Net Assessment.* London: International Institute for Strategic Studies, 2007.

Forman, Shepard. "Recommendation for Grant/FAP Action. Partial Support for the 1997 Preparatory Session of the Review Conference of the Nuclear Nonproliferation Treaty" (1996). Internal memo, *reel 7448, Ford Foundation Grants—U to Z. Rockefeller Archive Center,* Sleepy Hollow, NY.

Gavin, Francis J. *Nuclear Statecraft: History and Strategy in America's Atomic Age.* Ithaca, NY: Cornell University Press, 2012.

———. "Strategies of Inhibition: US Grand Strategy, the Nuclear Revolution, and Nonproliferation." *International Security* 40, no. 1 (2015): 9–46.

Geldenhuys, Deon. *Deviant Conduct in World Politics.* Houndmills, Basingstoke, UK: Palgrave Macmillan, 2004.

"Gemeinsame Aktion Zur Vorbereitung Der NVV-Konferenz (Joint action in preparation for the NPT conference)" (June 10, 1994). *Political Archive of the German Federal Foreign Office (selected documents),* Berlin.

Gerzhoy, Gene. "Alliance Coercion and Nuclear Restraint: How the United States Thwarted West Germany's Nuclear Ambitions." *International Security* 39, no. 4 (2015): 91–129.

Gheorghe, Eliza. "Proliferation and the Logic of the Nuclear Market." *International Security* 43, no. 4 (2019): 88–127.

Gibbons, Rebecca Davis. *American Hegemony and the Politics of the Nuclear Non-Proliferation Regime. PhD diss.,* Georgetown University, 2016.

———. "The Humanitarian Turn in Nuclear Disarmament and the Treaty on the Prohibition of Nuclear Weapons." *Nonproliferation Review* 25, no. 1–2 (2018): 11–36.

———. "Can This New Approach to Nuclear Disarmament Work?" *War on the Rocks,* January 23, 2019. https://warontherocks.com/2019/01/can-this-new-approach-to-nuclear-disarmament-work/.

Gibler, Douglas M. *International Military Alliances, 1648–2008.* Washington, DC: CQ Press, 2008.

Gleditsch, Kristian Skrede. "Expanded Trade and GDP Data." *Journal of Conflict Resolution* 46, no. 5 (2002): 712–24.

Goddard, Stacie E. "Embedded Revisionism: Networks, Institutions, and Challenges to World Order." *International Organization* 72, no. 4 (2018): 763–97.

Goosen, Peter. *"The Consequences of the 1995 Conference for the NPT: The Yardsticks for Non-Proliferation and Disarmament."* PPNN paper Cg18/7. Programme for Promoting Nuclear Nonproliferation, Southampton, UK, 1995.

———. "Nuclear Non-Proliferation Treaty (NPT): South African Position and Preparations for the NPT Review and Extension Conference" (February 24, 1995). Archives of the *Department of International Relations and Cooperation (DIRCO), Pretoria*, 1995.

———. *Interview by Michal Onderco,* 2017. 1995 NPT RevCon Oral History Project, NPIHP, Washington, DC.

Gore, Al. "Letter to Thabo Mbeki" (April 13, 1995). *Archives of the Department of International Relations and Cooperation (DIRCO), Pretoria.*

Gowa, Joanne, and Edward D. Mansfield. "Power Politics and International Trade." *American Political Science Review* 87, no. 2 (1993): 408–20.

Graham, Matthew. *The Crisis of South African Foreign Policy: Diplomacy, Leadership and the Role of the African National Congress.* London & New York: IB Tauris, 2015.

Graham, Thomas. *Interview by Michal Onderco,* 2017. 1995 NPT RevCon Oral History Project, NPIHP, Washington, DC.

———. *Disarmament Sketches: Three Decades of Arms Control and International Law.* Seattle: Institute for Global and Regional Security Studies; University of Washington Press, 2002.

Grand, Camille. *The European Union and the Non-Proliferation of Nuclear Weapons.* Chaillot Paper no. 37. Paris: European Union Institute for Security Studies, 2000.

Granovetter, Mark S. "The Strength of Weak Ties." *American Journal of Sociology* 78, no. 6 (1973): 1360–80.

Gregory, Barbara M. "Egypt's Nuclear Program: Assessing Supplier-Based and Other Developmental Constraints." *Nonproliferation Review* 3, no. 1 (1995): 20–27.

Hafner-Burton, Emilie M., Miles Kahler, and Alexander H. Montgomery. "Network Analysis for International Relations." *International Organization* 63, no. 3 (2009): 559–92.

Haim, Dotan A. "Alliance Networks and Trade: The Effect of Indirect Political Alliances on Bilateral Trade Flows." *Journal of Peace Research* 53, no. 3 (2016): 472–90.

Hamann, Hilton. *Days of the Generals: The Untold Story of South Africa's Apartheid-Era Military Generals.* Cape Town: Zebra, 2001.

Hardt, Heidi. "The Goldilocks Effect: Knowledge Networks in International Organizations." Working paper shared with the author, 2018.

Hart, Kathleen. "NPT Conference Opening Marred by Discord over Voting Rules."
Nucleonics Week 36, no. 16 (1995): 1.

Hasenclever, Andreas, Peter Mayer, and Volker Rittberger. *Theories of International
Regimes*. Cambridge Studies in International Relations. Cambridge & New York:
Cambridge University Press, 1997.

Hecker, Siegfried S, eds. *Doomed to Cooperate: How American and Russian Scientists
Joined Forces to Avert Some of the Greatest Post-Cold War Nuclear Dangers*. Los
Alamos, NM: Bathtub Row Press, 2016.

Henke, Marina E. "The Politics of Diplomacy: How the United States Builds Multilateral Military Coalitions." *International Studies Quarterly* 61, no. 2 (2017): 410–24.

———. "Buying Allies: Payment Practices in Multilateral Military Coalition-
Building." *International Security* 43, no. 4 (2019): 128–62.

———. *Constructing Allied Cooperation: Diplomacy, Payments, and Power in Multilateral Military Coalitions*. Ithaca, NY: Cornell University Press, 2019.

———. "Networked Cooperation: How the European Union Mobilizes Peacekeeping Forces to Project Power Abroad." *Security Studies* 28, no. 5 (2019): 901–34.

Heyes, Alan, Wyn Q. Bowen, and Hugh Chalmers. *The Global Partnership against
WMD: Success and Shortcomings of G8 Threat Reduction since 9/11*. Whitehall Paper
no. 76. London: RUSI, 2011.

Hibbs, Mark. "South Africa 'Moved Beyond NAM' in Support of Firm NPT Extension." *Nucleonics Week* 36, no. 19 (1995): 13.

Highsmith, Newell, and Mallory Stewart. "The Nuclear Ban Treaty: A Legal Analysis."
Survival 60, no. 1 (2018): 129–52.

Hoffmann, Wolfgang. "4.Prepcom Ueberpruefungs- Un Verlaengungskonferenzenz
Vom 23.1. Bis 27.1.1995: Allgemeine Aussprache (4.Prepcom review and extension
conference from January 23 until 27, 1995: general discussion)" (1995). *Political
Archive of the German Federal Foreign Office, row 675, box 48828*, Berlin.

———. "4.Sitzung Des Vorbereitungsausschusses Fuer Die NVV-Konferenz, New
York, 23–27.1.1995 (4.Meeting of the Preparatory Committee for the NPT Con-
ference, New York, January 23–27, 1995)" (1995). *Political Archive of the German
Federal Foreign Office, row 675, box 48828, Berlin.*

———."Koordinierungstreffen Der EU Und Der Westlichen Gruppe Sowie 'Treffen in Engerem Kreis' Am 20.01.1995 (Coordination meeting of the EU and
the Western group as well as 'Close circle meeting' on January 20, 1995)." 1995.
Political Archive of the German Federal Foreign Office, row 675, box 48828, Berlin.

Holum, John. "Holum Letter on Arms Control in 1995" (December 28, 1994).
*NPT–January 1995, box 2, OA/ID 720. Nonproliferation and Export Controls, the files
of Daniel Poneman, Clinton Presidential Records/NSC, Clinton Presidential Library/
NARA, Little Rock, AR.*

————. "South Africa NPT Extension Vote" (1994). *South Africa–1995, box 8, OA/ID872. African Affairs, the files of Donald Steinberg, Susan Rice, MacArthur DeShazer. Clinton Presidential Records/NSC, Clinton Presidential Library/NARA, Little Rock, AR.*

————. "NPT Extension. Meeting between Sri Lankan Ambassador Jayantha Dhanapala and ACDA Director Holum and Deputy Director Earle. Friday, March 31, 1995 (Washington, DC)" (1995). *NPT–March 1995, box 1, OA/ID720. Nonproliferation and Export Controls, the files of Daniel Poneman. Clinton Presidential Records/NSC, Clinton Presidential Library/NARA, Little Rock, AR.*

Hudson, John, and Paul Sonne. "Trump Administration Discussed Conducting First U.S. Nuclear Test in Decades." *Washington Post,* May 22, 2020. https://www.washingtonpost.com/national-security/trump-administration-discussed-conducting-first-us-nuclear-test-in-decades/2020/05/22/a805c904-9c5b-11ea-b60c-3be060a4f8e1_story.html.

International Campaign Against Nuclear Weapons. "Catastrophic Harm." Former text on ICAN website, 2013. http://www.icanw.org/the-facts/catastrophic-harm/.

————. "ICAN Statements to the Negotiating Conference." ICAN, 2016. https://www.icanw.org/ican_statements_to_the_negotiating_conference.

International Court of Justice. "Legality of the Threat or Use of Nuclear Weapons" (1996), Advisory Opinion of July 8, 1996, ICJ. https://www.icj-cij.org/en/case/95.

"Invitation to the Six Associated Countries About Troika Demarches." December 1, 1994. *Political Archive of the German Federal Foreign Office, row 537, box 37781,* Berlin.

"Istithnā' Isrā'īl Min Tawqī' Al-Mu'āhada Al-Nawawiyya Yuhaddidu Amn Wa Salām Al-Sharq Al-Awsaṭ Wa Ghayr Maqbūl (The League's Council Decides in Its Conclusion: Exclusion of Israel from the NPT Threatens Security and Peace in the Middle East and Is Unacceptable)." *Al Ahram,* March 24, 1995, 1.

Jabko, Nicolas, and Steven Weber. "A Certain Idea of Nuclear Weapons: France's Nuclear Nonproliferation Policy in Theoretical Perspective." *Security Studies* 8, no. 1 (1998): 108–50.

Jervis, Robert. "Cooperation under the Security Dilemma." *World Politics* 30, no. 2 (1978): 167–214.

Jo, Dong-Joon, and Erik Gartzke. "Determinants of Nuclear Weapons Proliferation." *Journal of Conflict Resolution* 51, no. 1 (February 1, 2007): 167–94.

Johnson, Rebecca. "Assessing the 2010 NPT Review Conference." *Bulletin of the Atomic Scientists* 66, no. 4 (2010): 1–10.

"Joint Action 'Preparation of NPT-Conference 1995.'" April 20, 1994. *Political Archive of the German Federal Foreign Office, row 242, box 37116/40,* Berlin.

Jonter, Thomas. *The Key to Nuclear Restraint: The Swedish Plans to Acquire Nuclear Weapons During the Cold War.* London: Palgrave, 2016.

Joyner, Daniel. *Interpreting the Nuclear Non-Proliferation Treaty.* Oxford & New York: Oxford University Press, 2011.

"July 8 Meeting of the Friends of NPT" (July 3, 1992). US Department of State, FOIA Virtual Reading Room, Case no. F-2008-02837.

Jurchewsky, Sven. *Interview by Michal Onderco*, 2017. 1995 NPT RevCon Oral History Project NPIHP, Washington, DC.

Karem, Mahmoud. *A Nuclear-Weapon-Free Zone in the Middle East: Problems and Prospects.* New York: Greenwood, 1988.

Kassenova, Togzhan. *Brazil's Nuclear Kaleidoscope: An Evolving Identity.* Washington, DC: Carnegie Endowment for International Peace, 2014.

Keller, Bill. "Building (and Dismantling) a Threat." *New York Times*, March 28, 1993, D2.

Keohane, Robert O. *After Hegemony: Cooperation and Discord in the World Political Economy.* Princeton, NJ: Princeton University Press, 1984.

Keukeleire, Stephan, and Tom Delreux. *The Foreign Policy of the European Union.* Basingstoke, UK: Palgrave Macmillan, 2014.

Kimball, Daryl G. "US Questions Russian CTBT Compliance." *Arms Control Today* 49, no. 6 (2019): 20–22.

———. "US Makes Noncompliance Charges." *Arms Control Today* 50, no. 4 (2020): 29–30.

Klijn, Erik Hans, Vicenta Sierra, Tamyko Ysa, Evan Berman, Jurian Edelenbos, and Don Y. Chen. "The Influence of Trust on Network Performance in Taiwan, Spain, and the Netherlands: A Cross-Country Comparison." *International Public Management Journal* 19, no. 1 (2016): 111–39.

Knopf, Jeffrey W. "After Diffusion: Challenges to Enforcing Nonproliferation and Disarmament Norms." *Contemporary Security Policy* 39, no. 3 (2018): 367–98.

———. "International Cooperation on Nonproliferation: The Growth and Diversity of Cooperative Efforts." In *International Cooperation on WMD Nonproliferation*, edited by Jeffrey W. Knopf, 1–22. Athens: University of Georgia Press, 2018.

Koremenos, Barbara. "Loosening the Ties that Bind: A Learning Model of Agreement Flexibility." *International Organization* 55, no. 2 (2001): 289–325.

———. "Contracting around International Uncertainty." *American Political Science Review* 99, no. 4 (2005): 549–65.

———. *The Continent of International Law: Explaining Agreement Design.* Cambridge: Cambridge University Press, 2016.

Koremenos, Barbara, Charles Lipson, and Duncan Snidal. "The Rational Design of International Institutions." *International Organization* 55, no. 4 (2001): 761–99.

Kratochwil, Friedrich. "Thrasymmachos Revisited: On the Relevance of Norms and the Study of Law for International Relations." In *The Puzzles of Politics: Inquiries into the Genesis and Transformation of International Relations*, edited by Friedrich Kratochwil, 83–98. Abingdon, UK: Routledge, 2011.

Krause, Joachim. "The Future of the NPT: A German Perspective." In Pilat and Pendley (1995), *1995: A New Beginning for the NPT?* 135–50.

Kreczko, Alan. "Legal Analysis of NPT Extension Options" (January 19, 1995).

NPT–January 1995, box 1, OA/ID720. Nonproliferation and Export Controls, the files of Daniel Poneman. Clinton Presidential Records/NSC, Clinton Presidential Library/ NARA, Little Rock, AR.

Kristensen, Hans M., and Robert S. Norris. "Global Nuclear Weapons Inventories, 1945–2013." *Bulletin of the Atomic Scientists* 69, no. 5 (2013): 75–81.

Kubbig, Bernd W., and Christian Weidlich. *A WMD/DVs Free Zone for the Middle East: Taking Stock, Moving Forward Towards Regional Security.* Frankfurt: Peace Research Institute Frankfurt, 2015.

Lake, Anthony. "Confronting Backlash States." *Foreign Affairs* 73, no. 2 (1994): 45–55.

———. "Holum Letter on Arms Control in 1995" (1995). *NPT–January 1995, box 2, ID720. Nonproliferation and Export Controls, the files of Daniel Poneman. Clinton Presidential Records/NSC, Clinton Presidential Library/NARA, Little Rock, AR.*

Lake, David A. *Hierarchy in International Relations.* Ithaca, NY: Cornell University Press, 2009.

Lantis, Jeffrey S. "Irrational Exuberance? The 2010 NPT Review Conference, Nuclear Assistance, and Norm Change." *Nonproliferation Review* 18, no. 2 (2011): 389–409.

Ledogar, Stephen. "Keeping up with the 'Principles' 2 May (Memorandum for Norman Wulf)" (1995). *NPT–March 1995, box 2, OA/ID720. Nonproliferation and Export Controls, the files of Daniel Poneman. Clinton Presidential Records/NSC, Clinton Presidential Library/NARA, Little Rock, AR.*

Leonard, James. "Steps toward a Middle East Free of Nuclear Weapons." *Arms Control Today* 21, no. 3 (1991): 10–14.

Lewis, Patricia M. "A Middle East Free of Nuclear Weapons: Possible, Probable or Pipe-Dream?" *International Affairs* 89, no. 2 (2013): 433–50.

Lewis, Patricia, Heather Williams, Benoit Pelopidas, and Sasan Aghlani. "Too Close for Comfort: Cases of Near Nuclear Use and Options for Policy." *Chatham House Report.* (London: Chatham House, April 2014). https://www.chathamhouse.org/ sites/default/files/field/field_document/20140428TooCloseforComfortNuclearU seLewisWilliamsPelopidasAghlani.pdf.

Litwak, Robert. *Rogue States and U.S. Foreign Policy: Containment after the Cold War.* Washington, DC: Woodrow Wilson Center Press, 2000.

Lyman, Princeton N. *Partner to History: The U.S. Role in South Africa's Transition to Democracy.* Washington, DC: US Institute of Peace Press, 2002.

———. *Interview by Michal Onderco,* 2017. 1995 NPT RevCon Oral History Project/ NPIHP, Washington, DC.

Maggi, Giovanni, and Massimo Morelli. "Self-Enforcing Voting in International Organizations." *American Economic Review* 96, no. 4 (2006): 1137–58.

Maitre, Emmanuelle. "French Perspectives on Disarmament and Deterrence." In *Europe's Evolving Deterrence Discourse,* edited by Amelia Morgan and Anna Péczeli, 51–65. Livermore, CA: Center for Global Security Research, Lawrence Livermore National Laboratory, 2021.

Maitre, Emmanuelle, and Pauline Lévy. "Becoming a Disarmament Champion: The Austrian Crusade against Nuclear Weapons." *Nonproliferation Review* 26, no. 5–6 (2019): 537–57.

"Majlis Al-Jāmiʿa Al-Arabiyya Yakhtatimu Dawratahu Al-ʿādiya Al-Yawm (The Arab League Council Concludes Its Regular Meeting Today)." *Al Ahram*, March 23, 1995, 6.

Malan, Magnus. *My Life with the SA Defence Force*. Pretoria: Protea Book House, 2006.

Mallard, Grégoire, and Paolo Foradori. "The Middle East at a Crossroads: How to Face the Perils of Nuclear Development in a Volatile Region." *Global Governance: A Review of Multilateralism and International Organizations* 20, no. 4 (2014): 499–515.

Mallea, Rodrigo, Matias Spektor, and Nicholas J. Wheeler, eds. *The Origins of Nuclear Cooperation: A Critical Oral History of Argentina and Brazil*. Rio de Janeiro & Washington, DC: Fundação Getúlio Vargas & Wilson Center, 2015.

Maoz, Zeev. *Networks of Nations: The Evolution, Structure, and Impact of International Networks, 1816–2001*. Cambridge & New York: Cambridge University Press, 2011.

Marin-Bosch, Miguel. "The 1995 NPT Review and Extension Conference." *Irish Studies in International Affairs* 6 (1995): 23–31.

Markram, Thomas. *A Decade of Disarmament, Transformation and Progress: An Assessment of the Development and Implementation of Policy on Disarmament, Non-Proliferation and Arms Control in South Africa 1994–2004*. Pretoria: SaferAfrica, 2004.

Marten, Kimberly. "Reconsidering NATO Expansion: A Counterfactual Analysis of Russia and the West in the 1990s." *European Journal of International Security* 3, no. 2 (2018): 135–61.

Martin, Lisa L. *Coercive Cooperation: Explaining Multilateral Economic Sanctions*. Princeton, NJ: Princeton University Press, 1992.

———. "Interests, Power, and Multilateralism." *International Organization* 46, no. 4 (1992): 765–92.

Masiza, Zondi, and Chris Landsberg. "Fission for Compliments? South Africa and the 1995 Extension of Nuclear Non-Proliferation." *Policy: Issues and Actors* 9, no. 3 (1996).

Mbeki, Thabo. "Letter to Vice-President Al Gore" (April 10, 1995). *Archives of the Department of International Relations and Cooperation (DIRCO), Pretoria*.

Mearsheimer, John J. "The False Promise of International Institutions." *International Security* 19, no. 3 (1994): 5–49

———. *The Tragedy of Great Power Politics*. New York: W.W. Norton, 2001.

———. "Bound to Fail: The Rise and Fall of the Liberal International Order." *International Security* 43, no. 4 (2019): 7–50.

Meerts, Paul. *Diplomatic Negotiation: Essence and Evolution*. Den Haag, The Netherlands: Clingendael, 2015.

Mehta, Rupal N, and Rachel Elizabeth Whitlark. "The Benefits and Burdens of Nuclear Latency." *International Studies Quarterly* 61, no. 3 (2017): 517–28.

Meunier, Sophie, and Kalypso Nicolaïdis. "The European Union as a Trade Power." In *International Relations and the European Union*, edited by Christopher Hill and Michael Smith. Oxford & New York: Oxford University Press, 2005.

———. "The European Union as a Conflicted Trade Power." *Journal of European Public Policy* 13, no. 6 (2006): 906–25.

Mian, Zia, and A. H. Nayyar. "Playing the Nuclear Game: Pakistan and the Fissile Material Cutoff Treaty." *Arms Control Today* 40, no. 3 (2010): 17–24.

Miller, Nicholas L. *Stopping the Bomb: The Sources and Effectiveness of US Nonproliferation Policy.* Ithaca, NY: Cornell University Press, 2018.

Ministry of Foreign Affairs of Ukraine. "Possible Consequences of Alternative Approaches to Implementation of Ukraine's Nuclear Policy (Analytical Report)" (February 3, 1993). Nuclear Proliferation International History Project (NPIHP)/ CCNY. https://digitalarchive.wilsoncenter.org/document/144983.

Minty, Abdul Samad. "Keynote Address." In *The Nuclear Debate: Policy for a Democratic South Africa, 7–15. Proceedings of a conference sponsored by ANC Western Cape Science and Technology Group / The Environmental Monitoring Group.* Cape Town, South Africa, 1994.

———. Interview by Sue Onslow, 2017. Commonwealth Oral History Project, Institute of Commonwealth Studies, University of London. https://sas-space.sas.ac.uk/6531/1/abdul_minty_transcript.pdf.

Mitchell, Sara McLaughlin, and Paul R. Hensel. "International Institutions and Compliance with Agreements." *American Journal of Political Science* 51, no. 4 (2007): 721–37.

"Miṣr Wa 107 Duwal Ghayr Munḥāza Tunāqishu Qaḍiyya Al-Mu'āhada Al-Nawawiyya Fī Bāndūnj Al-Usbū' Al-Qādim (Egypt and 107 Non-Aligned Countries Discuss the NPT in Bandung Next Week)." *Al Ahram*, April 16, 1995, 1.

"Miṣr Wa Isrā'īl Tatabādalāni Al-Muqtaraḥāt Li-Taswiyya Al-Khilāf Ḥawla Al-Barnāmij Al-Nawawī Al-Isrā'īlī (Egypt and Israel Exchange Suggestions to Resolve the Dispute around the Israeli Nuclear Program)." *Al Ahram*, March 25, 1995, 1.

Monterey Institute of International Studies. "The 1995 Review and Extension Conference of Parties to the Non-Proliferation Treaty: Assessment and Implications for the Future. A Workshop Conducted on 27–29 July 1995" (1995). *Reel 9159, Ford Foundation Grants—U to Z, Rockefeller Archive Center,* Sleepy Hollow, NY.

Montgomery, Alexander H. "Centrality in Transnational Governance: How Networks of International Institutions Shape Power Processes." In *New Power Politics: Networks, Governance, Global Security*, edited by Deborah Avant and Oliver Westerwinter. Oxford: Oxford University Press, 2015.

Möser, Robin. "'The Major Prize': Apartheid South Africa's Accession to the Treaty on the Non-Proliferation of Nuclear Weapons, 1988–91." *Nonproliferation Review* 26, no. 5–6 (2019): 559–73.

Moussa, Amr. *Kitābiyah (My Testimony)*. Cairo: Dār al-Shurūq, 2017.

———. *Interview by Michal Onderco*, 2019. 1995 NPT RevCon Oral History Project/ NPIHP, Washington, DC.

Moyer, Jonathan D., David K. Bohl, and Sara Turner. "Diplomatic Representation Data Codebook [Diplometrics]." Frederick S. Pardee Center for International Futures, Josef Korbel School of International Studies, University of Denver, CO, 2016. https://pardee.du.edu/diplomatic-representation-data-codebook.

Mpofu-Walsh, Sizwe. *"Obedient Rebellion: Nuclear-Weapon-Free Zones and Global Nuclear Order, 1967–2017."* PhD diss., Oxford University, 2020.

Mukhatzhanova, Gaukhar, Chen Kane, Miles Pomper, Leonard Spector, and Avner Cohen. "Fissile Material Cut-off Treaty: History and Status." Report no. OSRD 20011 030. Defense Threat Reduction Agency, Advanced Systems and Concepts Office, Fort Belvoir, VA, October 2010. https://www.hsdl.org/?view&did=716221.

Müller, Harald. "Smoothing the Path to 1995: Amending the Nuclear Non-Proliferation Treaty and Enhancing the Regime." In *Nuclear Non-Proliferation: An Agenda for the 1990s*, edited by John Simpson, 123–37. Cambridge: Cambridge University Press, 1987.

———, ed. *European Non-Proliferation Policy 1993–1995*. Brussels: European Inter-university Press, 1993.

———. "The Internalization of Principles, Norms and Rules by Governments: The Case of Security Regimes." In *Regime Theory and International Relations*, edited by Volker Rittberger, 361–90. Oxford: Clarendon, 1993.

———. "Arguing, Bargaining and all that: Communicative Action, Rationalist Theory and the Logic of Appropriateness in International Relations." *European Journal of International Relations* 10, no. 3 (2004): 395–435.

———. "A Treaty in Troubled Waters: Reflections on the Failed NPT Review Con-ference." *International Spectator* 40, no. 3 (2005): 33–44.

———. "The 2010 NPT Review Conference: Some Breathing Space Gained, but No Breakthrough." *International Spectator* 45, no. 3 (2010): 5–18.

———. "A Nuclear Nonproliferation Test: Obama's Nuclear Policy and the 2010 NPT Review Conference." *Nonproliferation Review* 18, no. 1 (2011): 219–36.

———. "Beyond 1995: The NPT and Europe." In Pilat and Pendley (1995), *1995: A New Beginning for the NPT?* 151–61.

———. *Interview by Michal Onderco*, 2017. 1995 NPT RevCon Oral History Project/ NPIHP, Washington, DC: Nuclear Proliferation International History Project.

———. "Justice and the Nonproliferation Regime." In *Behavioral Economics and Nuclear Weapons*, edited by Anne Harrington and Jeffrey W. Knopf, 135–58. Athens: University of Georgia Press, 2019.

Müller, Harald, and Daniel Druckman. "Introduction Justice in Security Negotiations." *International Negotiation* 19, no. 3 (2014): 399–409.

Müller, Harald, David Fischer, and Wolfgang Kötter. *Nuclear Non-Proliferation and Global Order.* Oxford: Oxford University Press, 1994.

Müller, Harald, and Wolfgang Kötter. *Germany, Europe & Nuclear Non-Proliferation, PPNN study no. 1.* Southampton, UK: Mountbatten Centre for International Studies, 1991.

Müller, Harald, and Lars van Dassen. "From Cacophony to Joint Action: Successes and Shortcomings of the European Nuclear Non-Proliferation Policy." In *Common Foreign and Security Policy: The Record and Reforms*, edited by Martin Holland, 52–72. London: Pinter, 1997.

Müller, Harald, and Carmen Wunderlich, eds. *Norm Dynamics in Multilateral Arms Control: Interests, Conflicts, and Justice.* Studies in Security and International Affairs. Athens: University of Georgia Press, 2013.

NATO. "Final Communique" (October 21–22, 1992). Nuclear Planning Group *(NPG) of the North Atlantic Alliance*, Gleneagles, Scotland. https://www.nato.int/cps/en/natohq/official_texts_23977.htm?selectedLocale=en.

———. "Statement on Russia's Failure to Comply with the Intermediate-Range Nuclear Forces (INF) Treaty." North Atlantic Council, Brussels, February 1, 2019. https://www.nato.int/cps/en/natohq/news_162996.htm.

Nincic, Miroslav. *Renegade Regimes: Confronting Deviant Behavior in World Politics.* New York: Columbia University Press, 2005.

"9. Deutsch-Russische NV-Konsultationen, Moskau, 03–06.05.1994 (9th German-Russian NPT consultations, Moscow, May 3–6, 1994)" (April 26,). *Political Archive of the German Federal Foreign Office, row 242, box 37116/40*, Berlin.

"1995 NPT Conference—Depositaries Meeting with France" (September 19, 1992). US Department of State, FOIA Virtual Reading Room, Case no. F-2008-02837.

"Non-Paper for SAG on NPT" (1995). *South Africa–1995, box 6, OA/ID872. African Affairs, the files of Donald Steinberg, Susan Rice, MacArthur DeShazer. Clinton Presidential Records/NSC, Clinton Presidential Library/NARA, Little Rock, AR.*

"NPT 95—PrepCom 1: Egypt Wants to Consult with US on Security Assurances in Advance of the 1995 NPT Conference" (May 17, 1993). US Department of State, FOIA Virtual Reading Room, Report no. M-2008-02837.

"NPT 95—First Session of the NPT Preparatory Committee (PrepCom): Wrap-Up" (June 3, 1993). US Department of State, FOIA Virtual Reading Room, Case no. F-2008-02837.

"NPT 95—Western Group Meeting in Geneva, April 2, 1993" (April 28, 1993). US Department of State, FOIA Virtual Reading Room, Case no. M-2008-02837.

"NPT 1995—Follow-up on Issues Raised at November US-EU Troika Consultations" (n.d.). *Political Archive of the German Federal Foreign Office, row 537, box 37781*, Berlin.

"NPT 1995—Preparing for January PrepCom Meeting" (December 30, 1993). US Department of State, FOIA Virtual Reading Room, Case no. F-2008-02837.

"NPT Consultations on the Margins of the June IAEA Board of Governors Meeting" (June 29, 1992). US Department of State, FOIA Virtual Reading Room, Case no. F-2008-02837.

"NPT Depositaries Meeting—Soviet Paper on Possible Non-Proliferation Cooperation" (June 6, 1991). US Department of State, FOIA Virtual Reading Room, Case no. M-2008-02837.

"NPT Depositaries Meeting—Points on Agenda" (June 7, 1993). US Department of State, FOIA Virtual Reading Room, Case no. F-2008-02837.

"NPT Depositaries Meeting—September 22 and 23, 1992" (September 28, 1992). US Department of State, FOIA Virtual Reading Room, Case no. F-2008-02837.

"NPT Depositaries Meeting" (August 4, 1992). US Department of State FOIA, Virtual Reading Room, Case no. F-2008-02837.

Nuti, Leopoldo. "'A Turning Point in Postwar Foreign Policy': Italy and the NPT Negotiations, 1967–1969." In *Negotiating the Nuclear Non-Proliferation Treaty: Origins of the Nuclear Order*, edited by Roland Popp, Liviu Horovitz, and Andreas Wenger, 77–97. Abingdon, UK: Routledge, 2017.

"NVV-Konferenz: Treffen Der Core Group (NPT Conference: Meeting of the Core Group)." (February 10, 1995). *Political Archive of the German Federal Foreign Office, row 675, box 48828*, Berlin.

"NVV-Überprüfungs - Und Verlängungskonferenz 1995. Treffen Der Core Group Am 10.02.1995 (NPT Review and Extension Conference 1995. Core Group meeting on February 10, 1995)" (1995). *Political Archive of the German Federal Foreign Office, row 675, box 48828*, Berlin.

"NVV-Verlängungskonferenz. Positionen Der Vertragstaaten (NPT extension conference. Positions of the States Parties)" (April 6, 1995). *Political Archive of the German Federal Foreign Office, row 675, box 48828*, Berlin.

"NVV Konferenz: Treffen Der Core-Group Am 10.02.1995 in Genf (NPT Conference: Meeting of the Core Group on February 10, 1995, in Geneva)" (February 13, 1995). *Political Archive of the German Federal Foreign Office, row 675, box 48828*, Berlin.

"NVV Verlängerungskonferenz: Treffen Der Core Group Und Westlicher Gruppe (NPT Extension Conference: Meeting of the Core Group and Western Group)" (March 25, 1995). *Political Archive of the German Federal Foreign Office, row 675, box 48828*, Berlin.

"NVV Vertrag: Stand Der Vorbereitungen Ein Halbes Jahr Vor Der Konferenz (NPT Treaty: Status of Preparations Half a Year Before the Conference)" (November 17,

1994). *Political Archive of the German Federal Foreign Office, row 675, box 48828,* Berlin.

"NVV: Core-Group Zur Vorbereitung Der Verlängerungsentscheidung (NPT: Core-Group on the preparation of the extension decision)" (January 28, 1995), *Political Archive of the German Federal Foreign Office, row 675, box 48828,* Berlin.

"NVV: Treffen Der Core Group NVV Am 20/21.03.95 in Genf (NPT: Meeting of the NPT Core Group on March 20/21, 1995, in Geneva)" (March 22, 1995). *Political Archive of the German Federal Foreign Office, row 675, box 48828,* Berlin.

"NVV: Treffen Der Core Group Und Treffen Der Westlichen Gruppe (NPT: Meetings of the Core Group and Meetings of the Western Group)" (March 22, 1995). *Political Archive of the German Federal Foreign Office, row 675, box 48828,* Berlin.

"NVV: Überprüfungs- Und Verlängerungskonferenz (NPT: Review and Extension Conference)" (March 24, 1995). *Political Archive of the German Federal Foreign Office, row 675, box 48828,* Berlin.

Nzo, Alfred. "Letter to Edward Bwanali, Minister of External Affairs of Malawi" (April 13, 1995). Archives of the *Department of International Relations and Cooperation (DIRCO), Pretoria.*

———. "The Statement by the Foreign Minister of the Republic of South Africa, Mr. Alfred Nzo. The 1995 Review and Extension Conference of the Parties to the Treaty on the Non-Proliferation of Nuclear Weapons" (April 19, 1995). *Archives of the Department of International Relations and Cooperation (DIRCO), Pretoria.*

Office of the Chief State Law Adviser (International Law) of the Republic of South Africa. "South African Legal Opinion on Article X.2 of the NPT" (December 27, 1994). *Archives of the Department of International Relations and Cooperation (DIRCO), Pretoria.*

Office of the Vice President. "Trip of the Vice President to New York, NY April 19, 1995" (1995), *box 010, Vice President's trip to New York City to attend NPT Conference. NARA, Washington, DC.*

Onderco, Michal. "Variation in Delegation Size in Multilateral Diplomacy." *British Journal of Politics and International Relations* 21, no. 2 (2019): 421–38.

———. "The Programme for Promoting Nuclear Non-Proliferation and the NPT Extension." *International History Review* 42, no. 4 (2020): 851–68.

———. "Collaboration Networks in Conference Diplomacy: The Case of Non-Proliferation Regime." *International Studies Review* 22, no. 4 (2020): 739–57.

Onderco, Michal, and Leopoldo Nuti, eds. *Extending the NPT: A Critical Oral History of the 1995 Review and Extension Conference.* Washington, DC: Woodrow Wilson International Center for Scholars, 2020.

Onderco, Michal, and Paul van Hooft. "Why Is the Proliferation Security Initiative a Problematic Solution?" *Chinese Journal of International Politics* 9, no. 1 (2016): 81–108.

Onderco, Michal, and Anna-Mart Van Wyk. "Birth of a Norm Champion: How South Africa Came to Support the NPT's Indefinite Extension." *Nonproliferation Review* 26, no. 1–2 (2019): 23–41.

Oneal, John R., Frances H. Oneal, Zeev Maoz, and Bruce Russett. "The Liberal Peace: Interdependence, Democracy, and International Conflict, 1950–85." *Journal of Peace Research* 33, no. 1 (February 1, 1996): 11–28.

Oneal, John R., and Bruce Russett. "Assessing the Liberal Peace with Alternative Specifications: Trade Still Reduces Conflict." *Journal of Peace Research* 36, no. 4 (1999): 423–42.

Onslow, Sue, and Anna-Mart van Wyk, eds. *Southern Africa in the Cold War, Post-1974.* Critical Oral History Conference Series. Washington, DC: Woodrow Wilson International Center for Scholars, 2013.

Orlov, Vladimir A. "*Konferenciya 1995 Goda Po Rassmotreniyu I Prodleniyu Sroka Deystviya Dogovora O Nerasprostranenii Yadernogo Oruzhiya: Osobennosti, Rezul'taty, Uroki (1995 Review and Extension Conference of the Treaty on the Non-Proliferation of Nuclear Weapons: Features, Results, Lessons)*" (1999). Scientific Notes no. 11, PIR Center, Moscow.

Oye, Kenneth A. "Explaining Cooperation under Anarchy: Hypotheses and Strategies." *World Politics* 38, no. 1 (1985): 1–24.

Pabian, Frank V. "South Africa's Nuclear Weapon Program: Lessons for U.S. Nonproliferation Policy." *Nonproliferation Review* 3, no. 1 (1995): 1–19.

Padgett, John F., and Christopher K. Ansell. "Robust Action and the Rise of the Medici, 1400–1434." *American Journal of Sociology* 98, no. 6 (1993): 1259–319.

Panda, Ankit. "What's in Russia's New Nuclear Deterrence 'Basic Principles'? A New Document Sheds Insight on Old Debates." *Diplomat* (July 9, 2020). https://thediplomat.com/2020/06/whats-in-russias-new-nuclear-deterrence-basic-principles/.

Patty, John W., and Elizabeth Maggie Penn. "Network Theory and Political Science." In *The Oxford Handbook of Political Networks*, edited by Jennifer Nicoll Victor, Alexander H. Montgomery and Mark Lubell, 147–71. Oxford: Oxford University Press, 2018.

Pelopidas, Benoît. "Nuclear Weapons Scholarship as a Case of Self-Censorship in Security Studies." *Journal of Global Security Studies* 1, no. 4 (2016): 326–36.

Perkovich, George. *India's Nuclear Bomb: The Impact on Global Proliferation.* Berkeley: University of California Press, 1999.

Peterson, John, and Elizabeth E. Bomberg. *Decision-Making in the European Union.* European Union Series. New York: St. Martin's Press, 1999.

Pevehouse, Jon, and Bruce Russett. "Democratic International Governmental Organizations Promote Peace." *International Organization* 60, no. 4 (2006): 969–1000.

Pilat, Joseph F. "Future of the NPT." In *Kernwaffenverbreitung Und Internationaler Systemwandel: Neue Risiken Und Gestaltungsmöglichkeiten (Nuclear Weapons Proliferation and Change in International System: New Risks and Policy Options)*, edited by Joachim Krause, 443–57. Baden-Baden, Germany: Nomos Verlagsgesellschaft, 1994.

———. "The NPT's Prospects." In Pilat and Pendley (1995), *1995: A New Beginning for the NPT?* 47–61.

———. *A World without the NPT Redux.* Geneva: UNIDIR, 2020.

Pilat, Joseph F., and Robert E. Pendley, eds. *Beyond 1995: The Future of the NPT Regime.* Boston: Springer, 1990.

———. *1995: A New Beginning for the NPT?* Boston: Springer, 2012.

Pollins, Brian M. "Conflict, Cooperation, and Commerce: The Effect of International Political Interactions on Bilateral Trade Flows." *American Journal of Political Science* 33, no. 3 (1989): 737–61.

Poneman, Daniel. "South Africa and NPT" (1995). *South Africa–1995, box 6, OA/ID872. African Affairs, the files of Donald Steinberg, Susan Rice, MacArthur DeShazer. Clinton Presidential Records/NSC, Clinton Presidential Library/NARA, Little Rock, AR.*

———. "SVTS Meeting on NPT Extension" (February 8, 1995). *NPT–February 1995, box 1, OA/ID 720. Nonproliferation and Export Controls, the files of Daniel Poneman. Clinton Presidential Records/NSC, Clinton Presidential Library/NARA, Little Rock, AR.*

———. "Thabo Cover Note" (1995). *South Africa–1995, box 8, OA/ID872. African Affairs, the files of Donald Steinberg, Susan Rice, MacArthur DeShazer. Clinton Presidential Records/NSC, Clinton Presidential Library/NARA, Little Rock, AR.*

Popp, Roland. "The Long Road to the NPT: From Superpower Collusion to Global Compromise." In *Negotiating the Nuclear Non-Proliferation Treaty: Origins of the Nuclear Order,* edited by Roland Popp, Liviu Horovitz and Andreas Wenger, 9–36. Abingdon, UK: Routledge, 2017.

Portela, Clara. *The Role of the EU in the Non-Proliferation of Nuclear Weapons: The Way to Thessaloniki and Beyond. PRIF Report no. 65.* Frankfurt: Peace Research Institute Frankfurt, 2004.

Posner, Eric A., and Alan O. Sykes. "Voting Rules in International Organizations." *Chicago Journal of International Law* 15, no. 1 (2014): 195–228.

Potter, William C. "The NPT Review Conference: 188 States in Search of Consensus." *International Spectator* 40, no. 3 (2005): 19–31.

———. "The NPT & the Sources of Nuclear Restraint." *Daedalus* 139, no. 1 (2010): 68–81.

———. "The Unfulfilled Promise of the 2015 NPT Review Conference." *Survival* 58, no. 1 (2016): 151–78.

Potter, William C., and Gaukhar Mukhatzhanova. *Nuclear Politics and the Non-Aligned Movement: Principles Vs. Pragmatism.* London: Routledge, 2012.

Pouliot, Vincent. *International Security in Practice: The Politics of NATO-Russia Diplomacy.* Cambridge: Cambridge University Press, 2010.

Pouponneau, Florent, and Frédéric Mérand. "Diplomatic Practices, Domestic Fields, and the International System: Explaining France's Shift on Nuclear Nonproliferation." *International Studies Quarterly* 61, no. 1 (2017): 123–35.

Powell, Colin. "Letter to Nelson Mandela" (February 8, 1995). *Folder South Africa–1995, box 9. Clinton Presidential Records/NSC, Clinton Presidential Library/ NARA, Little Rock, AR.*

"Preparation De La Conference De Prorogation Du TNP En 1995" (June 24, 1994). *Political Archive of the German Federal Foreign Office (selected documents)*, Berlin.

"Preparation of NPT Conference of 1995. Swiss Position/Joint Action" (June 22, 1994), *Political Archive of the German Federal Foreign Office (selected documents)*, Berlin.

"Preparation of the NPT Conference 1995 (Joint Action/Swiss Position)" (June 21, 1994), *Political Archive of the German Federal Foreign Office, row 242, box 37116/40*, Berlin.

"Preparing for the 1995 NPT Conference" (December 15, 1993). US Department of State, FOIA Virtual Reading Room, Case no. M-2008-02837.

"Presidential Thank-You for NPT Extension Effort" (May 23, 1995). US Department of State, FOIA Virtual Reading Room, Case no. M-2017-11533.

Programme for Promoting Nuclear Non-Proliferation. "The New Europe and Nuclear Non-Proliferation: A Seminar for Senior Government Officials" (1992). *MS424 A3079/1/1/13 f1, Archives of the University of Southampton, Southampton, UK.*

———. "Issues at the 1995 NPT Conference: An International Seminar for Government Officials. General Report" (July 9–12, 1993). *Reel 7448, Ford Foundation Grants—U to Z, Rockefeller Archive Center*, Sleepy Hollow, NY.

———. "Issues at the 1995 NPT Conference: An International Seminar for Government Officials. List of Participants" (July 9–12, 1993). *Special Collections, box MS 424 A3079/1/1/15, Archives of the University of Southampton, Southampton, UK.*

Rabinowitz, Or. *Bargaining on Nuclear Tests: Washington and Its Cold War Deals.* Oxford: Oxford University Press, 2014.

Rabinowitz, Or, and Nicholas L. Miller. "Keeping the Bombs in the Basement: U.S. Nonproliferation Policy toward Israel, South Africa, and Pakistan." *International Security* 40, no. 1 (2015): 47–86.

Rauf, Tariq. *Interview by Michal Onderco*, 2017. 1995 NPT RevCon Oral History Project/NPIHP, Washington, DC.

———. "The 2000 NPT Review Conference." *Nonproliferation Review* 7, no. 1 (2000): 146–61.

———. "An Unequivocal Success? Implications of the NPT Review Conference." *Arms Control Today* 30, no. 6 (2000): 9.

Rauf, Tariq, and Rebecca Johnson. "After the NPT's Indefinite Extension: The Future of the Global Nonproliferation Regime." *Nonproliferation Review* 3, no. 1 (1995): 28–42.

Reaching Critical Will. "History of the NPT 1975–1995." Reaching Critical Will website, n.d. https://www.reachingcriticalwill.org/disarmament-fora/npt/history-of-the-npt-1975-1995.

Reif, Kingston. "UN Approves Start of Nuclear Ban Talks." *Arms Control Today* (November 2016). https://www.armscontrol.org/ACT/2016_11/News/UN-Approves-Start-of-Nuclear-Ban-Talks.

———. "Trump to Withdraw U.S. from INF Treaty." *Arms Control Today* (November 2018). https://www.armscontrol.org/act/2018-11/news/trump-withdraw-us-inf-treaty.

"Resolution on the Middle East." In *1995 Review and Extension Conference of the Parties to the Treaty on the Non-Proliferation of Nuclear Weapons. Final Document, Part I—Organization and work of the Conference.* NPT/CONF.1995/32, Annex. New York: United Nations, 1995. https://unoda-web.s3-accelerate.amazonaws.com/wp-content/uploads/assets/WMD/Nuclear/1995-NPT/pdf/Resolution_MiddleEast.pdf.

Ritchie, Nicholas Edward, John Borrie, Tim Caughley, and Wilfred Wan. "Negotiation of a Nuclear Weapons Prohibition Treaty: The New Treaty; Taking Stock." United Nations Institute for Disarmament Research, 2017. http://eprints.whiterose.ac.uk/121920/1/2017_Aug_UNIDIR_TPNW_The_New_Treaty_Taking_Stock.pdf.

Ritchie, Nick (Nicholas Edward). "Pathways to Nuclear Disarmament: Delegitimising Nuclear Violence." Paper presented at the UNGA Open-ended Working Group on "Taking forward multilateral nuclear disarmament negotiations," Palais de Nations, Geneva, May 11, 2016.

———. "A Hegemonic Nuclear Order: Understanding the Ban Treaty and the Power Politics of Nuclear Weapons." *Contemporary Security Policy* 40, no. 4 (2019): 409–34.

Roberts, Cynthia. "Revelations About Russia's Nuclear Deterrence Policy." *War on the Rocks,* June 19, 2020. https://warontherocks.com/2020/06/revelations-about-russias-nuclear-deterrence-policy/.

Rockefeller, David, Jr. "Letter to President Clinton" (1993). *WHORM-Subject File-General, box 02284, OA/ID23306, folder FO 009. Clinton Presidential Records/NSC, Clinton Presidential Library/NARA, Little Rock, AR.*

Rockwood, Laura. "The IAEA's Strengthened Safeguards System." *Journal of Conflict and Security Law* 7, no. 1 (2002): 123–36.

———. "How the IAEA Verifies If a Country's Nuclear Program Is Peaceful or Not: The Legal Basis." *Bulletin of the Atomic Scientists* 74, no. 5 (2018): 317–25.

Rockwood, Laura, and Larry Johnson. "Verification of Correctness and Completeness in the Implementation of IAEA Safeguards: The Law and Practice." In *Nuclear Non-Proliferation in International Law. Vol. 2, Verification and Compliance,* edited by Jonathan L. Black-Branch and Dieter Fleck, 57–94. The Hague: T.M.C. Asser Press, 2016.

Rublee, Maria Rost. "Egypt's Nuclear Weapons Program: Lessons Learned." *Nonproliferation Review* 13, no. 3 (2006): 555–67.

"Rūsiyā Tuṭālibu Min Isrāʾīl Al-Inḍimam Li-Muʿāhada Manʿ Al-Intishār Al-Nawawī (Russia Asks Israel to Join the NPT)." *Al Ahram* April 4, 1995, 1.

Russett, Bruce, and John R. Oneal. *Triangulating Peace: Democracy, Interdependence, and International Organizations.* New York: Norton, 2001.

Ruzicka, Jan. "Behind the Veil of Good Intentions: Power Analysis of the Nuclear Non-Proliferation Regime." *International Politics* 55, no. 3 (2018): 369–85.

Sabet, Farzan. "The April 1977 Persepolis Conference on the Transfer of Nuclear Technology: A Third World Revolt against US Non-Proliferation Policy?" *International History Review* 40, no. 5 (2018): 1134–51.

"Sachbestand: Ergebnisse Der 2. Sitzung Des Verbeitungsauschusses (State of play: Results of the 2nd meeting of the Preparatory Committee)" (January 27, 1994). *Political Archive of the German Federal Foreign Office, row 242, box 37116/40,*Berlin.

Sagan, Scott D. "Why Do States Build Nuclear Weapons? Three Models in Search of a Bomb." *International Security* 21, no. 3 (1996): 54–86.

———, ed. *Inside Nuclear South Asia.* Redwood City, CA: Stanford University Press, 2009.

———. "The Causes of Nuclear Weapons Proliferation." *Annual Review of Political Science* 14, no. 1 (2011): 225–44.

Sami, Mariam. "Egypt Loses Bid for Arab League Support on Nuclear Treaty" (1995).

Sanders, Ben, ed. *Newsbrief 2 (1995).* PPNN / Mountbatten Center for International Studies, University of Southampton.

———, ed. *Newsbrief 4 (1995).* PPNN / Mountbatten Center for International Studies, University of Southampton.

———. *NPT Review Conferences and the Role of Consensus. Issue review no. 4.* Southampton, UK: PPNN, 1995.

———. *"The Nuclear Non-Proliferation Regime after the NPT Conference."* PPNN paper Cg18/8. Programme for Promoting Nuclear Nonproliferation, Southampton, UK, 1995.

———, ed. *Newsbrief 2 (1997).* PPNN / Mountbatten Center for International Studies, University of Southampton.

———. "1995: A Time for Optimism?" In Pilat and Pendley (1995), *1995: A New Beginning for the NPT?* 77–89.

———. *Interview by Michal Onderco,* 2017. 1995 NPT RevCon Oral History Project/ NPIHP, Washington, DC.

Sarkar, Jayita. "U.S. Policy to Curb West European Nuclear Exports, 1974–1978." *Journal of Cold War Studies* 21, no. 2 (2019): 110–49.

"Sarnia Symposium on the International Nuclear Non-Proliferation Regime in the 1990s." *MS424 A3079/1/1/1. Archives of the University of Southampton, Southampton, UK,* 1986.

Sauer, Tom. "It's Time to Outlaw Nuclear Weapons." *National Interest,* April 18, 2016. http://nationalinterest.org/feature/its-time-outlaw-nuclear-weapons-15814?page=show.

"Schedule and Taskings on Engagement/Nonproliferation Roll-out" (February 24, 1995). *NPT–February 1995, box 2, OA/ID720. Nonproliferation and Export Controls, the files of Daniel Poneman. Clinton Presidential Records/NSC, Clinton Presidential Library/NARA, Little Rock, AR.*

Schlosser, Eric. *Command and Control: Nuclear Weapons, the Damascus Accident, and the Illusion of Safety.* London: Penguin, 2014.

"Schlussbericht Des 2.VA (Final report of the 2nd PrepCom)" (January 21, 1994). *Political Archive of the German Federal Foreign Office, row 242, box 37116/40,* Berlin.

"The Secretary's Meeting with Egyptian Foreign Minister Moussa, Budapest, December 4, 1994" (December 5, 1994). US Department of State, FOIA Virtual Reading Room, Case no. M-2017-11694.

"Secretary's Meeting with French Foreign Minister Alain Juppe, March 22, 1995, Paris" (March 23, 1995). US Department of State, FOIA Virtual Reading Room, Case no. M-2017-11622.

Sha, Zukang. *Interview by Katrin M. Heilmann,* 2016. 1995 NPT RevCon Oral History Project/NPIHP, Washington, DC.

Shaker, Mohamed Ibrahim. *The Nuclear Non-Proliferation Treaty: Origin and Implementation, 1959–1979.* London & New York: Oceana, 1980.

———"The Legacy of the 1985 Nuclear Non-Proliferation Treaty Review Conference: The President's Reflections." In *Nuclear Non-Proliferation: An Agenda for the 1990s,* edited by John Simpson, 9–23. Cambridge: Cambridge University Press, 1987.

Shetty, Shatabhisha, and Heather Williams. "The P5 Process: Opportunities for Success in the NPT Review Conference." European Leadership Network, June 30, 2020. https://www.europeanleadershipnetwork.org/report/the-p5-process-opportunities-for-success/.

Shultz, George P., William J. Perry, Henry A. Kissinger, and Sam Nunn. "A World Free of Nuclear Weapons." *Wall Street Journal,* January 4, 2007. https://www.wsj.com/articles/SB116787515251566636.

Signorino, Curtis S., and Jeffrey M. Ritter. "Tau-B or Not Tau-B: Measuring the Similarity of Foreign Policy Positions." *International Studies Quarterly* 43, no. 1 (1999): 115–44.

Simpson, John, and Darryl Howlett. "The NPT Renewal Conference: Stumbling toward 1995." *International Security* 19, no. 1 (1994): 41–71.

Slaughter, Anne-Marie. "A Grand Strategy of Network Centrality." In *America's Path: Grand Strategy for the Next Administration*, edited by Richard Fontaine and Kristin M. Lord, 43–56. Washington, DC: Center for New American Security, 2012.

———. *The Chessboard & the Web: Strategies of Connection in a Networked World.* New Haven, CT: Yale University Press, 2017.

Smetana, Michal. "Stuck on Disarmament: The European Union and the 2015 NPT Review Conference." *International Affairs* 92, no. 1 (2016): 137–52.

———. *Nuclear Deviance: Stigma Politics and the Rules of the Nonproliferation Game.* London: Palgrave, 2020.

Smith, Mark. "Disarmament in the Anglo-American Context." In *Nuclear Weapons after the 2010 NPT Review Conference (Chaillot Paper no. 2010)*, edited by Jean Pascal Zanders, 71–86. Paris: European Union Institute of Security Studies, 2010.

Solingen, Etel. "The Domestic Sources of Regional Regimes: The Evolution of Nuclear Ambiguity in the Middle East." *International Studies Quarterly* 38, no. 2 (1994): 305–37.

———. "The Political Economy of Nuclear Restraint." *International Security* 19, no. 2 (1994): 126–69.

Sotomayor, Arturo. *"Mexico en el TNP en Momentos de Cambio."* Master's thesis, Instituto Tecnologico Autonomo de Mexico, Mexico City, 1997.

"South Africa's Position on the Extension of the Nuclear Non-Proliferation Treaty" (April 3, 1995). *Archives of the Department of International Relations and Cooperation (DIRCO)*, Pretoria.

"South Africa: Response to Letter from President Clinton to President Mandela" (1995). *South Africa–1995, box 9, OA/ID872. African Affairs, the files of Donald Steinberg, Susan Rice, MacArthur DeShazer. Clinton Presidential Records/NSC, Clinton Presidential Library/NARA, Little Rock, AR.*

Steinberg, Gerald M. "Middle East Peace and the NPT Extension Decision." *Nonproliferation Review* 4, no. 1 (1996): 17–29.

Stoiber, Carlton. "The Evolution of NPT Review Conference Final Documents, 1975–2000." *Nonproliferation Review* 10, no. 3 (2003): 126–66.

Stone, Diane. "Global Public Policy, Transnational Policy Communities, and Their Networks." *Policy Studies Journal* 36, no. 1 (2008): 19–38.

Stone, Randall W. *Controlling Institutions: International Organizations and the Global Economy.* Cambridge: Cambridge University Press, 2011.

Taliaferro, Jeffrey W. *Defending Frenemies: Alliances, Politics, and Nuclear Nonproliferation in US Foreign Policy.* Oxford: Oxford University Press, 2019.

"Tansīq Al-Mawāqif Al-'arabiyya Ḥawla Al-Mu'āhada Al-Nawawiyya (Coordination of Arab Positions on NPT)." *Al Ahram*, March 23, 1995, 1.

Taylor, Ian. "South Africa and the Nuclear Non-Proliferation Treaty." In *The New Multilateralism in South African Diplomacy*, edited by Donna Lee, Ian Taylor and Paul Williams, 159–81. Houndmills, Basingstoke, UK: Palgrave Macmillan, 2006.

"Telefonat Brengelmann/Guellil Am 6.4.94 (Telephone call Brengelmann/Guellil on April 6, 1994)" (April 7, 1994). *Political Archive of the German Federal Foreign Office, row 242, box 37116/40*, Berlin.

Thakur, Vineet. "Foreign Policy and Its People: Transforming the Apartheid Department of Foreign Affairs." *Diplomacy & Statecraft* 26, no. 3 (2015): 514–33.

Timerbaev, Roland. "Statement by Roland Timerbaev at the NGO Meeting During the 4th NPT Prepcom," January 25, 1995. Personal communication, 2016.

"TNP/Position De Certains Pays Arabes Et Maghrebins (NPT/Position of Certain Arab and Maghreb Countries)" (1995). *Political Archive of the German Federal Foreign Office, row 675, box 48828*, Berlin.

Trager, Eric. "The Throwback: Meet the Anti-Israel Demagogue Who Will Likely Be Egypt's Next President." *New Republic*, April 29, 2011. https://newrepublic.com/article/87607/moussa-biography-egypt-arab-league-mubarak.

Treaty on the Non-Proliferation of Nuclear Weapons (NPT). UN Office for Disarmament Affairs, New York, July 1, 1968. https://www.un.org/disarmament/wmd/nuclear/npt/text/.

Turque, Bill. *Inventing Al Gore: A Biography.* Boston: Houghton Mifflin, 2000.

United Nations. "Draft Resolution Submitted by Algeria, Bahrain, Egypt, Iraq, Jordan, Kuwait, the Libyan Arab Jamahiriya, Mauritania, Morocco, Qatar, Saudi Arabia, the Sudan, Tunisia and Yemen." In *1995 Review and Extension Conference of the Parties to the Treaty on the Non-Proliferation of Nuclear Weapons, Final Document, Part II—Documents issued at the Conference.* NPT/CONF.1995/L.7. United Nations, New York, 1995. https://documents-dds-ny.un.org/doc/UNDOC/GEN/N95/167/92/IMG/N9516792.pdf?OpenElement.

———. "Extension of the Treaty on the Non-Proliferation of Nuclear Weapons—Democratic People's Republic of Korea, Indonesia, Iran (Islamic Republic of), Jordan, Malaysia, Mali, Myanmar, Nigeria, Papua New Guinea, Thailand and Zimbabwe: draft decision." In *1995 Review and Extension Conference of the Parties to the Treaty on the Non-Proliferation of Nuclear Weapons*, L.3, 234. UN Office for Disarmament Affairs, New York, May 5, 1995. http://daccess-ods.un.org/access.nsf/Get?OpenAgent&DS=NPT/CONF.1995/32(PARTIII)&Lang=E.

———. "Mexico: Draft Resolution." In *1995 Review and Extension Conference of the Parties to the Treaty on the Non-Proliferation of Nuclear Weapons.* UN Office for Disarmament Affairs, New York, May 5, 1995. https://digitallibrary.un.org/record/199290/files/NPT_CONF.1995_L.1-EN.

———. *1995 Review and Extension Conference of the Parties to the Treaty on the Non-Proliferation of Nuclear Weapons. Final Document, Part III—Summary and Verbatim Records. NPT/CONF.1995/32.* United Nations, New York, 1995. https://documents-dds-ny.un.org/doc/UNDOC/GEN/N96/216/75/IMG/N9621675.pdf?OpenElement.

———. *2010 Review Conference of the Parties to the Treaty on the Non-Proliferation of*

Nuclear Weapons. Final Document. Part I—Review of the operation of the Treaty, as provided for in its Article VIII (3), taking into account the decisions and the resolution adopted by the 1995 Review and Extension Conference and the Final Document of the 2000 Review Conference and the Final Document of the 2000 Review Conference. Conclusions and Recommendations for follow-on actions. NPT/CONF.2010/50, vol. *1**. United Nations, New York, 2010.

United Nations General Assembly. *Resolution adopted by the General Assembly on 7 December 2015. 70/48, Humanitarian pledge for the prohibition and elimination of nuclear weapons.* A/Res/70/48. UNGA, New York, December 11, 2015. http://www.un.org/ga/search/view_doc.asp?symbol=a/res/70/48.

———. Resolution 73/546, *Convening a Conference on the establishment of a Middle East zone free of nuclear weapons and other weapons of mass destruction.* UNGA, New York, December 23, 2018. https://www.un.org/disarmament/wp-content/uploads/2019/10/Decision-A_73_546.pdf.

———. *Resolutions Adopted by the General Assembly.* 49/75 F, *General and complete disarmament.* UNGA, New York, January 9, 1995. https://undocs.org/en/A/RES/49/75.

———. "Result of the Exchange of Views on the Review and Extension Conference on the NPT (Appendix to the Communiqué from the Ministerial Meeting of the Coordinating Bureau of the Non-Aligned Countries in Bandung, Indonesia, 25–27 April 1995." Letter dated April 27, 1995, in Bandung. UNGA Security Council, New York, April 27, 1995, 36–37. https://undocs.org/A/49/920.

US Department of State. "Press Conference with President Hosni Mubarak and Secretary of State Warren Christopher" (1995). *NPT–March 1995, box 2, OA/ID720. Nonproliferation and Export Controls, the files of Daniel Poneman. Clinton Presidential Records/NSC, Clinton Presidential Library/NARA, Little Rock, AR.*

———. "Secretary Blinken's Remarks to the Conference on Disarmament." Remarks at the High-Level Segment of the Conference on Disarmament , virtual presentation (February 22, 2021). https://www.state.gov/video-remarks-to-the-conference-on-disarmament/.

Van Der Merwe, Frederick A. "Arms Control and Disarmament in South Africa after the Cold War." *Strategiese Oorsig vir Suider-Afrika (Strategic Review for Southern Africa)* 25, no. 1 (2003): 53–87.

Van Doren, Charles. "Avoiding Amendment of the NPT." In Pilat and Pendley (1995), *1995: A New Beginning for the NPT?* 179–91.

van Wyk, Anna-Mart (Martha). *The 1977 United States Arms Embargo against South Africa: Institution and Implementation to 1997.* PhD diss., University of Pretoria, 2006.

———. "Sunset over Atomic Apartheid: United States–South African Nuclear Relations, 1981–93." *Cold War History* 10, no. 1 (2009): 51–79.

———. "South African Nuclear Development in the 1970s: A Non-Proliferation Conundrum?" *International History Review* 40, no. 5 (2018): 1152–73.

van Wyk, Jo-Ansie. "Nuclear Diplomacy as Niche Diplomacy: South Africa's Post-Apartheid Relations with the International Atomic Energy Agency." *South African Journal of International Affairs* 19, no. 2 (2012): 179–200.

———. *South Africa's Nuclear Diplomacy, 1990–2010: Securing a Niche Role through Norm Construction and State Identity.* PhD diss., University of Pretoria, 2013.

———. "From Apartheid to Ubuntu: Transition, Transaction and Transformation in South Africa's Post-Apartheid Foreign Ministry." *South African Journal of International Affairs* 26, no. 3 (2019): 413–34.

van Wyk, Jo-Ansie, and Anna-Mart van Wyk. "From the Nuclear Laager to the Non-Proliferation Club: South Africa and the NPT." *South African Historical Journal* 67, no. 1 (2015): 32–46.

Verdier, Daniel. "Multilateralism, Bilateralism, and Exclusion in the Nuclear Proliferation Regime." *International Organization* 62, no. 3 (2008): 439–76.

"Verlängerung Des NVV: Amerikanische Demarche Durch Botschafter Hunter (Extension of the NPT: American Démarche through Ambassador Hunter)" (April 6, 1995). *Political Archive of the German Federal Foreign Office, row 675, box 48828,* Berlin.

"Vertrag Ueber Die Nichtverbreitung Von Kernwaffen (NVV). Britische Haltung (Treaty on the Non-Proliferation of Nuclear Weapons (NPT). British position)" (1995). *Political Archive of the German Federal Foreign Office, row 675, box 48828,* Berlin.

Volpe, Tristan A. "Atomic Inducements: The Case for 'Buying out' Nuclear Latency." *Nonproliferation Review* 23, no. 3–4 (2016): 481–93.

———. "Atomic Leverage: Compellence with Nuclear Latency." *Security Studies* 26, no. 3 (2017): 517–44.

von Hippel, Frank N. "The Decision to End U.S. Nuclear Testing." *Arms Control Today* 49 (December 2019). https://www.armscontrol.org/act/2019-12/features/decision-end-us-nuclear-testing.

von Wielligh, Nic, and Lydia von Wielligh-Steyn. *The Bomb: South Africa's Nuclear Weapons Programme.* Pretoria: Litera, 2015.

Walker, William. "Nuclear Order and Disorder." *International Affairs* 76, no. 4 (2000): 703–24.

———. "Nuclear Enlightenment and Counter-Enlightenment." *International Affairs* 83, no. 3 (2007): 431–53.

Ward, Libby. "US Text (Fax to Daniel Poneman)" (1995). *NPT–May 1995, box 2, OA/ID721. Nonproliferation and Export Controls, the files of Daniel Poneman. Clinton Presidential Records/NSC, Clinton Presidential Library/NARA, Little Rock, AR.*

Ward, Libby, and Robert Einhorn. "Draft (Fax to Daniel Poneman)" (1995). *NPT–May 1995, box 2, OA/ID721. Nonproliferation and Export Controls, the files of Daniel Poneman. Clinton Presidential Records/NSC, Clinton Presidential Library/NARA, Little Rock, AR.*

Way, Christopher, and Karthika Sasikumar. *"Leaders and Laggards: When and Why Do Countries Sign the NPT?"* Working paper, Research Group in International Security (REGIS), Montreal 2004.

Welsh, Susan B. "Delegate Perspectives on the 1995 NPT Review and Extension Conference." *Nonproliferation Review* 2, no. 3 (1995): 1–24.

Westdal, Christopher. *Interview by Michal Onderco*, 2017. 1995 NPT RevCon Oral History Project/NPIHP, Washington, DC.

Weston, Michael. "Principles: Discussion with South Africans: 1 May" (1995). *NPT–March 1995, box 2, OA/ID720. Nonproliferation and Export Controls, the files of Daniel Poneman. Clinton Presidential Records/NSC, Clinton Presidential Library/NARA, Little Rock, AR.*

White House, The. "President Clinton Fact Sheet on Nonproliferation and Export Control Policy" (September 27, 1993). Office of the Press Secretary. Reference Documents Concerning the RERTR Program, Nuclear Science and Engineering Division/Argonne National Laboratory, 1993. https://www.rertr.anl.gov/REF-DOCS/PRES93NP.html.

———. *A National Security Strategy of Engagement and Enlargement.* NSS report, Washington, DC, July 1994. https://nssarchive.us/wp-content/uploads/2020/04/1994.pdf.

———. *The National Security Strategy of the United States of America.* NSS report, Washington, DC, March 2006. https://nssarchive.us/wp-content/uploads/2020/04/2006.pdf.

———. *National Security Strategy.* NSS report, Washington, DC, 2010. https://nssarchive.us/wp-content/uploads/2020/04/2010.pdf.

———. *National Security Strategy.* NSS report, Washington, DC, February 2015. https://nssarchive.us/wp-content/uploads/2020/04/2015.pdf.

Whitlark, Rachel Elizabeth, and Rupal N. Mehta. "Hedging Our Bets: Why Does Nuclear Latency Matter?" *Washington Quarterly* 42, no. 1 (2019): 41–52.

Williams, Heather. "A Nuclear Babel: Narratives around the Treaty on the Prohibition of Nuclear Weapons." *Nonproliferation Review* 25, no. 1–2 (2018): 51–63.

———. "CEND and a Changing Global Nuclear Order." European Leadership Network, 2020. https://www.europeanleadershipnetwork.org/commentary/cend-and-a-changing-global-nuclear-order/.

Winecoff, William Kindred. "Structural Power and the Global Financial Crisis: A Network Analytical Approach." *Business and Politics* 17, no. 3 (2015): 495.

———. "'The Persistent Myth of Lost Hegemony,' Revisited: Structural Power as a Complex Network Phenomenon." *European Journal of International Relations* 26, no. 1, suppl. (2020): 209–52.

Wohlforth, William C. "The Stability of a Unipolar World." *International Security* 24, no. 1 (1999): 5–41.

Wulf, Norman A. "Observations from the 2000 NPT Review Conference." *Arms Control Today* 30, no. 9 (2000): 3–9.

Wunderlich, Carmen. *Rogue States as Norm Entrepreneurs: Black Sheep or Sheep in Wolves' Clothing?* Cham, Switzerland: Springer, 2020.

Wunderlich, Carmen, Andrea Hellmann, Daniel Müller, Judith Reuter, and Hans-Joachim Schmidt. "Non-Aligned Reformers and Revolutionaries: Egypt, South Africa, Iran and North Korea." In Müller and Wunderlich (2013), *Norm Dynamics in Multilateral Arms Control.*

Zelnick, Robert. *Gore: A Political Life.* Washington, DC: Regnery Publishing, 1999.

Index

Bundy, McGeorge, 33, 113
Bunn, George, 5, 27, 29, 117n15, 124n50
Bunn–Van Doren extension. *See* red-
light rolling extension of NPT
Burk, Susan, 67
Bush, George H. W., 31, 84
Bush, George W., 98, 102, 106
Butler, Richard, 59–60, 136n66

Campaign for the Non-Proliferation
Treaty, 5, 79
Canada: nonproliferation policies of, 78;
support for indefinite extension of
NPT by, 66–67, 71
Caracciolo, Roberto, 20
Caribbean, nuclear-weapon-free zone
in, 101
Carnegie Corporation, 5
CEND (Creating an Environment for
Nuclear Disarmament), 101
Center for Nonproliferation Studies, 95
Central Asia: EU influence in, 47;
nuclear-weapon-free zone in, 102
centrality in networks, 39–41; of United
States, 44–45, 47, 110–13
CFSP (Common Foreign and Security
Policy of EU), 52; Joint Action Deci-
sion on NPT extension (Decision
94/509/CFSP), 52, 54
Chemical Weapons Convention, 4
China: diplomatic network of, 44; on
indefinite extension of NPT, 35; rati-
fication of NPT by, 4
Christopher, Warren, 86, 87, 147n39
Cirincione, Joseph, 5, 79
CISAC (Center for International Se-
curity and Cooperation, Stanford
University), ix
civil society, campaigns for extension of
NPT by, 5

Clinton, Bill, 61, 126n78; lobby-efforts
on NPT indefinite extension by, 71,
72, 73, 89–90, 148n63; nonproliferation policies of, 31–32, 33–34; on
nuclear testing, 126n75
coercion, IR theory on, 7–8
Cold War, end of, 64
collective action problem, nonproliferation as, 36–37
communities, cooperation between, 39
conditional extension of NPT, 10, 18,
27, 29–30
consensus decision-making, NPT
regime of, 24, 37. *See also* voting,
absence of
Considine, Laura, 108
constructivist IR theory, on indefinite
extension of NPT, 9–10
conventional arms agreements, 4
Cooley, Alexander, 111
cooperation: between communities,
39; East-West, at NPT RevCons,
23; between states, 18–19; US-EU,
viii, 14, 48, 49, 50–52, 59–62, 111–
12; US-Soviet Union/Russia, 24,
50–51
Critical Oral History Conference Rotterdam (2018), 11–12
CTBT (Comprehensive Test Ban
Treaty), 103–4; absence of, 25–26;
negotiations on, 23, 54, 78, 108; US
attitude towards, 33
CTBTO (Commission for the Comprehensive Nuclear-Test-Ban Treaty
Organization), 104
Cuba, ratification of NPT by, 101

democratization, in South Africa, 65,
143n79
Deutsch, Karl, 44

Sagan, Scott, x, 119n41
sanctions, against South Africa, 73,
    142n60
Sanders, Ben, xi, 5, 12, 66, 94, 97,
    116n12, 122n30
SCFA (Sub-Council on Foreign Affairs,
    South Africa), 65, 139n12
semistructured interviews, 11
Shaker, Mohamed, 20, 21, 24, 25, 120–
    21n8
Shalikashvili, John, 126n75
side payments, in international rela-
    tions, 43
Simpson, John, 4, 66
Slaughter, Anne-Marie, 110–11
Smetana, Michal, 125n67
social network theory, 3; application to
    diplomacy/international relations
    of, 38–41, 111; application to NPT
    indefinite extension of, 13–14, 15, 41–
    47, 61, 110
Solingen, Etel, 145n5,12
Sonn, Franklin, 74
Sotomayor, Arturo, 123n43
South Africa: democratization in, 65,
    143n79; foreign policy of, 65, 139n16;
    NAM membership of, 63; nonprolif-
    eration policies of, 65, 76; and NPT
    extension, 12, 66–71, 75, 76–78, 79,
    80, 139n25, 141n49, 142n72; nuclear
    program of, 24, 63, 64; opposition
    to NPT indefinite extension by, 14,
    27, 28–29, 63–64, 69–71, 73–75, 80,
    140n46; ratification of NPT by, 4,
    63, 64; sanctions against, 73, 142n60;
    support for NPT indefinite exten-
    sion by, 7, 12, 14–15, 60, 65, 67, 71–
    81, 87, 139n25; US influence on, 14–
    15, 67, 71–75, 80–81, 143–44n88,90

Southeast Asia, nuclear-weapon-free
    zone in, 102
South Pacific, nuclear-weapon-free zone
    in, 101
Soviet Union: cooperation with US, 24;
    limited duration of NPT supported
    by, 21; nuclear arms of, 4, 31, 32;
    withdrawal from Africa of, 64. See
    also Russia
Spektor, Matias, x
START (Strategic Arms Reduction
    Treaty) I, 4
START (Strategic Arms Reduction
    Treaty) II, 4, 33
START (Strategic Arms Reduction
    Treaty) New, 112
states in international system, 18–19;
    and collective action problems, 36;
    and social network theory, 39, 40–41;
    society of states/ties between states,
    38, 41–47
Suharto, Haji Muhammad, 59
superpowers: realist IR theory on, 7. See
    also great powers
Sweden, nonproliferation policies of,
    49, 121–22n22
Switzerland: EU pressure on, 135n50;
    support for limited duration of NPT
    by, 21
symbiosis, of United States and its al-
    lies on indefinite extension of NPT,
    41–42

Tammany Society (New York City),
    136n64
Taylhardat, Adolfo, 7
Taylor, Ian, 140n45
technological developments, uncertainty
    of, 19, 20